Blaine Palque
APRIL 2014

THE FIRES
OF OCTOBER

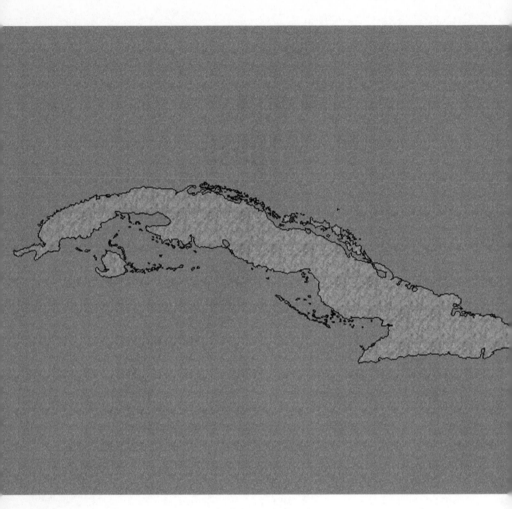

The island of Cuba.

THE FIRES
OF OCTOBER

THE PLANNED US INVASION OF CUBA
DURING THE MISSILE CRISIS OF 1962

BLAINE L. PARDOE

FONTHILL

Fonthill Media Limited
Fonthill Media LLC
www.fonthillmedia.com
office@fonthillmedia.com

First published in 2013

ISBN 978-1-78155-196-7

Typeset in 9.5pt on 13pt Sabon LT
Printed and bound in England

Connect with us
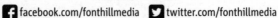facebook.com/fonthillmedia twitter.com/fonthillmedia

Contents

Dedication

To the marines, sailors, airmen, infantry, paratroopers, tankers, and support personnel that nearly went to war in late October 1962. Your service and near-sacrifice has not been forgotten. For the first time, this is a glimpse of what you would have faced.

To my dad David Pardoe, who was stationed at Continental Army Command, Fort Monroe, VA, in October/November 1962, and was spared the trip to Florida because my mother was about to give birth to me.

Acknowledgments

There are a lot of people and organizations that contributed to this project. The following are the ones that stand out:

Tammy T. Horton, Air Force Historical Research Agency
The Alderman, Library of the University of Virginia
Virginia Military Institute
The College of William and Mary
Donna Tabor, historian, XVIII Airborne Corps
Frank R. Shirer, chief, Historical Research Branch, US Army Center of Military History
Janis Jorgensen, manager of the Heritage Collection, US Naval Institute
Richard L. Baker, MA (MSgt, USAF ret.), senior technical information spec. GS-11
US Army Military History Institute, Army Heritage and Education Centre
Malea Walker, reference librarian, Newspaper & Current Periodical Reading Room, Library of Congress
Jean Armstrong, Wings Over The Rockies Museum, Denver Colorado
The Earth Sciences and Map Library, University of California, Berkeley
Matthew J. Seelinger, chief historian/editor, *On Point*, Army Historical Foundation
Paul Nergelovic, reference librarian, United States Military Academy Library
Robert Hanshew, US Navy Historical Research Center
David Fort, US National Archives
Nathaniel Patch, US National Archives
Cathy Cox, archivist, AFHRA/RSA
Kevin Burge, archivist, AFHRA/RS
Tim Densham
Tom Hickcox
Fred Epler
Jennifer M. Halpern, archives technician, National Declassification Center, US National Archives
Roslyn Pachoca, Newspaper & Current Periodical Room, Library of Congress

Amie V. Stone, MLS, research librarian, US Army War College Library
Ken Schlessinger, US National Archives
Lena Kaljot, reference historian, Marine Corps History Division
Ann Robson, Culpeper County Library
Stephen Plotkin, reference archivist, John F. Kennedy Presidential Library
Dwight Zimmerman, author and member of The Military Writers Society of
    America
Dino Brugioni, author and witness to the events in October of 1962
Earth Sciences and Map Library, University of California, Berkeley

Author's Foreword

When asked about the invasion that did not happen: 'Number one,' says a Navy officer, 'we would not have made any mistakes. We could not let it look like we couldn't beat Russia if we had to. We would have subjected Cuba to intensive bombardment.' 'First, you knock out the targets that can hurt you,' says a Navy man. 'We'd sterilize the island,' said a Marine flier. 'Neutralize 'em,' said the Army. 'De-sanitize them,' said the Air Force.[1]

The Cuban Missile Crisis. The mention of it used to stir ripples of fear in people. Most people alive today were not even born when the crisis took place. They have no frame of context for it. They were raised in a world that was free from the persistent and horrific threat of nuclear holocaust. To the three generations that have emerged that have no memory of the crisis, it is merely a footnote in history; a fact to be studied and forgotten when the class is over. To them, it was a surreal non-event. Their world is more dominated by the images of the World Trade Center collapsing. They should consider themselves fortunate. The War on Terror, while frightful on its own, pales in comparison to the fear of total annihilation that the Cold War presented.

I myself have no memory of the incident. My father was stationed at Fort Monroe, Virginia, when the crisis broke out. At the time, my mother was in her ninth month of pregnancy with me. Having been born on 6 November 1962, I was brought into the world a few days after the world stepped back from the brink of nuclear war. I was surprised as I did my research to learn that my birthday could very well have been the day that the invasion of Cuba would have taken place. I was raised fearing and respecting the Russians; always cognizant they possessed a vast arsenal of nuclear weapons pointed at my country. They were not as much an enemy as a looming threat. Films like *Red Dawn* and *The Day After* taught my and earlier generations that we needed to be constantly watchful, constantly prepared, ever vigilant.

In the last twenty years, more and more information has been declassified and made available about the missile crisis. New books, which thankfully presented those new details, have still managed to captivate readers. Why? What is our fascination with the crisis? What is it that compels us to look at it?

The answer is simple: It was the closest we ever came to unleashing the Third World War. We actually toyed with setting in motion a series of events, starting with air strikes and the invasion of Cuba, which could have sent the USA and the USSR on a nuclear collision course. The missile crisis represents the one event in our history where, if it had played out, the potential exists that the world would be a different place entirely. Even more tantalizing is that the image of that world was so horrible to contemplate that both sides stepped away from that precipice and opted for peace.

But what if we hadn't stepped away from war? What would have happened? How might events have unfolded? Would the war have engulfed the world in nuclear winter, or would it have been a regional conflict like Vietnam a few years later – one closer to America's shores? If nuclear weapons were employed, would they have been an all-out slugfest between the superpowers, or would it have been limited to the theatre of operations?

This was the thinking that fascinated me over the years. The books of Michael Dodd, Aleksandr Fursenko, and Timothy Naftali were not just history books; they were tense thrillers. I began to accumulate materials related to the planned invasion of Cuba. I pressed for materials to be declassified and made available. I wanted to know for myself what would have happened if calmer minds had *not* prevailed in late October of 1962, and the US had unleashed its military on the tiny island of Cuba.

The invasion of Cuba has remained one of the great 'what ifs' of the Cold War. There is no way to perfectly determine how events would have unfolded that autumn. Even those closest to the events had no idea what their reactions might have been to circumstances that never happened. Some were too terrible to contemplate, while others were simply impossible to game out. The attack and invasion of Cuba was detailed in its planning and conception. It was also based on falsifies and a lack of information. Despite the debacle of the Bay of Pigs only a year earlier, the US still believed that Cuba was an 'imprisoned island', and there were large numbers of non-Communist sympathizers that would rush to join the US in overthrowing Castro. They seemed to ignore the fact that the Cuban military was skilled in guerilla and irregular warfare. They also did not fully realize just how much training and how many modern arms had been provided to the Cuban Army. Some military planners, such as General Cutis LaMay, felt that the invasion was going to be easy, a 'walk-in'.[2] Some saw Fidel Castro's army as a rag-tag group that would fold quickly once the full might of the US military was brought to bear.

Despite its incredible level of detail, the invasion plans dramatically underestimate the number of Soviet troops on the island, or their relative combat experience. While the US estimated there were 12,000 Russians in Cuba, there were over 40,000. Military planners underestimated the number and types of conventional tanks, artillery, and other arms that they may have had to face during an invasion.

US planners did not factor in, until the very last days prior to the invasion, that the Soviet forces would have tactical nuclear weapons on the island. Even when they did take those into account, they treated it more as a footnote in their planning rather than the realization that Russian military doctrine would have called for their use. Unlike the invasions at Inchon or Iwo Jima, the Americans landing in Cuba would have potentially faced a tactical nuclear response that could have decimated some of the landing attempts.

What we do have is plans, and the dispositions of some of the combatants. It is possible to extrapolate responses based on known historical events however. This book will, for the first time, detail what might have happened if the US invaded Cuba and the ramifications around the world of such an action. This is not counterfactual history or speculative – this is based on the invasion plans themselves.

In researching this book, I was faced with a daunting task. First, was that many materials relating to the missile crisis and the state of the US and USSR military, even after five decades, remain classified. Getting access to some of these materials has proven challenging. Where gaps have existed, I have had to rely on a wide range of sources.

In some cases, the materials have been lost. As one archivist put it to me, the planned invasion (OP Plan 316-62) was never executed. If it had been, it would have been properly archived. Because it was simply a contingency plan that never happened, individual unit copies of the plan were treated as disposable material. Some branches, such as the Marine Corps, preserved their copies. Some, like the Army copies of plans, were either disposed of or are buried in boxes in holding facilities for the National Archives, and may yet one day emerge to the light of day. Other plans have been so heavily redacted that they are difficult to use. This is the case with the United States full nuclear strike plan: SIOP 62. Specific targets and damage estimates by cities are obscured. When I tried to get some of this material declassified, I was told that the US has never declassified these lists and never would. As hard as it is to believe, the 1962 nuclear attack plan details are still considered sensitive because there is a fear that modern-day terrorists might be able to leverage them.

I was fortunate enough to find enough copies of the invasion plan to painstakingly piece together the full invasion. This was no small task, and devoured my home office space with maps, plans, reams of printed material, and countless notes.

America's changing attitude to Cuba also has factored in. One archivist told me I would be facing an uphill battle to get some of the material declassified because releasing the invasion plans for Cuba, at a time when we are attempting to get to more normal relations with Cuba, might inflame some individuals. I appreciated the warning. At the same time, I think it is safe to say that in the last fifty years, the Cubans were damned well aware that we were going to invade them. It was in the newspapers and on television around the world. The details of the invasion were not likely, in my mind, to cause any sort of international incident.

The air of tension is quite real though, so their concerns are somewhat valid. In reality, the US military has never stopped planning for the invasion of Cuba. Contingency plans have been drawn up at least eleven times, as late as the year 2000, detailing for the invasion of the island.[3] I am quite sure from my probing in the archives that the Department of Defense most likely has invasion plans for every country in some way, shape, or form. But Cuba is likely one of the most active plans.

Among the challenges I faced in writing this book was the incredible amount of military acronyms used for the widespread commands and authorities involved with such an operation. It was easy to see why other authors shied away from this undertaking. The buzzwords, lingo, and acronyms make some of the invasion plan documents almost unreadable and subject to translation. For the readers of this book, I will expose these terms for context, but I have strived to keep this book readable for both laymen and historians alike.

The Cuban archival information remains mostly elusive. The missile crisis in Cuba was both a moment in the international spotlight and one of frustration and embarrassment. My requests for information from the Cuban authorities were politely ignored.

Most authors of the missile crisis attack the issue along three axis of perspective. First, the crisis is viewed through the lens of the diplomatic, political, and geopolitical implications. This is by far the most actively area of study and the most traditional route. The second axis has grown in popularity over the years; the decision-making implications of the crisis. The events in Cuba in 1962 are often cited as a case study for how leadership decision-making is executed. Third is the military aspect of the events that took place. These have almost entirely been focused on the planning for an attack and the risks of the confrontation expanding to a global thermonuclear war.

Oddly enough, the military aspects tend to be seen not on their own, but as the impetus to drive the decisions that were made. This casts the role of the military as the antagonist in the crisis. Even films from the era, such as *Dr Strangelove* and the more contemporary *Thirteen Days*, paints the military planners as evil, unbalanced men with schemes bent on igniting a global war for the sheer fun of it. This is not fair or just. It also has clouded the study of the military aspects of the crisis in regards to the invasion of Cuba. It overshadows the invasion with the ominous cloud of World War Three.

It is because of this and my strong curiosity that I opted to dig into this aspect for this work. It is this military study of the war that never was; the invasion of Cuba and its long-term implications – that is the focus of this book.

Much of the work has to be drawn upon by extrapolation and the known plans/estimates. It is impossible to factor in the individual acts of heroism and cunning that might turn the course of a battle. Indeed, this book will present a probable course of events in the invasion. It will be for future scholars in unborn generations to determine how accurate these events might be.

There was a temptation to not write the book until all of the relevant information was available, located, or declassified. But that would mean the book never would have been ready to write. After three years of gathering what information I could on the events in late 1962, the time was right to tell this story. Few authors have tried to describe the crisis in military terms and implications, and it is a field where the interest is high. Also, with the fiftieth anniversary of the events coming at the time of this publication, it is clear that this new perspective – a military one – is needed to fully understand the events that *almost* happened.

For those of you reading this book, you are in for an incredible journey. It is my intent to put you on the ground in Cuba to experience events that were forestalled through diplomacy and pure luck. Prepare to experience a series of battles that would have altered the US involvement in the Cold War.

Blaine Pardoe

CHAPTER ONE

Planning for War

We shall always have a Cuban problem.

John Quincy Adams

Origins

Logic might say, 'You don't plan the invasion of another country without a damned good reason to do it.' Reality however, points out that it is best to be prepared for any potential eventuality. In the case of the plan to invade Cuba in the autumn of 1962, it was a mix of these two concepts. There was the contingency aspect of the plan; a need to have a plan just in case a plan was ever needed. There was also the motivation aspect. The political situation in Cuba was a nagging political and diplomatic pain for the United States.

The origins of the plan to invade Cuba are important to understand. It provides a perspective as to why they were drawn up, their objectives and intended outcomes, and why they were conceived. It is this 'why', the historical background, that is of importance in the plan formulation.

Most people erroneously focus on the tension between Kennedy administration and the Castro regime. The central issues dealing with the Cuban Missile Crisis reached their pinnacle in 1962, but in reality, have their origins embedded with the Eisenhower administration.

The United States became entangled with Cuba as a result of the Spanish American War. It was on this island that Theodore Roosevelt led his Rough Riders on the charge up San Juan Hill, eventually leading to Spain being driven out of Cuba. In kicking Spain out of Cuba, America assumed an uninvited role as protector of the island. The US ended up with the base at Guantánamo in the south-east of Cuba; a perfect base in the coming decades for protecting its interests in the Panama Canal.

In exchange for including it in its sphere of influence, America took a hands-off approach with the country that it liberated. Some referred to it as America's 'good neighbor' policy – where we had a vested interest in the affairs of Cuba, but did not use our influence to protect her people.[1] Indeed, the relationship between the two countries was friendly, with American businesses investing heavily in Cuba, and the Cuban Government warmly welcoming them and the influx of tourist dollars.

Things changed in 1958, when the then Cuban President Batista was ousted from power. His downfall would mar the region for years to come. The Atlantic and Caribbean, which had been so stolid in the postwar years, suddenly changed overnight.

An Island in Turmoil

Fulgencio Batista was a character out of central casting when it came to filling the role of a Third World despot and dictator. He slid into power during a coup, first taking on the position of the Cuban Army chief of staff – using his power to sway and influence, manipulate and control several Cuban leaders. Batista purged his own officers' corps to ensure only men loyal to him were in posts of authority. Finally, after wielding power for years from behind the scenes, he became Cuba's President in 1940 and led the tiny island nation through the Second World War.

In an almost cliché style, he used his position to loot the Cuban treasury and exploit her people. His hand-picked successor took over when the people turned against him. Batista fled for a long period to the United States, but then returned to run again for the presidency in 1952. When it appeared that he would not win, his solution was to stage another coup to seize the office. Corrupt to the core, he became a pawn of organized crime and an enemy to the Cuban people. With the mob's backing, he turned Havana into a massive tourist trap, with casinos, plush hotels, and stunning beaches – while his own people slid further and deeper into poverty. American businesses found a willing ally in Batista and poured millions of dollars into the tiny island. While the President lined his own pockets, the common person in Cuba found their quality of life diminishing every year. For those that spoke out against him, Batista ordered arrests, summary executions, and retributions against family members.

After another rigged election in 1956, Batista was nearly overthrown by the Army in their own coup. He once more purged the officer ranks; in the end a horrible mistake given that the resistance against his regime was beginning to become more organized.

A young law student, Fidel Castro, eventually led a rebellion against the corrupt Batista. With his customary brutality, the President attempted to wipe out those that supported Castro – which only gave him more supporters. Until March of 1958, the US supported Batista, selling him arms to fight the insurrection. Popular support for Castro grew, and through his own manipulation of an election, he rose to power as Prime Minster of Cuba in late 1958. Batista fled for Dominican Republic, having plundered the Cuban Government.

The Castro Issue

Fidel Castro was not just a revolutionary leader, but one with Socialist leanings. Castro was well educated and highly motivated by the plight of the Cuban people. He favored the traditional course of Communism to come to power through violent revolution. In his native Cuba, he found the ideal grounds for such a revolt. The vast majority of the population was oppressed by the Batista regime, supported by the Capitalist US. Castro set up a sophisticated, cell-based revolutionary group called 'The Movement'. Their staged attacks against the Batista Government were not largely successful, but garnered popular support from the oppressed Cuban people. Castro led these operations from a concealed base at Gran Piedra in the rugged Sierra Maestra Mountains.

He was eventually apprehended for coordinating an attack on an army barracks, and in a show-trial, he was sentenced to prison. Batista underestimated Castro's influence and eventually released him, only to have Castro reorganize his cells and revolt against the Government. For two years, Fidel, his brother Raul, and Che Guevara waged war against Batista and his people. By 1958, most of the Oriente Province, especially the mountainous areas, was under the control of Castro and his revolutionaries. Batista had no choice but to come down on the revolt, sending in 10,000 soldiers against Castro's paltry band of 300.

Castro refused to fight fair. They did not engage in a straight up confrontation with their opponents, instead they laid land mines, staged careful ambushes – they fought and ran rather than engage in the kind of battle that favored their enemy. After weeks of battling and slow bleeding losses, the Batista military withdrew.

Fidel was not the only revolutionary leader in Cuba at the time. With Batista's fall, another leader, General Cantillo, attempted to stage a military junta, in the process betraying Castro. Fidel's manipulation of the events saved Cuba from simply changing from Batista to another oppressive leader, and for that, the Cuban people saw him as a savior of sorts. On 6 February 1959, Fidel was named Cuban Premier.

As he consolidated power, Castro initiated land reforms to give property ownership to the poor, something they had been denied under the previous regime. This only fueled his popularity, but was the first hint of his Marxist tendencies to the world. By 1959, Castro began to nationalize industries in Cuba, stripping ownership from US-based companies such as Shell and Standard Oil. The US was Cuba's largest importer, mostly of their sugar production. When Castro began to strip American companies of their assets, the US Government responded by restricting the amount of sugar that was imported. Castro responded with a massive agrarian reform and nationalized Cuba's sugar production as well, further hurting US interests. Land was taken from the corporations and provided to the people. When he began making overtures to the USSR, it became clear that the US was facing a Communist Government at its own back door.

The tit-for-tat between the two Governments reached a diplomatic peak in October 1960 when the Eisenhower administration imposed a partial embargo on

Cuba. Fidel Castro realized that his primary source of income (sugar) and all of his imported oil supplies were at risk of crushing his already fragile economy. Castro needed international friends, and he turned to the Soviet Union for assistance.

Castro's Socialist leanings were not new, but he began to see the need to solidify his relationship with the USSR. As the US stepped up its harsher tones toward his policies, he realized that irritating the large neighbor to the north might come back to bite him.

To say that Fidel Castro's support with the people was unanimous would have been a gross exaggeration. There was a portion of the population that did not like the Socialist list to the left of the Government. Other dissidents were those that had been profiting under the Batista regime and longed for a return to those days. Those that could afford it fled Cuba, many heading to Florida and the states of the Gulf Coast. This led to even more tension with the US Government, which now had to deal with this unexpected influx of immigrants. The dissatisfied that could not afford to leave simply remained and waited, assuming that at some point the Castro Government would be replaced by coup or election; coups had become so common in Cuba and the rest of Latin America that it was a reasonable expectation.

In February 1960, the Castro brothers and their trusted aide Ché Guevara finally persuaded the Soviets to send a delegation, under the leadership of Deputy Premier Anastas Mikoyen, to visit Cuba. The pretext for these talks was to solidify the relationship between the two nations. While the USSR saw potential in Cuba, the Castro regime simply seemed too good to be true – a potential Communist satellite nation only a few miles off the coast of America. It was a possibility that was too tempting to ignore. There were also concerns as to just how Socialist Fidel Castro was. To the press, the story was that the visit was to promote Cuban and Soviet friendship; in reality, it began a series of events that would eventually lead to the missile crisis.[1]

Early Invasion Planning

Contingency planning has always been a part of military preparation. Contingency plans are designed to be operational missions that can be pulled out in certain circumstances and employed. The Pentagon planners have a wide range of contingency plans dealing with almost every country on the planet.

Such contingency plans often lack specific objectives, but are designed to simply get 'boots on the ground' in a country. Military and political objectives are often designated later, after an initial invasion. The intent is that in the event of an emergency, such as, 'Mexico becomes a hostile Communist state,' the plans are broken out and used as the starting point to plan invasions and occupations. Contingency plans differed from war plans (referred to as the Strategic Capabilities Plan) in that the war plans were designed to achieve the suppression and destruction of a specific enemy to wage war. Most contingency plans, except for those against known enemies of the United States, are deliberately vague and do not go into details beyond ten to fifteen days after an invasion.

In the case of Cuba, there had been no contingency plans drawn up prior to 1959. It was most likely not seen as necessary given the friendliness of the Batista Government to America. However, with Castro's rise to power, that attitude changed significantly. The need for some sort of potential plan for invading Cuba needed to be at least considered.

Since 1947, the responsibility for Cuba fell in the geographic boundaries of the US Atlantic Command. Specifically, the responsibility for any military operations involving Cuba fell to the commander in chief of the Atlantic Command, or CINCLANT. CINCLANT was charged with the preparation of strategic and logistic plans, strategic and operation direction of his assigned forces, conduct of combat operations, and any other necessary function of command required to accomplish his mission.[3]

The CINCLANT in 1962 was Admiral Robert L. Dennison. Dennison was an old-school naval officer. The Pennsylvania native was a 1923 graduate of the US Naval Academy. Dennison was extremely intelligent. He secured a master's degree from Pennsylvania State College in 1930, and a doctorate in engineering from John Hopkins University five years later. As a younger officer, Dennison had commanded the USS *Ortlan*, the submarine USS *Cutterfish*, and the destroyer USS *John Ford* up until the outbreak of the Second World War. He rose in position to be the chief of staff to the commander of Allied Naval Forces, East Australia.

As the war continued on, Dennison became the chief of staff to the commander of the amphibious force of the Pacifica Fleet (9th Amphibious Force). In this role, he helped plan and execute the invasions of Attu and Kiska in the Aleutian Islands. While relatively small amphibious operations, these landings proved to be logistically challenging.

Dennison's intelligence drew him to work on the Joint Chiefs of Staff in the Joint War Plans Committee for the bulk of the war. After the surrender of Japan, he commanded the battleship USS *Missouri*, which gave him the chance to meet, and apparently impress, President Truman. The President was so impressed he named Dennison as his naval aide.

After the Truman administration, Dennison was promoted to Admiral and put in command of the Pacific First Fleet. In 1959, he was placed into his role as commander in chief of the Atlantic Command.[4] Such a role, even in the postwar era, was not seen as an overly demanding position. If war broke out, it would take a lot of fighting before the Soviet Union became a real threat in the Atlantic. Aside from both sides, Dennison's role in commanding the Atlantic was one that *should* have led to a relatively comfortable position. As a person, Dennison was a true navy man. On his desk, his nameplate read, 'Bob Dennison, Sailor.' The Admiral enjoyed a good golf game and topped of his evenings with a stiff drink.[5] Posting to Norfolk, Virginia, in peacetime should have been a quiet and peaceful way to end a distinguished career. That would change in 1962. In his role, pulling together a contingency plan for dealing with an invasion of Cuba fell onto his shoulders. If that plan was executed, Bob Dennison would have been the man to command the forces.

In terms of Cuba, the initial planning in late 1959 was based on the premise of three circumstances that might trigger a US invasion. First was that the United States, acting under the terms of the Inter-American Treaty of Reciprocal Assistance, would be engaged to protect either Haiti or the Dominican Republic if they found themselves attacked by Cuba or Venezuela. The second trigger was a series of events that would be seen as falling short of a full, general war – to deploy to any country in the region quickly in order to support a broader military plan. It was this second trigger that became the crux of CINCLANT's invasion plans drawn up in 1959.[6]

Drawn up in mid-1959, OP Plan (Operational Plan) 310-60 was intended to address the broad contingency plan for the entire Caribbean, including Cuba.[7] This version of the plan was incomplete and dealt mostly with mobilization of forces rather than any specific invasion plans.

Admiral Dennison and his staff realized quickly that to fulfill the objectives of such a plan and deal specifically with Cuba as an invasion target, it required a joint-services task force. In 1959, the thought was that it would involve the forces that fell under the commander of the US 2nd Fleet and the necessary Air Force and Army units. Command of the Army forces would be the commanding general of the XVIII Airborne Corps out of Fort Bragg, North Carolina.

The Army planning group began work on a plan, working somewhat in isolation, to address an invasion to Cuba. By late 1959, the headquarters of the XVIII, under Lieutenant General Howze, drew up their own plan – STRAC OP Plan (Standards in Training Commission Operational Plan) 51-59.[8] This plan called for the invasion of Cuba by an airborne force, consisting of elements of the 82nd Airborne Division augmented by elements of the 101st Airborne. The airborne troops would assault two airports outside of Havana: the Jose Marti International Airport (known at the time as Batista Airfield) and San Antonio de los Banos Airport. These airfields were to the south and south-west of Havana.

Once these two airfields were secured, additional forces could be landed by transport aircraft to reinforce and resupply the airborne troops. Both divisions would drive through Havana proper to the port of Regla and the harbor fortifications at Morro Castle. Regla was seen as an important aspect of the plan since it ensured that heavier (armored) troops could be safely landed to assist the airborne troops. Once a surface echelon was brought in at Regla, it would be able to move using the network of highways out of Havana to the south-east to link up with American forces at Guantánamo Bay.[9]

The headquarters of the XVIII Airborne Corps felt that the forces they planned for the mission, two reinforced battle groups under a division command, and control from the 82nd Airborne Division alone was going to be enough to handle the job.[10] Reality was that in 1959, with the Cuban military and Government in turmoil, that might have been the case. But there were risks; a fighting force of lightly reinforced infantry moving through an urban combat environment like Havana could potentially become bogged down and bottlenecked.

Admiral Dennison's staff requested a variant of STRAC OP Plan 51-59 in December 1959. Rather than simply two battle groups, the suggestion was made to include the entire 82nd Airborne Division and that the deployment would need to be done on short notice. Also, the need for armored forces was seen as important, so the plans were altered to include the landing of a squadron of armored cavalry that would be flown into the secured airports. The armored force that was designated for this plan was the 2nd Armored Division. This plan, OP STRAC OP Plan 51-59A, required a much larger commitment from the Air Force's TAC (Tactical Air Command), specifically the 19th Air Force, and required approval from the Joint Chiefs of Staff, since it involved the deployment of the entire 82nd Airborne Division.[11]

As Castro began to consolidate power and demonstrate his Communist leanings, it became clear that the plans as outlined in STRAC OP Plan 51-59A were not going to suffice. By January of 1961, the Cuban Government was seen as 'Communist-controlled,' and 'in open league with the Soviet Union and Communist China.'[12] CIA reports were indicating a flow of conventional arms and armor to Cuba from the Soviet Union as Fidel Castro reshaped and rearmed the Cuban Armed Forces. It was becoming clear that a single airborne division attempting to seize a port might not be sufficient to deal with this rising military power. A new plan was needed to deal with invading Cuba.

In December 1960, in a conference room in Norfolk, Virginia, Admiral Dennison convened a larger conference to plan for a contingency invasion of Cuba. Representatives from US CONARC (Continental Army Command), Tactical Air Command, the US Second Fleet, Fleet Marine Force Atlantic, and the Atlantic Amphibious Force were assumed to tackle the complicated task. The conference arrived at pulling together two revised plans. First was a version of OP Plan 51-59A on steroids – also designed as OP Plan 312-60. Two full divisions of airborne infantry reinforced by air-landed light armor would be used to seize the port at Regla, where the rest of the surface echelon would be landed. The second plan retained the essence of OP Plan 51-59A – using the airborne forces to secure airfields, augmented by a simultaneous amphibious assault.[13] Both plans had merits depending on the circumstances, so neither one was favored over the other. While both plans had potential flaws, in many respects they would become the core of what would be the eventual invasion plan for Cuba two years later.

The Less-Than-Covert War Begins

President Dwight Eisenhower's administration was the first that was forced to deal with the premise of a Socialist Government in the western hemisphere. President

Eisenhower initiated two efforts – one covert, one military. On 17 March 1960, the President approved a recommendation from the 5412 Committee at a meeting of the US National Security Council (NSC). The 5412 Committee was a 'Special Group' tasked with outlining and coordinating Government covert operations. Their plan outlined:

A Program of Covert Action Against the Castro Regime

1. Objective: The purpose of the program outlined herein is to bring about the replacement of the Castro regime with one more devoted to the true interests of the Cuban people and more acceptable to the US in such a manner as to avoid any appearance of US intervention. Essentially, the method of accomplishing this end will be to induce, support, and so far as possible direct action, both inside and outside of Cuba, by selected groups of Cubans of a sort that they might be expected to and could undertake on their own initiative. Since a crisis inevitably entailing drastic action in or toward Cuba could be provoked by circumstances beyond control of the US before the covert action program has accomplished its objective, every effort will be made to carry it out in such a way as progressively to improve the capability of the US to act in a crisis.

2. Summary Outline: The program contemplates four major courses of action:

a. The first requirement is the creation of a responsible, appealing, and unified Cuban opposition to the Castro regime, publicly declared as such and therefore necessarily located outside of Cuba. (Remainder redacted.)

b. So that the opposition may be heard and Castro's basis of popular support undermined, it is necessary to develop the means for mass communication to the Cuban people so that a powerful propaganda offensive can be initiated in the name of the declared opposition. The major tool proposed to be used for this purpose is a long and short wave broadcasting facility, probably to be located on Swan Island. (Remainder redacted.)

c. Work is already in progress in the creation of a covert intelligence and action organization within Cuba, which will be responsive to the orders and directions of the exile opposition. (Remainder redacted.)

d. Preparations have already been made for the development of an adequate paramilitary force outside of Cuba, together with mechanisms for the necessary logistic support of covert military operations on the Island. Initially, a cadre of leaders will be recruited after careful screening and trained as paramilitary instructors. In a second phase, a number of paramilitary cadres will be trained at secure locations outside of the US so as to be available for immediate deployment into Cuba to organize, train, and lead resistance forces recruited there, both before and after the establishment of one or more active centers of resistance. The creation of this capability will require a minimum of six months and probably closer to eight. In the meanwhile, a limited air capability for resupply and for infiltration and exfiltration already exists under CIA control, and can be rather easily expanded if and when the situation requires. Within two months, it is hoped to parallel this with a small air resupply capability under deep cover as a commercial operation in another country.[14]

In this sweeping set of actions, the US stepped down a path that caused the missile crisis, and set in motion the need to prepare for an invasion of Cuba. The full scope of covert operations waged against the Castro regime remain classified even today. Several highly public incidents did occur that could be attributed to such activities. The freighter *La Coubre*, filled with Belgium arms and ammunition, exploded in Havana harbor on 4 March 1960. The explosion killed between 75 and 100 people, and left more than 200 injured.[15] Fidel Castro firmly believed that this was an act of sabotage by the United States, even going so far as to say that it was a crime as infamous as the sinking of the USS *Maine* – which had been the spark that had ignited the Spanish American War. If the covert war was designed to intimidate the Government in Havana, it only seemed to galvanize it.

The CIA, under Alan Dulles, initiated plans to use the refugee community to perhaps overthrow or oust Fidel Castro from power. The plan they conceived, at least on paper, seemed to be sound. Assuming that there were many Cubans on the island that would welcome the chance to rise up against Castro if the opportunity presented itself, the US would fund and support arming a brigade of Cuban refugees and assist them with the invasion of their home country. This 'liberation' of the Cuban people would be backed by the US military, who would also logistically support the effort.

Active recruitment commenced and training bases were established in the US and other Latin American countries, complete with CIA instructors. Detailed planning was undertaken. The plan called to land the brigade (Brigade 2506) at Trinidad, Cuba, south and east of Havana. The city had a good port facility and was considered to be close to where forces acting against Castro were operating. The 20,000 plus population of Trinidad was thought to have fragile loyalties to the new Castro Government, which would help the invaders. The beaches where the assault would take place were easily defensible, and should the operation fail, the Escambray Mountain were close enough for Brigade 2506 to fall back into to carry on the fight as guerillas.

Brigade 2506 was initially conceived as being made up of a paratrooper battalion, three infantry battalions, and a heavy-weapons battalion armed with mortars, recoilless rifles, and heavy machine guns. The unit was also supposed to have an armored infantry battalion equipped with armored trucks and a tank company outfitted with new US Army M 41 tanks. These numbers were modified downward, again with the aim of limiting the international exposure of the United States.

The key to the entire operation was air superiority. The CIA would be providing the Cubans with Second World War surplus B-26 bombers, which were intended to attack Castro's airfields at the start of the campaign. They were intended to wipe out the Cuban Air Force, which would take some pressure off of the landings. The US would poise several ships off of the base at Guantánamo Bay to create the illusion that the invasion would be taking place there, hopefully misleading Castro's forces.

Things changed in 1960 when John F. Kennedy was elected President. One of President Eisenhower's last acts in office in January 1961 was to formally sever diplomatic relations with Cuba – leaving the new President to deal with the Cuban situation. Also in January 1961, President Kennedy was fully briefed on the planned operation. The State Department had reservations about the landing site being so close to Havana; Castro's epicenter of power. The new President asked that an alternate landing site be chosen in March 1961. President Kennedy preferred a low-key night time invasion that did not closely link the US with the brigade's efforts. The new landing beaches, located at Bahía de Cochinos, Playa Giròn (the Bay of Pigs), were on the south side of Cuba.[16]

Even by this point, the flaws in the plan were starting to emerge. Firstly, within the CIA, questions were being raised about whether the timing had already passed for such an action. In a memo entitled, 'Is time on our side in Cuba?' CIA officials point out that Castro's power was not weakening over time, but growing.[17] His reforms socially and economically were only cementing him in power, rather than sowing the seeds of counter-revolution. Since a general uprising of the Cuban people was crucial to removing Castro from power, even in the ranks of the CIA the premise of the operation was being called into question.

Secondly, the Joint Chiefs of Staff were internally questioning the soundness of the invasion. A Pentagon team that inspected Brigade 2506 pointed out that, 'An aircraft armed with 50-calibre machine guns could sink all or most of the invasion force.'[18] Even their positive words were thin at best. In a message from the Joint Chiefs of Staff to Secretary of Defense McNamara, their evaluation of the operation concluded that, 'Since the Cuban Army is without experience in coordinated offensive action, the invasion force should be able to successfully resist the initial attacks,' but, 'Lacking a popular uprising or substantial follow-on forces, the Cuban Army could eventually reduce the beachhead.' They went on to say that, '… The operation as presently envisaged would not necessarily require overt US intervention.' 'The Joint Chiefs of Staff consider that timely execution of this plan has a "fair" chance of ultimate success, and even if it does not achieve the full results desired, could contribute to the eventual overthrow of the Castro regime.'[19]

Thirdly, the location chosen for the landing of the brigade at the Bay of Pigs was filled with geographic pitfalls. The nearest sizeable airfield that the brigade could potentially secure was 60 miles away. They were almost the same distance from the mountains that they intended to use as their base of operations against Fidel Castro. The bay itself posed issues; there were deep salt marshes on one flank, which would bog them down from moving inland and hem them in when counter-attacked. At the time planning was underway, it was seen as useful terrain, for the marshland would hinder a Cuban attack from that sector. Fourthly, the assault beach was so far from Havana, it would provide Castro time to mobilize and organize a strong counter-attack.

Finally, the CIA had failed to maintain intelligence of their activities in preparing to invade. Even as early as November 1960, the *New York Times* was reporting on the CIA training camps in Guatemala, and *The Nation* magazine ran an article, 'Are We Training Cuban Guerrillas?'[20]

Also, members of the Cuban national community were freely discussing the recruitment efforts taking place in their community. Leaks were everywhere, alerting the Cuban Government that some sort of invasion was forthcoming. Of equal importance, the coming invasion was being funded and prepared by the United States Government.

The exiles invasion plan was based on the premise of surprise; establishing a foothold on Cuba before the Castro Government could mobilize an effective counter-attack. The change of locations, the leaks, and press coverage hamstrung those efforts even before the invasion was initiated.

The Bay of Pigs Debacle

The Eisenhower administration had left the ultimate decision for going ahead with the invasion with the new Kennedy administration. Despite all of the flaws, the CIA still felt that the attempt would be worthwhile. If it was not immediately successful, it might spark counter-revolution in Cuba and topple Castro. At best it was a blind hope; one that not even the entire community at the CIA subscribed to.

President Kennedy's stipulations as to relocating the landing site and minimizing the exposure to the United States had dire consequences that few of his advisers voiced. The CIA pushed strongly for the invasion to take place, despite the growing body of evidence showing that the attempt had little chance of success.

Fidel Castro was aware that an invasion was coming, although he did not know where, or if it would be the United States Marines/Army coming. He sent his army to probable invasion beaches and took the precaution of camouflaging or outright dispersing of his air force, knowing that an air attack would precede any invasion.[21]

On 15 April 1961, eight B-26 bombers of the 'Cuban Expeditionary Force' struck at key Cuban airbases. Commanded by the refugees of the invasion force, it was initially thought they had crippled the Cuban Air Force. Fidel's concealment efforts had paid off, however, and a significant number of planes survived.

On 17 April, the landing force came ashore in the Bay of Pigs. The operation called for a follow-up series of air strikes to finish off the Cuban Air Force, but President Kennedy put that element of the operation on hold, at the last minute. This effort effectively left the men of Brigade 2506 landing with no immediate air cover or support.

The Cuban defenders at the Bay of Pigs was initially 900 militia men from a nearby sugar mill, but Castro quickly reinforced them with a battalion of militia in Matanzas Province, including three mortar batteries. Three additional battalions were thrown onto the two major highways needed by the invaders to drive inland. They were effectively bottled-up on the beach.

At first light, the refugees dropped 177 of their paratroopers south of the Australian sugar mill on the road to Palpite and Playa Larga. Their mission, tagged 'Operation Falcon', was to seize the road and block it to prevent the Cuban militia and regular troops from reaching the beach. Operation Falcon was botched from the moment the paratroopers jumped. Thirty of them landed in the swamps, as did all of their heavy equipment that was necessary to take out Cuban tanks. The result was that the paratroopers were unable to block the road or even hinder access. The beaches lay wide open for the Cuban Armed Forces to drive down on the still landing amphibious forces.

The Cuban Air Force struck at first light, catching some of the landing forces as they hit the beaches. Fidel Castro had armed his old T-33 aircraft, something that the CIA had not known or factored into their planning. The forces in the Bay of Pigs withered under bombs and strafing runs. The supply freighter *Rio Escondido* was attacked and sunk by a rocket hit from a Cuban fighter. The ship was loaded with ten days of reserves of ammunition and the majority of food, hospital supplies, and gasoline to be used by the landing force. The other key supply freighter used by the expeditionary force, the *Houston,* was also sunk by the Cuban Air Force. Its loss sealed the fates of the counter-revolutionaries trying to get off of the beaches.

The Cuban Armed Forces moved in tanks on the roads leading to the encircled beachhead. Even though they were Second World War surplus, they were more than what Brigade 2506 could hope to muster. With air supremacy on Castro's side, the American-backed forces were hemmed in by the swamps and the increasing number of Cuban Army troops. The CIA had war-gamed this type of scenario, but always under the assumption that the Brigade had all of its supplies and ammunition ashore. With the loss of their principle supply ships, the counter-revolutionary force could not hope to penetrate inland to wage any sort of guerilla war.

A call went out for direct American military intervention – both by air and by sea. Forces were poised to go in, but President Kennedy was concerned about how the international community might view such a blatant use of force. It would have been seen as yet another episode of the American Yankees imposing their will on a tiny Latin American country. Pleas on the behalf of the US military were made to send in fighters to take out the Cuban Air Force that was pummeling the men on the beach, but in the end, the President held his hand and ordered a withdrawal.

By the early morning of 19 April, the remnants of the expeditionary force were surrounded, and 'under artillery fire with tanks and vehicles to both the east and west'.[22] The order went out to the US Navy to evacuate all of the invasion force that could be safely extracted. When the Navy departed that evening, only 14 of the brigade had been rescued. Another 1,189 were forced into surrender, handing Fidel Castro a significant military and political victory.

The Change to a Covert War

The Bay of Pigs debacle was one that was destined to have long term implications for Cuba and the relations with the United States. From a military standpoint, the changes that the White House had made to the planning, such as insisting on a change of landing site, restricting the use of US military force, etc., had all but ensured disaster for the Cubans landing to remove Castro. From the White House perspective, the disastrous invasion had been recommended by the CIA and the Pentagon, and the President felt he had been given assurances as to the probability of success that were at best, fictitious. With all parties pointing at each other for the failure, it created an atmosphere that was to cloud thinking, decisions, and actions going forward for the next year and a half.

In the post-Bay of Pigs thinking, Cuba was a threat that deserved even more attention. A message from the White House to the secretaries of defense and state, and the director of the CIA, outlined the risks that Cuba still presented, which was identified as 'The Five Threats':

a. It might join with the USSR in setting up an offensive air or missile base.

b. It might build up sufficient conventional military strengths to trigger an arms race in the hemisphere and threaten the independence of other Latin American nations.

c. It might develop its covert subversive network in ways which would threaten other Latin American nations from within.

d. Its ideological contours are a moral and political offence to us; and we are committed, by one means or another, to remove that offence, including our commitment to the Cuban refugees among us.

e. Its ideological contours and success may tend to inflame disruptive forces in the rest of Latin America, accentuating existing economic, social, and political tensions, which we, in any case, confront.[23]

The CIA began planning for the covert overthrow of Fidel Castro, since outright invasion seemed off the plate. The problem was that the White House was less than enthusiastic about another CIA-sponsored initiative so close on the heels of the Bay of Pigs. The CIA saw few risks in attempting to kill or overthrow Fidel Castro. If it succeeded, the region would be stabilized. If it failed, they would have successfully established an underground network in Cuba that might prove useful in future operations.

On 30 November 1961, a variant of the plan, code named 'Operation Mongoose', was approved by President Kennedy. There were some restrictions on the management of the operation. It was to be led by General Edward Lansdale – a man that the CIA considered something of a loose cannon. The leadership of Operation Mongoose was to be done by the Special Group Augmented (SGA), an inter-agency task force led by the President's brother attorney General Robert Kennedy. The CIA-managed operation was being led by someone the agency would not have chosen, and was being directed outside of the CIA. It was going to take some time for the agency to move out of the shadows of the Bay of Pigs debacle.

Lansdale's operation had broad parameters, all aimed at toppling Fidel Castro from power or otherwise disposing of him. Some acts were minor, such as organizing and encouraging work slow-downs. Most were more open, such as establishing and arming guerilla bands and a hard intelligence network on the island. Demonstrations were to be organized and the Government and military were to be infiltrated by 'freedom fighters.' Lansdale believed that Mongoose would eventually lead to outright revolution. He still believed that in the final stages of any uprising, US military force might need to be called upon.[24] As such, the continued planning for an invasion of Cuba remained important from a military perspective.

In terms of a covert program, Operation Mongoose was both a success and a failure. It would eventually involve over 400 Americans and 2,000 Cubans:

A private navy of speedboats, and an annual budget of some $50 million. Task Force W carries out a wide range of activities, mostly against Cuban ships and aircraft outside Cuba (and non-Cuban ships engaged in Cuban trade), such as contaminating shipments of sugar from Cuba and tampering with industrial products imported into the country.[25]

Despite these activities, by 25 July 1962, General Lansdale was reporting that, 'Time is running out for the US to make a free choice on Cuba.' President Kennedy was given several options, including cancelling Operation Mongoose. In a meeting with the SGA, he opted to, 'Exert all possible diplomatic, economic, psychological, and all other pressures to overthrow the Castro/Communist regime without overt employment of the US military.'[26]

By August 1962, the CIA prepared a list of potential assassination targets in Cuba. But as Lansdale noted, the window of opportunity for the US intervention in Cuba was narrowing. While there were some stunning public bombings and sabotage efforts, there was little support for a broad public uprising in Cuba. Fidel Castro's grip on power was growing stronger, rather than weaker. Mongoose was still an active program by the time of the Cuban Missile Crisis a few months later.

Refining the Military Plans

Only a few days after the Bay of Pigs, Admiral Dennison's staff asked for a revised contingency plan to be drawn up. On 28 April 1961 (following the break in diplomatic relations with Cuba), CINCLANT drafted a separate contingency plan for Cuba, OP Plan 312-61.[27] This plan was still vague in its execution, but relied on using a simultaneous airborne and amphibious assault of Cuba. One of its most significant changes was a shift to an extended air campaign prior to an invasion. Previous OP Plans had opted more for a quick-strike, with the air war unfolding at the same time as the landings, or just slightly before. OP Plan 312-61 increased the Air Force's role in the operation significantly. The proposed bombing campaign to neutralize the Cuban Air Force and destroy ground troops and targets was scheduled to last for a minimum of four days, with a maximum of eighteen, before the landing of troops on the island.

OP Plan 312-61 was much more robust in terms of the weight of forces the US would be bringing to bear against Cuba. The Army element was designated as Task Force 125. It was to consist of the entire 82nd Airborne Division, an infantry brigade, an armored cavalry regiment, a medium tank battalion, and an artillery battalion (with 8-inch howitzers). The plan called for as much of the 82nd Airborne that military transport could carry to be dropped in one wave. There were no specific plans for how the remaining forces would be landed, although the plan called for the capture of Regla.

The nexus of OP Plan 312-61 was that the assault on Cuba would be both by airborne and amphibious assaults, with the seaborne marine contingent landing at the resort beach of Tarará, east of Havana. The heavier armor and artillery would come ashore at the Port of Regla, which the 82nd Airborne was tasked with securing only a few hours after their initial assault. OP Plan 312-61 was designed to seize and cut-off Havana, presumably capturing Castro or his military command in the process – though he was not named specifically.

No sooner than OP Plan 312-61 was drawn up, CINCLANT ordered a revision. The intelligence reports brought in by the CIA Mongoose teams indicated that the Cubans were being equipped with Soviet tanks and artillery. The new plan, OP Plan 312-61 (revised) added the 101st Airborne Division back into the mix and elements of the 2nd Marine Division. Furthermore, the armored cavalry regiment was replaced by the 1st Armored Division. These additions were to counter not only the increased Cuban fire power now believed to be on the island, but to add additional objectives for the Task Force 125 elements; in this case, the airfield at Baracoa and the Port of Mariel some 25-miles west of Havana.[28]

The staff of the XVIII Airborne Corps, assigned to command Task Force 125, began to work on adjusting their detailed plans. As they worked on these plans, they began to leverage the work done earlier in the Army's STRAC OP Plan 51-59. This plan was suddenly considered viable again, despite the Bay of Pigs debacle. Before they could reign in these often duplicative plans, the Army updated STRAC

Evolution of the Planned Invasion of Cuba

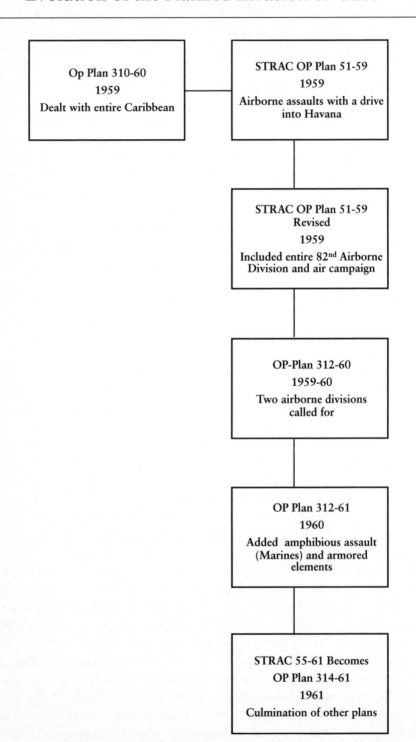

OP Plan 55-61. While maintaining a predominantly Army-centered view towards the invasion, the update was filed 5 October 1961, a full year before the missile crisis.[29]

The updates to both of these plans (STRAC OP Plan 55-61 and OP Plan 312-61 (revised)) were drawn up with almost no reliance on a general uprising by the Cuban population. One thing the Bay of Pigs had shown was that the Cuban populace was not laying in wait for an invasion force to throw off the shackles of Communism. If the US gained nothing from the Bay of Pigs, it was a better understanding of the political leanings of the Cuban people.

The culmination of all of this planning and re-planning was a consolidated invasion plan developed between July 1961 and October 1962, when STRAC OP Plan 55-61was re-designated, at the behest of the CINCLANT, as OP Plan 314-61. Once approved by Admiral Dennison, Army Staging Area Command conducted surveys of Homestead, McCoy, McDill, and Patrick Air Force bases in Florida, with eyes on turning them into forward bases for operations against Cuba.[30] These Army needs were not coordinated at all with the Air Force's planning, which also saw these bases as critical for their operations.

All of these changes reflected the tensions and international pressures that the Kennedy administration and the Pentagon were facing. The Berlin Crisis of 1961 had forced a major revision of war plans and contingencies to deal with the possible scenarios regarding the divided city of Berlin. Korea was still a relatively fresh wound in the minds of military planners. There was also a wave of planning associated with another far eastern country, Vietnam, which was beginning to draw the interests of the United States. Military planning was being stretched to the limits, and keeping all of these contingencies straight was a tricky job all on its own. With minor adjustments, OP Plan 314-61 would serve as the basis of the final plans that would be leveraged for the intended invasion of Cuba during the missile crisis.[31]

The US Government was not the only one to begin to undertake changes based on the Bay of Pigs fiasco. The Castro regime had come to realize through the Bay of Pigs and the covert war of sabotage and subterfuge of Operation Mongoose that the US focus on Cuba was not waning. It was destined to force the Cubans to turn to the USSR for military support – and would lay the foundation for the coming crisis.

CHAPTER TWO

The Arming of Cuba

The United States had already tried to topple Castro by supporting the Bay of Pigs invasion, and next time, Khrushchev surmised, it would certainly do the job correctly. Khrushchev also thought Kennedy weak and easily pressured into action by hard-liners in the CIA and the Pentagon, who no doubt were maneuvering him closer to an invasion every day.[1]

The Inevitable

In some respects, the eventual placement of strategic missiles, bombers, and Soviet troops in Cuba was inescapable. Its roots were intertwined with several events in the early Cold War years, especially the Berlin Crisis of 1961.

Berlin had been a troublesome spot for the victors of the Second World War almost from the outset. Thanks to the terms of the agreement at the Yalta Conference of 1945, Germany was carved up among the Allies. Berlin fell within the Soviet zone of occupation, but the city itself was further divided by the Allies. Most of the Governments recognized the words of Lenin: 'Whoever controls Berlin controls Germany, and whoever controls Germany controls Europe.'

While Berlin was nestled in what would eventually become East Germany, there was a great deal of reluctance to turn the capital of Germany over to Communist influence. The idealist intent of the Western Allies was that the city would be needed one day when Germany was ready to reunite, something that the war-torn Soviets were deeply opposed to.

The first Berlin Crisis was in 1948, when Joseph Stalin attempted to strong-arm control of the city from his former Allies. His blockade of Berlin's road, railroads, and canals was aimed at forcing the Western Allies to turn to the USSR for supplies to keep the population alive, essentially turning over control of the city to the Soviets and their puppet East German Communist Government. Stalin was counting on the fact that the Allies would not risk going to war over the still war-shattered city and would relinquish it to him eventually.

The Americans, British, and French mobilized a response to Stalin's blockade with the Berlin Airlift. Led by the Americans, transport aircraft flew around the clock to keep the citizens in the city fed and fueled. It was a strain, but it was a move that Stalin had no counter to, short of shooting down the transport aircraft. The USSR found itself facing the same problem that the Western Allies did; they did not want to go to war over Berlin – especially with the United States having such a superior edge in terms of a nuclear arsenal. By April 1949, the Soviets ended the blockade with little fanfare; what did not disappear was the desire for Berlin to come under their control.

With the ascent of Nikita Sergeyevich Khrushchev as Stalin's successor, he found himself facing the same unresolved desire when it came to Berlin. By 1960, Berlin was becoming more of a problem than ever before. The Marshall Plan and the recovery of Western Germany, along with the portion of Berlin that the Western Allies controlled, was much more rapid and prosperous than that of the Soviet-dominated portions. Berlin had gone from being just a splintered city in the heart of East Germany to a hub of emigration to the west. Hundreds of thousands of East Germans or East Berliners migrated to the west seeking better paying jobs and a better lifestyle. Communist-controlled portions of Germany were hemorrhaging some of their best and brightest people, and the pressures on Khrushchev were mounting.

In 1958, the Soviet Premier attempted to turn his Berlin problem into a resolution of the goals that Stalin and pressed for in 1948. He issued an ultimatum to make Berlin a free and demilitarized city, turning over its administration to the East German Government. The Western Allies would have access to the city, but it would in essence fall under Communist domination.

To the Western Allies, this demand, and the overt dissolving of the existing treaty regarding Berlin, was unacceptable. By 1959, the Soviets withdrew their ultimatum after their former Allies turned it down. As Eisenhower described the Soviet threats, 'All outstanding international questions should be settled, not by the application of force, but by peaceful means through negotiations.'[2] All that this did was leave the matter unresolved by the time that John Kennedy was elected as the new American President in 1960. With a new administration stepping in, Premier Khrushchev saw an opportunity to once more force the Berlin issue to the forefront. At the Vienna summit on 4 June 1961, he once more asserted his threat to recognize the East German Government and end the four-power control of Berlin. President Kennedy's response was to call for more troops to be drafted, and more spending on conventional weapons. He did not pledge to go to war over Berlin, or even offer a tangible counterproposal to the USSR short of additional talks. Kennedy reaffirmed that he would not surrender Berlin, having secured its rights in fighting the Germans and by treaty at the end of the Second World War.

Khrushchev was a seasoned politician, having risen up through the ranks in the oppressive and brutal Stalinist USSR. Kennedy was young and inexperienced in terms of international diplomacy. It is clear that Khrushchev sensed this. In the events that would follow, his interpretation of Kennedy and his softness would play a key role.

The East German President Walter Ulbricht persuaded Khrushchev that only the use of force could stem the exodus of East Germans across the border to the West or into Berlin. The plan he called for was to physically block off East Germany and Berlin by erecting a wall. President Ulbricht had his Government covertly began stockpiling the materials necessary for such a barrier – concrete, barbed wire, etc. Khrushchev felt that the wall might force the issue once more with the Western Allies, but if not, the wall alone solved the issue.

The American sector of Berlin was defended lightly, with only a half-dozen tanks with infantry support. Being surrounded by Communist East Germany, the conventional thinking was that defending Berlin was going to be nearly impossible. Short of all-out war, the best course of action to reinforce the Western-controlled portions of the city was to send troops and tanks into East Germany, down the autobahn; an action that was likely to start a war.

On 12 August 1961, the order to proceed was given by Present Ulbricht, and the sealing of the border commenced; the construction of the iconic Berlin Wall began. The Soviet influence on the action was not even discreetly hidden, as their tanks were brought into play to secure the wall's construction. American and Soviet tanks squared off a few yards from each other at what would eventually become 'Checkpoint Charlie'. People valiantly attempted to emigrate to West Berlin before the wall was completed; many were successful, some were not. Methodically, Berlin became a walled-in city and the German border became sealed.

The Kennedy administration, like the rest of the world, was caught off guard by the move. The only course of action was to send in military force to attempt to tear down the wall. But the East Germans and their Soviet allies had not violated the agreements regarding Berlin. Access to the city by the Western Allies was allowed – the Western-controlled portions of the city was simply sealed off from the rest of the city and the rest of Germany. There was little that the new American President could do but allow the wall to go up. No one was prepared to go to war over Berlin.

Words were offered to counter the concrete and barbed wire, but little more. This solidified Khrushchev's thinking of the new American President as inexperienced and weak. It laid the stage for the missile crisis just over a year later.

Distant Cousins

For its part, the USSR initially viewed the Castro's (Fidel and Raul) with skepticism. After all, it seemed too good to be true; a Communist nation right off the shores of the United States, in perfect position to influence all of Latin America. Not only that, it would provide potential naval and air bases with rapid access to the United States and the strategic Panama Canal. Despite all of the potential strategic advantages, the Soviet Union was not quick to embrace the Castro regime. There were concerns about just how Socialist the new Government was. There were also suspicions that Fidel Castro was turning to the USSR as a potential ally solely because of the political, economic, and diplomatic tensions with the United States.

Ironically, what drove the USSR to offer military assistance to Cuba was the abortive Bay of Pigs invasion. It was clear that the US had been the driving force behind the invasion, and there was a real fear on the part of Fidel Castro that the United States was planning, at some point, on invading his country. Based on the planning in Norfolk and the Pentagon, such plans were indeed underway, although there is no indication that Castro possessed any hard intelligence of this. If such an invasion were to take place, it would cost the USSR its best chance at securing a friendly satellite nation in the western hemisphere. What the Kennedy administration had hoped to resolve with the Bay of Pigs – preventing a stronger connection to the Soviet Union – was actually the *result* of their actions.

The initial help for Cuba came in the form of what were classed as 'defensive weapons', i.e. conventional arms and armor. Intelligence estimates of the exact amounts of weapons vary. On 1 January 1961, Cuba held a third anniversary of the Regime Military Parade, which the CIA paid close attention to in hopes of pinning down types and numbers of equipment.

Table 2-1: Conventional Arms Sold to Cuba by USSR[3]

US Intelligence Numbers	Models	Notes
25-30 *	JS-2 Heavy Tanks	Mounts 122-mm gun; weighs 51 tons
104-120 *	T-34/85 Medium Tanks	Mounts 85-mm gun, weighs 25 tons
50	SU 100 Self-Propelled guns	100-mm gun mounted on a T-34 chassis, weighs 35 tons
50	122-mm artillery pieces	Powerful long range (22,747 yards) artillery, duel wheel mounted
50	122-mm howitzers	Range of 13,000 yards. Mounted on same carriage as the 152-mm US M 1943 howitzer
72	85-mm anti-tank guns	Lightweight, dual purpose weapon (anti-tank and anti-personnel), range of 18,000 yards
120	76-mm anti-tank guns	Lightweight weapon, dual purpose weapon, range of 14,545 yards
30	37-mm AA guns	Single 37-mm manual drive gun on four-wheel carriage. Vertical range 19,685 feet, horizontal range of 8,748 yards

200	Quad 12.7-mm Anti-Aircraft guns	Four 12.7 machinegun in quad mount on two wheel trailer
12+ **	Katyusha rocket launching trucks	Truck mounted WWII-era rocket launchers
200	82-mm mortars	Range of 90 to 3,320 yards. Unit breaks into three parts for pack transportation
70	120-mm mortars	Range of 50 to 6,500 yards, transported by jeep or towed
500	7.62 light machineguns	Shoulder fired light machinegun supported by bipod
220,000	7.62 submachineguns PPSH-41	Shoulder fired submachinegun
Unknown	Czech L-25 submachineguns	Pistol gripped submachinegun
Unknown	Czech Model 52 rifles	Semi-automatic rifle with folding bayonet
26,000	Belgian FN (7-48) rifles	Similar to American BAR

* Discrepancies in sources have been factored into these numbers.
** Seen in the 2 January 1962 parade in Havana. These antiquated systems were still highly mobile, easy to conceal, and effective against enemy infantry.

Other intelligence analysis at the time painted an even grimmer picture – with an additional 167,000 rifles, 7,250 machine guns, and considerable amounts of ammunition, explosives, grenades, mines, and other material.[4] One thing was sure: in a few short months, Cuba had gone from being weakly defended to being a place where any attacker would be bled. The Soviets also sent advisers to Cuba to provide training to the Cuban Army. These 300-500 advisers were not sent in to fight, but to turn the Cuban Army into something that could potentially defend itself against any further American incursions. These forces were in place by early 1960, meaning that by the time of the pending missile crisis, the Cuban Army would have had training in using their new armored forces and some expertise in modern infantry tactics.

The Revolutionary Army

American intelligence of the Cuban Army was remarkably limited, despite the penetration of the island during Operation Mongoose. Cuba was divided into six military districts, each following the same lines of demarcation as the provinces.[5]

Overall control of these provinces was placed under three Territorial Army commands. Overall, the Revolutionary Army (FTC) had a standing strength (immobilized) of 75,000 men. It possessed a ready-reserve strength of 100,000. On top of this, the Revolutionary Army had approximately 100,000 force of militia. These militia troops were marginally trained and designed to augment the police force.[6] The militia and reserve forces were organized under the umbrella organization called the Revolutionary National Militia. The territorial commands of the army were the Army of the East, including Oriente Province. The Central Army included Camaguey and Los Villias provinces. The Army of the East included the Pinar Del Rio, Matanzas, and Habana provinces, and the Isle of Pines, which was just off the southern coast of the island nation.[7] Each of these territorial commands were responsible for all forces in their regions, including the Revolutionary Air Force. Within each army command were corps and division headquarters. These headquarters had no operational roles, but did control internal security and 'static defence'.[8]

Within the three armies, two corps, three military regions, and forty-four divisions have been identified. All of these headquarters have administrative control, but no apparent operational status; however, as the reported reorganization of the ground forces progresses, divisions to be deployed as operational units.[9]

Internal organization follows the usual lines of subordination. There is evidence, however, that the armed forces of the general staff has either been done away with, or at least stripped of many of its control functions. The army and militia now report direction to the minister of the armed forces. The division between the tactical combat forces (the regular army) and the Revolutionary National Militia (the reserve and volunteer forces) is becoming more and more nebulous.[10]

The armored forces of the Cuban Army also included a number of Second World War surplus US armored vehicles and tanks, which had been sold to the Batista Government. This included a dozen M3A1 Stuart light tanks, the M4A1/76 Sherman tanks mounted with 76-mm cannons, and a number of M-8 armored cars. Also in the mix were a few British armored vehicles, consisting of the COMET medium tank with a 77-mm main armament.[11]

A 'typical' Cuban Regular Army battalion was broken down as follows:

Headquarters and Service company: 1 officer, 152 enlisted personnel
- Headquarters, communications, medical and quartermaster platoons

Four Special Infantry companies: 1 officer, 154 enlisted personnel
- 4 rifle platoons with 27 Czech or PH 7.62 automatic rifles
- 1 machine gun platoon with 6 7.62-mm Czech machine guns
- 1 submachine gun platoon with 24 Czech submachine guns

One Light Infantry Company: 1 officer, 106 enlisted personnel
- 3 rifle platoons with 24 7.62-mm Czech or FN automatic rifles
- 1 submachine gun platoon with 24 submachine guns

One Mortar Company: 1 officer, 66 enlisted personnel, 8 82-mm mortars
- 1-10 men Headquarters Section
- 3-18 man platoons with three sections each

One Mine Sapper Platoon: 26 enlisted personnel
- Mine detectors and submachine guns

One Reconnaissance Platoon: 1 officer, 28 enlisted personnel
- 28 Czech submachine guns[12]

The Cuban Army was a relatively mobile force. There were over 43,000 trucks on the island of Cuba that could be pressed into action if needed. This had happened during the Bay of Pigs invasion and helped account for some of the rapid response by the Cuban military to the landings. While the Regular Army would get priority use of such vehicles, militia units were expected to fend for themselves.[13]

The Cuban Revolutionary Air

Prior to the Bay of Pigs, the Cuban Revolutionary Air Force existed more on paper than in reality. The equipment it was armed with was old, obsolete aircraft that were poorly maintained. Pinning down the exact number of fully functional aircraft for the Revolutionary Air Force is difficult, but the approximate size by late spring of 1961 was as follows:

Table 2-2: Cuban Revolutionary Air Force Combat Aircraft, Post Bay of Pigs, Before Russian Reinforcement[14]

US Intelligence Numbers	Models	Notes
5-10	T-33	Jet training aircraft Armaments: two .50 caliber machineguns. Speed: 504/7,000 ft Range: 1,086 nautical miles/381 kts
1	F51 Mustang	Propeller-driven fighter aircraft Armaments: six .50 caliber machineguns. Speed: 435kts/22,700 ft Range: 1,720 nautical miles/236 kts

3	F-47	Propeller driven fighter bomber Armaments: eight .50 caliber machineguns. Speed: 390 kts/35,000 ft Range: 2,020 nautical miles/244 kts
4	Sea Fury	Armaments: four .20-mm guns; 12-2" rockets; 2-500 lb bombs Speed: 390kts/20,000 ft Range: 915 nautical miles/245 kts
10-15	B-26	Propeller driven, twin-engine attack bomber Armaments: eleven .50 caliber machineguns Speed: 250 kts/5,000 ft Range: 1,490 nautical miles/185 kts
6	TBM 35	Propeller driven anti-submarine aircraft Armaments: three .50 caliber machineguns; one .30 caliber machinegun Speed: 235 kts/16,500 ft Range: 1,510 nautical miles/128 kts Ceiling: feet
2	PBY-5A	Propeller driven, twin engine seaplane Armaments: three .50 caliber machineguns; two .30 caliber machineguns Speed: 160 kts/17,000 ft Range: 2,214 nautical miles/102 kts
1	H-19	Sikorsky helicopter (US) Speed: 101 mph Range: 405 miles Note: Can carry 12 troops

In addition to these aircraft, the Revolutionary Air Force maintained a number of unarmed transport aircraft; C-54s, C-47s, C-46s, and light Scouts (Cessna 310s), most of which were the Second World War surplus.[15] It should also be noted that the PBYs and TBMs, while designed primarily for ASW, (Anti-Submarine Warfare), were not capable of performing these duties at night time.[16]

The attack by the Cuban Expeditionary Force's aircraft and their failure to destroy the Revolutionary Air Force on the ground during the Bay of Pigs was a mistake that the United States was not likely to make should it sponsor or lead an attack again. The Soviets realized that any conventional arming of Cuba was going to have to include substantial fighter aircraft as well. Like the arms they provided to the Army, the USSR did not give their top-of-the-line weapons in great quantity to the Revolutionary Air Force. Their was one exception was in the inclusion of the more contemporary MIG 21 fighter.

The following table outlines the increases to the Cuban Revolutionary Air Force in terms of defensive aircraft:

Table 2-3: Soviet Defensive Aircraft Provided the Cuban Revolutionary Air Force[17]

US Intelligence Numbers	Models	Notes
40	MIG 21	Jet fighter aircraft Armaments: one 3-mm cannon, two air-to-air missiles or two 500-kg bombs Speed: 1,385 mph Range: 981 miles
30-50	MIG 15	Jet fighter aircraft Armaments: one 37-mm cannon, two 23-mm cannon Speed: 572/sea level Range: 430 nautical miles
Unknown	MIG 17	Jet fighter aircraft Armaments: one 37-mm cannon, two 23-mm cannon Speed: 625/sea level Range: 1,100 nautical miles
1-10	MIG 19	Jet fighter aircraft Armaments: two 23-mm cannon Speed: 675/sea level Range: 1,400 nautical miles
12	MI-4	Helicopter Armaments: None Speed: 116 mpg Range: 313 nautical miles Note: Can carry 16 troops
10	MI-1	Helicopter Armaments: None Speed: 115 mpg Range: 268 nautical miles

The stationing of the Revolutionary Air Force provided coverage around the island. The following table breaks down the American intelligence understanding as to where the principle equipment, all Soviet, was placed.

Table 2-4: Cuban Revolutionary Air Force Placement[18]

Strength	Airfield	Aircraft
One Fighter Regiment	San Antonio De Los Banos	MIG 15s, 17s, and 19s
Two Fighter Squadrons	Santa Clara	MIG 15s, 17s, and 21s
One Fighter Squadron	Camaguey	MIG 15s and 17s
One Utility Air Unit	Playa Baracoa	IL-14s (posted during offensive build-up), MI-1s, and MI-4s

It is worth noting that at the time of the invasion of Cuba, intelligence did not have information on the non-Soviet aircraft that the Cubans were known to possess. The assumption was that these aircraft had been moved to hangars, retired (scrapped), or concealed.

The base commander at the American military base at Guantánamo Bay prepared a detailed analysis of airfields that were capable to handling jet aircraft. This list does not take into account the large number of airfields where transport aircraft could be landed or used, of which there were nearly a dozen other fields. This list was specifically for identifying fields where the more sophisticated fighter jets and bombers could be used.

Table 2-5: Cuban Airfields Capable of Handling Jet Aircraft[19]

Airfield	Remarks
Los Canos	Commercial field for Guantánamo. 8,100-ft runway
Antonio Maceo	Commercial field for Santiago. B-26 and Sea Fury aircraft had been sighted at this strip in the past but were not visible by October of 1962. 7,000-ft runway
Coronel Pasqual (sic)	7,400-ft runway
Camaguey International	Commercial field for Camaguey. 8,000-ft runway
San Antonio de Los Banos	Major military airfield. 7,220-ft runway
Holguin	Near completion. 8,000-ft runway
Santa Clara International	Commercial airfield. 9,600-ft runway
Jose Marti International	Commercial airfield for Havana. 7,060-ft runway
El Jiqui	8,400-ft runway
Camo Libertad	Headquarters of the FAR. 6,790-ft runway

Note: This list was prepared by the commander of the American base at Guantánamo Bay just prior to the planned invasion. Omitted from the list are three other runways that could *have supported jet aircraft, the most substantial being San Julián Asiento, which was used as the primary base for the Soviet supplied IL-28 bombers.*

This list, while addressing commercial and military airfields, does not take into account improvised airfields. As learned during the Second World War, the Germans were able to leverage flat stretches of paved roads as makeshift runways. While such fields often lack the proper equipment for storage or repair, they were utilized. In the case of Cuba, where the key airfields were destined to be targets for bombing, this strategy may have been considered by the Revolutionary Air Force. Unfortunately, the Cuban military records were not available for verification.

The Soviets realized that introducing just the necessary aircraft alone was not enough to ensure the security of Cuba. As such, they arranged to have Cuban pilots trained alongside USSR pilots in their schools. While some of their models of MIG aircraft were nearing obsolescence, the aviators in Cuba were being trained with the same level of detail and expertise as Soviet aviators. This means that in a fight, while they lacked practical combat experience, they would represent a threat to any attacking American jets.

The Cuban Revolutionary Navy

What Fidel Castro inherited upon taking office was a navy that was made up, for the most part, from Second World War US surplus ships and a number of retired US Coast Guard Cutters. None of the ships were modern. While the Cuban Navy fielded somewhere between 4,000 and 5,000 personnel, it was not an offensive force by any means. This limited its roles to coastal patrol and defense. However, as soon as military assistance started coming into Cuba from the USSR, the key officers of the Cuban Revolutionary Navy were sent for several weeks' training with the USSR Navy.

Table 2-6: Cuban Naval Strength[20]

Hull Number	Name	District	Vessel Type	Remarks
Unknown	Cuba	West	Patrol Frigate	Cruise built in 1911 used primarily for training. Home port most likely Havana
F-301	Jose Marti	West	Patrol Frigate	Ex-USS *Eugene* (PF-40) Home port most likely Havana

F-302	Antonio Maceo	West	Patrol Frigate	Ex-USS *Peoria* (PF-67) Home port most likely Havana
F-303	Maximo Gomez	West	Patrol Frigate	Ex-USS *Grand Island* (PF-14) Home port most likely Havana
PE-201	Caribe	West	Coastal Patrol	Ex-USS *PCE 872*. Home port most likely Cardenas
PE-202	Siboney	West	Coastal Patrol	Ex-USS *PEC 893*. Home port most likely Batabano
PE-203	Baire	Unknown	Postal Gunboat	Sunk 19 April 1961. Raised and under repair
GC	Unknown	East	Covered Lighter	110-ft coast guard patrol boat of one officer and eighteen men. Home port most likely Antilla or Banes
GC-102	Donativo	Unknown	Patrol Craft	Non-operational
GC-103	Matanzas	Central	Patrol Craft	100-ft auxiliary coast guard patrol boat, reactivated 8 December 1960. Home port most likely Cienfuegos
GC-104	Oriente	West	Patrol Craft	Ex-USS *SC-1000*
GC-105	Camaguey	Unknown	Patrol Craft	Ex-USS *SC-1001*
GC-106	Las Villas	West	Patrol Craft	Hijacked in January 1962, returned to Cuba
GC-107	Habana	East	Patrol Craft	Ex-USS *SC-1291*. Home port unknown. Reported in October 1961 in Santiago for repairs
GC-108	Pinar Del Rio	Unknown	Patrol Craft	Ex-USS *SC-1301*
GC-11	Unknown	West	Patrol Craft	Ex-US CGC *83351* 83-ft former coast guard cutter
GC-12	Unknown	Unknown	Patrol Craft	Ex-US CGC *83386*.

GC-13	Unknown	West	Patrol Craft	Ex-US CGC *833585*. Home port most likely Santiago
GC-14	Unknown	West	Patrol Craft	Ex-US CGC *83395*. Home port most likely Cardenas
GC-31	Unknown	Unknown	Patrol Craft	Ex-US CGC *65189*
GC-32	Unknown	Unknown	Patrol Craft	Ex-US CGC *56191*
GC-33	Unknown	Unknown	Patrol Craft	Ex-US CGC *56190*
GC-34	Unknown	East	Patrol Craft	Ex-US CGC *56192*. Home port most likely Santiago
SV-1	Unknown	Unknown	Patrol Craft	SV-1 to SV-6 are 32-ft auxiliary patrol craft, speed 18 kts
SV-2	Unknown	Unknown	Patrol Craft	Home port most likely Batabano
SV-3	Unknown	Unknown	Patrol Craft	Home port most likely Batabano
SV-4	Unknown	Unknown	Patrol Craft	
SV-5	Unknown	East	Patrol Craft	Home port most likely Santiago
SV-6	Unknown	East	Patrol Craft	Home port most likely Santiago
SV-7	Unknown	East	Patrol Craft	SV-7 to SV-10 are 40-ft auxiliary patrol craft, speed 25 kts. Home port most likely Antilla
SV-8	Unknown	Unknown	Patrol Craft	
SV-9	Unknown	Unknown	Patrol Craft	
SV-10	Unknown	Unknown	Patrol Craft	
SV-11	Unknown	East	Patrol Craft	Last known operating area Antilla (November 1961)
SV-12	Unknown	West	Patrol Craft	
SV-13	Unknown	Unknown	Patrol Craft	
SV-14	Unknown	Unknown	Patrol Craft	
SV-15	Unknown	Unknown	Patrol Craft	

SV-16	Unknown	Unknown	Patrol Craft	
R-41	Unknown	Unknown	Patrol Craft	Ex-US *PT 715*
R-42	Unknown	West	Patrol Craft	Ex-US *PT 716*. Home port most likely Batabano
RS-210	10 De Octobre	West	Rescue Tug	Ex-US *ATR 43*. Home port most likely Havana
RS-211	20 De Mayo	Unknown	Rescue Tug	Ex-US ATR 3
None	Enrique Collazo	Unknown	Tender	Ex-merchantman fitted as lighthouse and buoy-tender

Khrushchev's military advisers realized the weaknesses of the Cuban naval assets in the event that the United States might attempt an invasion. The solution they employed was to provide the Cubans with twelve KOMAR guided missile boats. These were introduced in the USSR's Navy in the 1950s, but were still considered state of the art at the time. At 25.4 m in length, with speeds capable of 44 knots, these ships packed the kind of punch that might make an amphibious assault force flinch. Armed with two 25-mm guns for defense, their primary weapons were a pair of P-15 Termit (NATO designation SS-N-2 Styx) anti-ship missiles. These 2,300-kg missiles packed the kind of punch that posed a risk to even capital ships. They had a range of 10-15 km, meaning that the KOMAR ships gave the Revolutionary Navy the ability to strike at any attacking invasion fleet. Also, the size of the vessels meant that they could be concealed in any number of coves and bays along the Cuban coast.[21]

Providing Offensive Capabilities

In the late spring of 1962, Premier Khrushchev's attention remained fixed on Cuba. It had only been a year since the failed Bay of Pigs invasion and attempt to remove Castro from power. Since that time, it was clear that the American Government was sponsoring a covert war in Cuba. The United States was not turning its gaze off of Cuba; nor could the USSR.

Khrushchev's desire was to provide a long-term deterrence to an invasion of Cuba. As he put it in his memoirs:

What would happen if we lose Cuba? I know it would be a terrible blow to Marxism-Leninism. It would gravely diminish our statue throughout the world, but especially in Latin America. If Cuba fell, other Latin American countries would reject us, claiming that for all of our might, the Soviet Union hadn't been able to do anything for Cuba expect to make empty protests to the United Nations. We had to think up some way of confronting America with more than words.[22]

The solution that he devised was to provide Cuba with an offensive capability. This offensive capability, dubbed Operation Anadyr, was to install thirty-six R-12 medium-range missiles, twenty-four R-14 intermediate-range nuclear missiles, twelve IL-28 jet bombers (with six nuclear bombs), and twenty-two surface-to-air missile batteries. Supporting this would be USSR troops to man the missile launch sites and four motorized rifle regiments for ground defence.[23] This was destined to be the largest and most complicated seaborne operation that the USSR had ever planned. By May 1962, discussions were held with Fidel Castro and extensive planning put into action to implement Operation Anadyr.

When the United States made such strategic deployments, such as the launch of its Polaris weapons systems, it did so very publicly so as to not catch the Soviet Union off-guard and provoke an unplanned and reckless response. Such was not the case with the USSR. They tended to make weapons deployments or announcements suddenly, so as to wreck havoc with their enemies. As such, there was no fanfare regarding the decision to move troops and offensive missiles to Cuba.

The Soviet forces initially planned to be sent to Cuba were broken down as follows:

Air and Anti-Aircraft Forces

2 anti-aircraft divisions (10th and 11th), each broken down into three surface-to-air missile (SAM) regiments with 4 launch complexes each

- Each division had 72 missile launchers
- The 10th Division was augmented with forty MIG-21 fighters under its command
- 2 cruise missile (FKR) regiments with 5 missiles/warheads for each of the regiment's 8 launchers for a total of eighty missiles. Warheads were a 5-12 kiloton yield
- A regiment of 33 MI-4 helicopters
- A squadron of 11 IL-28 bombers (for conventional weapons use) and 6 IL-28s specially outfitted to carry one nuclear bomb each
- A mixed squadron of 11 Li-2s and An-24s for non-combat, intra-island transport, and communications

Note: The Soviet's changed the numbering on their units as part of their security. The 10th and 11th anti-aircraft divisions were re-designated as 12th and 27th divisions respectively by the time of the missile crisis.

Infantry

Four motorized rifle regiments from the Leningrad Military District (74th, 134th, 146th, and 106th)

Each regiment was equipped as follows:

- 2,500 personnel
- 31 regular tanks (T-34s or T-55s)
- 3 amphibious tanks (PT-76)
- 10 self-propelled 100-mm cannon (SAU)
- 10 armored reconnaissance vehicles
- 9 120-mm mortars
- 9 anti-tank guided missiles
- 9 57-mm anti-aircraft machine guns
- 6 122-mm howitzers
- 60 armored personnel carriers
- 18 motorcycles
- 233 cars and trucks

Note: These regiments also appear as the 302nd, 314th, 400th, and 469th as part of the security measures applied by the Soviets.

The 74th, 134th, and 146th regiments were equipped with Luna rocket detachments from the Kiev Military District.

Each detachment was equipped with:

- 2 launchers
- 4 missiles

Navy

- 1 squadron of 11 submarines
- 1 squadron of surface ships
- 2 cruisers
- 2 missile-firing destroyers
- 2 regular destroyers
- 1 brigade of 16 torpedo boats
- 1 coast defense regiment with 6 Sopka missile launchers
- 1 naval-air regiment of twelve IL-28s: designated as a mine-torpedo aviation regiment
- Supporting this force would be 2 supply ships, 2 tankers, 2 bulk carriers and 1 repair ship[24]

The Soviets made changes to the units and hardware sent. The motorized infantry units were augmented, for example, with 3M6 Shmel (NATO Designation Snapper) anti-tank missile launchers. These rail-launched missiles could be truck-mounted, and packed a deadly punch against opposing armored units. They had a range up to 2.3 km and had a 5.4-kg HEAT (high explosive anti-tank) warhead. It was estimated by the United States that thirty-five of these anti-tank, missile-mounted scout cars were in place on Cuba.[25]

The number and designation of the IL-28s changed as well. Eventually, thirty-three would be scheduled for deployment. One squadron of IL-28 bombers comprised ten to twelve aircraft, including delivery and countermeasures aircraft, with a mobile PRTB and six atomic bombs (407N), each of 8-12 kilotons. This change was authorized personally by Premier Khrushchev.[26] The rest were designated for use with the mine-torpedo aviation regiment, comprising three squadrons with RAT-52 jet torpedoes (150 torpedoes), and air-dropped mines (150 mines) for destruction of surface ships.[27]

The motorized infantry units were armed with the new AKM assault rifle, the weapon that replaced the AK-47. Like its predecessor, it was a weapon that offered ease of maintenance and durability in almost any combat environment.

By July, the plan had been modified slightly to the following organization structure:[28]

Mobilizing such a massive force for deployment in a tropical environment was far from easy. In order to mislead the efforts, the Soviet personnel were to wear civilian clothing. Most of the movement across the island was done at night to avoid the probing eyes of the American over-flights – the primary means of gathering intelligence in the age prior to satellite coverage.

While trucks and missiles could potentially be concealed, it would be impossible to hide the launch complexes for the SAMs and the strategic missiles themselves. By mid-summer 1962, personnel and equipment was arriving at Cuban ports and construction began. The building of the SAM sites were first priority to ensure protection of the medium and intermediate-range strategic missiles.

The Soviet logic was centered on the concept of getting the missile complexes completed for the strategic missiles quickly, before the US could discover them. Once those missiles were in place and protected by a shield of SAM sites, the United States would not be willing to risk an invasion, or even an air strike. The missiles would become something that the US simply would have to come to live with.

The Soviet logic was sound in some respects. The US had placed medium-range Thor missiles in Great Britain and Jupiter intermediate-range missiles in Italy and Turkey. Turkey in particular was next door to the USSR. They had been forced to endure these threats on their border and had every reason to believe that the United States would also be willing to tolerate their presence.

The trip to Cuba was almost unbearable for the men involved. Temperatures hovered near 100 degrees Fahrenheit. The troops were confined below decks during the day and could only venture out at night to avoid being spotted. The refrigeration systems could not preserve the food adequately and the foodstuffs began to spoil. Furthermore, the Soviet troops had been stationed in a climate that was relatively cool in the summers and bitterly cold in the winters. They were now

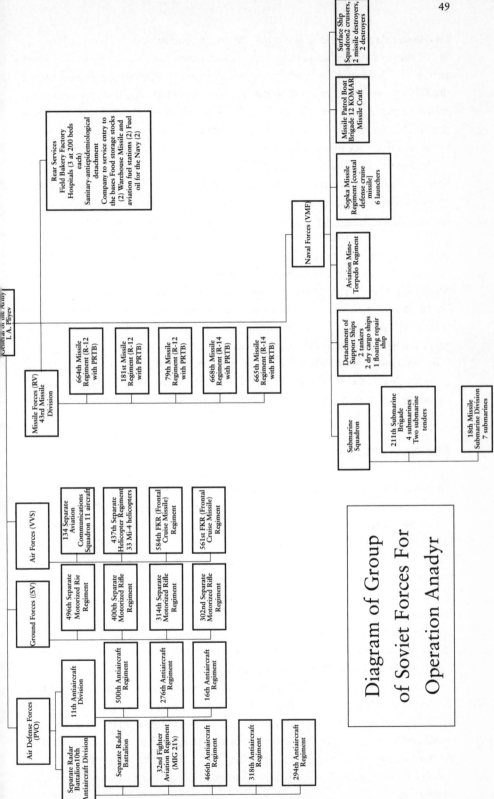

Diagram of Group of Soviet Forces For Operation Anadyr

49

travelling to a place that was almost always hot and humid. Starting in July, two Soviet supply and transport ships began to arrive at Cuban ports every day. Over 200 shiploads of supplies, fuel, hardware, and gear shuttled by 85 ships delivered the USSR troops.[29] Compared to the massive amphibious operations the United States waged in the second World War, this was a relatively small operation. It was remarkable for the USSR, given their lack of experience in such operations, as well as the fact that they managed to keep the true intent of the operation secret.

The Soviet headquarters was established at Managua, south of Havana. The 10th (12th) Anti-Aircraft Division was responsible for the SAM sites in the western part of Cuba while the 11th (27th) covered the rest of the island and the eastern portion. These sites were more than just missile launchers; they were part of a sophisticated air defense network that protected the island. Each was tied in with air search radar, target acquisition systems, and missile guidance radar stations.

With the exception of the KOMAR missile craft, the naval forces that were part of Operation Anadyr were scheduled to be the last elements to arrive at the island. Where the placement of the missile forces was done with a great deal of maskirovka (camouflage and deception), the Soviets realized that the arrival of the naval elements would be difficult to conceal.

By September, Khrushchev must have been concerned about such a large naval presence and he canceled most of the Navy deployment, including seven missile-launching submarines, with twenty-one nuclear ballistic missiles.[30]

The Soviet Command

The man designated to lead the USSR's forces on Cuba was Army General Issa Pliyev. The general staff had recommended another officer to head up the Soviet forces, but Khrushchev had overruled them. General Pliyev was a highly decorated cavalry officer who had commanded motorized rifle troops in the Far East during the Second World War. While he had experience leading ground troops, Pliyev had been given assignment over rocket troops, which required more than just tactical expertise; it required a level of technical complexity that he lacked. Another reason the general staff had not recommended him was that the posting in Cuba was not like a command in mother-Russia. The man that had to command the Soviet forces in Cuba had to also be a diplomat and emissary to Cuba. It was in these capacities that General Pliyev was markedly deficient.[31]

Other changes were made to the deployment seemingly at the last minute. A separate IL-28 squadron for nuclear bomb delivery (comprising nine aircraft) was included and assigned to the Holguin airbase in eastern Cuba.[32] Four atomic mines were originally scheduled for deployment to protect the naval assets; these too were removed from the hardware scheduled for the Soviet forces, along with the torpedo boats.[33]

The orders provided to Pliyev were daunting indeed for a man of his experience and background.

Memorandum, R. Malinovsky and M. Zakharov to Commander of Group of
Soviet Forces in Cuba, 8 September 1962
Top Secret
Special Importance

Copy No. 1

Personally To the Commander of the Group of Soviet Forces in Cuba.

The temporary deployment of Soviet Armed forces on the island of Cuba is necessary to insure joint defense against possible aggression toward the USSR and the Republic of Cuba. A decision on employment of the Soviet Armed Forces in combat actions in order to repel aggression and reinstatement [of the situation] will be made by the Soviet Government.

1. The task of the Group of Soviet Forces in Cuba is not to permit an enemy landing on Cuban territory from the sea or from the air. The island of Cuba must be turned into an impenetrable fortress. Forces and means: Soviet troops together with the Cuban Armed Forces.

2. In carrying out this task, the Commander of the Group of Soviet Forces on the island of Cuba will be guided by the following considerations:

a) With respect to Missile Forces:

The missile forces, constituting the backbone for the defense of the Soviet Union and Cuba, must be prepared, upon signal from Moscow, to deal a nuclear missile strike on the most important targets in the United States of America (list of targets included in Attachment No. 1) [Translator's Note: This attachment was not included in the Volkogonov Papers.]

Upon arrival of the missile division in Cuba, two R-12 [SS-4] regiments (539th and 546th) and one R-14 [SS-5] regiment (564th) will deploy in the western region, and one R-12 regiment (the 514th) and one R-14 regiment (the 657th) in the central region of Cuba.

The missile units will deploy to the positional areas and take up their launch positions; for R-12 missiles, not later than [illegible] days; for the R-14 missiles with fixed launch facilities, [illegible] period.

With the establishment of launchers on combat duty, [illegible – all?] regiments will maintain Readiness No. 4 [Translator's Note: The lowest level of combat readiness, and the least provocative.]

b) With Respect to Air Defense (PVO) Forces:

PVO forces of the Group will not permit incursion of foreign aircraft into the air space of the Republic of Cuba [illegible words] and strikes by enemy air against the Group, the most important administrative political [and industrial] centers, naval bases, ports [illegible]. Combat use of PVO forces will be activated by the Commander of the Group of Forces. The PVO divisions will be deployed:

• 12th Division [surface to air missiles] – the western region of Cuban territory [illegible]

- 27th Division [surface to air missiles] –the eastern region of Cuban territory [illegible]
- 213th Fighter Air Division will be deployed at Santa Clara airfield. After unloading in Cuba of the surface-to-air missiles and fighter aviation will be deployed [illegible] and organization of combat readiness

c) With Respect to the Ground Forces:

Ground forces troops will protect the missile and other technical troops and the Group command centre, and be prepared to provide assistance to the Cuban Armed Forces in liquidating [illegible] enemy landings and counter-revolutionary groups on the territory of the Republic of Cuba. The independent motorized rifle regiments (OMSP) will deploy:

- The 74th OMSP, with a battalion of Lunas, in the western part of Cuba in readiness to protect the Missile Forces [Translator's Note: in the San Cristobal and Guanajay areas] and to operate in the sectors Havana and Pinar del Rio.
- The 43rd OMSP, with a battalion of Lunas, in the vicinity of Santiago de Las Vegas in readiness to protect the Command of the Group of Forces and to operate in the sectors Havana, Artemisa, Batabano, and Matanzas.
- The 146th OMSP, with a battalion of Lunas, in the area Camajuani, Placetas, Sulu... [illegible], in readiness to protect the Missile Forces [Translator's Note: in the Sagua la Grande and Remedios areas] and to operate in the sectors: Caibarien, Colon, Cienfeugos, Fomento.
- The 106th OMSP in the eastern part of Cuba in the vicinity of Holguin in readiness to operate in the sectors Banes, Victoria de las Tunas, Manzanillo, and Santiago de Cuba.

d) With Respect to the Navy:

The Naval element of the Group must not permit combat ships and transports of the enemy to approach the island of Cuba and carry out naval landings on the coast. They must be prepared to blockade from the sea the US naval base in Guantánamo, and provide cover for our transport ships along lines of communication in close proximity to the island.

Missile-equipped submarines should be prepared to launch, upon signal from Moscow, nuclear missile strikes on the most important coastal targets in the USA. (List of targets in Attachment No. 1.)

The main forces of the fleet should be based in the region around Havana and in ports to the west of Havana.

One detachment of the brigade of missile patrol boats should be located in the vicinity of Banes.

The battalions of Sopka [coastal defense cruise missiles] should be deployed on the coast:

- One battalion east of Havana in the region of Santa Cruz del Norte
- One battalion south-east of Cienfuegos in the vicinity of Gavilan
- One battalion north-east of Banes in the vicinity of Cape Mulas

- One battalion on the island Piños [Isle of Pines] in the vicinity of Cape Buenavista

The torpedo-mine air regiment [IL-28s] will deploy at the airfield San Julian Asiento, and plan and instruct in destroying combat ships and enemy landings from the sea.

e) With Respect to the Air Force:

The squadron of IL-28 delivery aircraft will be based on Santa Clara airfield in readiness to operate in the directions of Havana, Guantánamo, and the Isle of Pines. [Translator's Note: This deployment was later changed to Holguin airfield] The independent aviation engineering regiments [OAIP] (FKR) [cruise missiles] [Translator's Note: The OAIP designation was a cover; the real designation was FKR regiments] will deploy:

- 231st OAIP—in the western region of Cuba, designated as the main means to fire on the coast in the north-eastern and northern sectors, and as a secondary mission in the direction of the Isle of Pines.
- 222nd OAIP – in the eastern part of the island. This regiment must be prepared, upon signal from the General Staff, in the main sector of the south-eastern direction to strike the US naval base at Guantánamo. Secondary firing sectors in the north-eastern and south-western directions.

The fighter aviation regiment armed with MiG-21 F-13 aircraft is included as a PVO [air defense] division, but crews of all fighters will train also for operations in support of the Ground Forces and Navy.

3. Organize security and economy of missiles, warheads, and special technical equipment, and all combat equipment in the armament of the Group of Soviet Forces in Cuba.

4. Carry out daily cooperation and combat collaboration with the Armed Forces of the Republic of Cuba, and work together in instructing the personnel of the Cuban Armed Forces in maintaining the arms and combat equipment being transferred by the Soviet Union to the Republic of Cuba.

5. Deploy the rear units and offices and organize all-round material, technical, and medical support of the troops.

Rear area bases will be located in the regions as follows:

- Main Base – comprising: the 758th command base, separate service companies, the 3rd automotive platoon, 784th POL fuel station, the 860th food supply, depot, the 964th warehouse, the 71st bakery factory, the 176th field technical medical detachment –Mariel, Artemisa, Guira de Melena, Rincon.
- Separate rear base – comprising: 782nd POL station, 883rd food supply depot, a detachment of the 964th warehouse, [the 1st] field medical detachment, a detachment of the 71st bakery factory – Caibarien, Camajuani, Placetas.
- Separate rear base – comprising: separate detachments of the 784th POL station, the 883rd food supply depot, the 964th warehouse, [the 71st bakery unit, and the 1st field medical detachment – Gibara, Holguin, Camasan.

Fuel stocks for the Navy will be:

- Depot No. 4472 – Mariel, a branch at Guanabacoa
- Depot No. 4465 – vicinity of Banes

Hospitals will be set up in the regions: Field hospitals No. 965 with blood transfusion unit – Guanajay; No. 121 – Camajuani, Placetas; No. 50 – Holguin.

The transport of material to be organized by troop transport means, and also do not use local rail or water transport.

6. The operational plan for the employment of the Group of Soviet Forces in Cuba should be worked out by 1 November 1962. [Translator's Note: Date filled in by a different hand; probably omitted for security reasons or for later decision by a higher authority.]

USSR Minister of Defense Marshal of the Soviet Union R. Malinovsky
Chief of the General Staff Marshal of the Soviet Union M. Zakharov[34]

The most significant aspect of these orders is that the USSR troops were to not permit an enemy landing. This would mean that the Soviet forces, when the Americans landed, would not be reactive forces relegated to defending themselves. They would actively attempt to repel an invasion.

The posting of the Soviet motorized rifle regiments were ultimately placed as follows:

74th Regiment: Near Artemisa (Note: This unit was equipped with Luna missiles)

134th Regiment: Near Managua (Note: This unit was equipped with Luna missiles)

106th Regiment: Near Holguin

146th Regiment: Near Santa Clara (Note: This unit was equipped with Luna missiles)

Headquarters: El Chico, south-west of Havana

The Headquarters of the Soviet forces was placed in a former boys' reform school at El Chico. With its dormitories, offices, converted classrooms, and pristine parade fields, it was well suited for General Pliyev and his staff.

The Soviet forces were not properly equipped or prepared for the tropical environment of Cuba. In order to preserve security, tropical uniforms had not been ordered for the troops, so many arrived with their heavy clothing. The locations for the strategic missile sites were isolated, with poor road networks leading to them, which made moving all of the necessary heavy equipment challenging. The areas with trees, which were thought to provide shelter from the Caribbean sun, were some of the more humid places to remain. Machinery and men all suffered from the heat and humidity. Work had to be done in short shifts to avoid heat exhaustion. The air conditioning units that the Soviets had in trailers were inadequate given the temperatures. At night, the men sweltered in tents, swarmed by mosquitoes and other insects. On the eastern part of the island, the Soviets learned that touching the guayaco trees native to the area caused breakouts and blisters on the skin.[35]

The maps the Soviets used were old, out of date, or simply inaccurate, which complicated matters even more. Few of the men spoke Spanish, which made interacting with their Cuban military counterparts and the locals clumsy and difficult. For their first attempt to deploy away from mother-Russia, the Soviets had picked a locale that was proving to be harsher than anticipated.

The Nuclear Forces on Cuba

The construction of the strategic missile launch sites began in earnest as the supplies arrived. Standard Soviet procedure was to attempt to conceal the sites with the use of trees and natural foliage, but in the case of Cuba, this was nearly impossible. The concrete pads necessary for launch, the mobile erectors, fuel trucks, hundreds of meters of thick cable, and the command and support buildings would be distinctly visible from the air. Attempts were made to conceal all of the heavy equipment, but it was in vain.[36]

Barbed wire encircled the launch facilities far enough out to keep away prying eyes. Just moving the all of the construction equipment and the missiles themselves (on trailers) was difficult to keep entirely secret. Maneuvering through small Cuban villages often resulted in trailers damaging buildings, which attracted unwanted attention. Cuban military personnel smoothed over such incidents, but the Soviets were concerned that their operation might be exposed to spies at any time.

The medium-range R-12 missile launch sites were established near Cristobal and Sangua La Grande. The Cristobal complex consisted of sixteen launchers and twenty-four missiles. The Sangua la Grande was established with eight launchers and twelve missiles. The R-12 missiles, (NATO designation SS-4 Sandal) had a range of 1,300 nautical miles and carried a 1-megaton nuclear warhead.

The intermediate-range R-14 missiles were placed in two complexes; one at Guanajay and one at Remedios. Both of these sites were to have eight launchers and twelve missiles each. The R-14s (NATO designation SS-5 Skean) had a range of 2,800 nautical miles and also carried a 1-megaton nuclear warhead. The storage of the nuclear warheads was separate from the missiles themselves; a standard Soviet procedure. The nuclear warhead was thus in a depot at Bejucal, 12 miles south-west of Havana. This facility was designed to be a temporary single repository, with a second depot planned at Santa Clara.

The R-12s had enough range to reach Washington DC and the southern states and airbases. The R14s were the most dangerous threats. These could reach most of the Continental United States, with the exception of Seattle.

The IL-28 bombers (NATO designation Beagle) and the MIG 21s were delivered in crates and had to be unpacked and assembled. The IL-28s were sent to San Julián Asiento and Holguin airfields.

The arsenal of nuclear weapons brought to Cuba was not limited to the strategic weapons. The FKR (Frontoviye Krilatiye Raketi) 'Sopka' cruise missiles (NATO designation SSC-2a Salish) were posted to the 561st and 584th frontal cruise missile (FKR) regiments. These were launched from a towed trailer and were designated for coastal defense. At first glimpse, the missiles appeared more like a jet (MIG 15) mounted on a trailer-mounted launch rail. In reality, the missiles were built on MIG 15 airframes as a building-block for the missiles. Each regiment had eight launchers and forty nuclear-capable missiles. Thirty-six of the nuclear warheads had been delivered to Cuba. The nuclear warheads were 14-15 kilotons each – the equivalent of the bomb that destroyed Hiroshima. The FKRs had a range of 50-60 miles, providing them the ability to potentially decimate any approaching invasion force.

The Soviets also possessed the Luna 3R9/10 (NATO designation FROG 3/5) short-range tactical battlefield rockets. The launch system was mobile, mounted on a PT-76 tank chassis. The Soviet Luna battalion was made up of three batteries, each with a pair of mobile launchers with six missiles. There were a total of twelve nuclear warheads available on Cuba by October 1962, four per battery. The Luna's did not pack much of a punch, armed with a 2-kiloton warhead. What made them more dangerous was their mobility and relative ease of concealment. Each Luna had a range of 18 miles.[37]

The strategic weapons posed a potential threat to the Continental United States. For an invasion force, however, it was the tactical nuclear weapons that presented the greatest risk – not just from the fire power that they brought to bear, but by the fact that the Soviet military doctrine differed from American doctrine in terms of tactical nuclear weapons. Soviet guidelines treated battlefield (tactical) nuclear weapons as a form of advanced artillery. They were usually not under stringent guidelines about release and use. In this respect, the Soviet ground commanders had been trained to treat their nuclear weapons as a tool to be used at their discretion, whereas American military commanders required permission to use nukes on the field of battle.[38]

Soviet doctrine was similar to the United States in that field commanders were under strict orders that tactical nuclear weapons were not to fall into enemy hands. The difference was that in the case of the Soviets, the opportunity to 'use it or lose it' was a potential option. In the case of being potentially overrun, they might be pressed into release of their weapons if they were at risk of falling into an invader's possession.

The Soviets built two nuclear weapon storage bunkers – one in Bejucal, and one outside of Managua. Their intention, per Soviet doctrine, was to keep the launch mechanisms (missiles/rockets) separate from the warheads until the time of launch.

In a matter of a few short months, Cuba was turning itself into the most heavily armed nation in the Caribbean after the United States.

CHAPTER THREE

The Battlefield: Cuba

The base (Guantánamo Bay) had become a 'two-edged sword' in America's hand. On one hand, it could become a dangerous pawn in super-power military and political conflict that might require a military commitment not commensurate with its strategic value as a military installation. At the same time, it could be a base from which to launch offensive operations against Cuba should the need arise.[1]

The Environment of Cuba

Cuba is an island with a wide range of environments and terrain. The island is 777-miles long and 187-miles wide. The beaches on the north side of the island tend to be long and flat, with scattered hills and ridges. They are thick with sand with a deep clay base.[2] On the south part of the island, there are smaller, white-sand beaches, and thick mangroves and marshes, which limit mobility, as the invaders at the Bay of Pigs encountered.

The rolling hills give way to more rugged rocky terrain further inland. The highest ground is the Sierra Maestra mountain at Pico Turquino, towering at 6,476 feet. This high point is the south-east of the island. The other three mountain ranges are the Sierra Cristal in the south-east, the Escambray range in the centre of the island, and the Sierra del Rosario in the north-west. A single rail line, the Cuban Hersey Railway, ran through the island from Havana, west to east, through the heart of the island. This line was put in to help get sugar cane crops in and supplies moved out from the ports at Havana and Mariel to the outlying communities. The rail line had some passenger capabilities, but it was a slow-moving line, and more equipped for the transportation of materials than men. The path of the railway provided a raised roadbed, which could provide cover, and railroad cuts, which would be choke points for movement. Cuba's road networks along the northern coasts and outlying key cities were paved and relatively well maintained. Once you got off of the key highways, however, the roads were often dirt trails; treacherous to navigate after a heavy rain.

The rivers of Cuba tend to be short, running only a few miles. In their tidal areas, they were usually very deep, but inland, they can run almost dry, yet turn into raging torrents with the arrival of a thunderstorm. This meant that the control of the bridges over the rivers became critical to military movement.

Outside of the mountains, there are deep valleys, often filled with dense jungle growth. The interior of Cuba had been cleared in many areas and supported large sugar cane plantations, cattle ranches, and small tropical forest copses. The condition of the cane fields depended on the season. During planting and in the winter, they would be perfect flat fields. At their peak, as many would be in October 1962, the fields would be thick with 10-foot-tall sugar cane stalks, which would block line of sight, and in the minds of military planners, would make movement through fields 'impassible to wheels or tracked traffic'.[3]

The Climate

Cuba has a mean average temperate of 78 degrees Fahrenheit, with a mean maximum of 86 degrees and a mean low of 74.6 degrees. Between May and October, the average temperature is 87.5 degrees Fahrenheit, with a low dipping only to 76.5 degrees. From November and December, these numbers only vary by 1 degree.[4]

Island winds are low, averaging 7 knots. High-wind periods are in March and April, with lows in June to September. The prominent direction of winds is south-east/north-west. Wind speeds during October and November are normally between 8-12 knots during the day, lowering to 3-5 knots at night.[5]

Rainfall on Cuba varies depending on the season. May through October is the wet season, usually ushered in during the tropical storm/hurricane season. The rainfall on the island varies from 5-6 inches during this period. November through April is the dry season, with rainfall dropping to 2-3 inches per month.[6] The rainfall amounts alone do not paint an accurate picture of the moisture. Being an island, Cuba has a relative humidity of over 75 percent year round.[7] In the island interiors and valleys where the air movement would be minimized by tropical growth, it is much higher. Visibility, with the exception of December, is 2.5 miles or more midday, except during thunderstorms. From April to November, morning fog is common, limiting visibility to feet rather than miles. Fog ceases to be an issue between December to March.

Cloudiness would factor in on any planned air operations by anyone executing military operations in Cuba. From September to January, the cloudiness was 44 percent.[8] Storms would also hinder operations on the ground or in the air. On roughly one-third of the days in October and November, thunderstorms occur, some of which are severe. Hurricane season, running from June to November, offered potential risks to both the Soviets on the island and the Americans that were eyeing Cuba as a potential target. Hurricane Ella formed over Cuba in mid-October, moving up the US East Coast. The storm did damage in Cuba, but what it represented was a risk to naval operations in the Caribbean around the island.

Hurricanes grounded air forces, forced cession of ground operations, and often disrupted communications and road networks.

Vegetation

Thick growths of Royal Poincianas, coconut, and dinner palm trees were common to the interior of the island. To the south, near Guantánamo Bay, the Cuban mahogany tree was more common. These large trees were deeply rooted and offered the most shade. The Royal Poinciana tree was imported to the island, and in May and June, the branches of these trees were a mass of flame-colored blossoms. Other forest/jungle growth included several species of rubber trees, banyans, and Spanish Laurel.

The beaches were often dotted with sea grape trees. These tall trees produce a berry that had taste marginally like that of grapes. These trees grow close to each other, often forming an impassible barrier where they were prominent.

Tropical fruits were common, including a range of mangoes. However, some varieties on the island caused allergic reactions that required hospitalization. Avocados, papayas, bananas, oranges, and grapefruit trees group plentifully. Lime trees, sour-sopes, guavas, and pomegranates grew in the south and east of the island.[9] The Cuban villages were able to sustain themselves in many cases.

Animal Life

The birds common to Cuba ranged from thrushes, orioles, flycatchers, belted kingfishers, the Cuban Green Woodpecker, turkey vultures, and the Cuban blackbirds (of which there were five different varieties). Wild Guinea were plentiful, as well the odd little Cuban Lizard Cuckoo, an awkward looking brown bird with a strange call. The rivers at the coastal basins were filled with ducks, herons, pelicans, and gulls.[10]

White-tailed deer ran wild in the interior and the Jutia, a tree-dwelling rodent that was as cross between a possum and a woodchuck. The locals found the Jutia to be a delicacy, but it was by most accounts an acquired taste.

Snakes of all varieties, including the Maja boa constrictor were plentiful, as were iguanas and a number of native lizards.

The real risk came not from the animal life on the island, but from the insects. There were tarantulas and black widow spiders that were common, but it was the mosquitoes and sand fleas that made life at night difficult. Mosquitoes were thick and some carried malaria. The insects made outdoor living nearly unbearable when combined with the heat and humidity.[11]

The Impact on Military Operations

The analysis of the US military on all of these factors on potential operations on the island of Cuba were broken down into three basic summaries:

a. Rain will adversely affect cross-country movement and movement on secondary roads. Flash floods can be expected in stream beds, barramoas, and drainage ditches.

b. The heat, humidity, and rain will result in a high factor of corrosion. Water consumption will increase considerably and preventive measures against heat exhaustion and sun stroke will be taken.

c. Conditions are generally favorable for air operations, aerial observation, and aerial photography, except during thunderstorms.[12]

The impact on the Cubans and their Soviet allies was seen as much less: 'The effects on the enemy will be similar to on our operations, due to his familiarity and acclimation to the area he will not be affected to the same degree'.[13]

The Curse and Blessing: Guantánamo Bay

La Bahia de Guantánamo, Guantánamo Bay, was and remains the lone American foothold on the Communist island of Cuba. Christopher Columbus entered the bay on his second voyage on the evening of 30 April 1494 at a spot now referred to as Fisherman's Point. He named the Bay 'Puerto Grande'.

During the heydays of the Spanish Main, the bay at Guantánamo was a pirate stronghold. The famed pirates Naum, Sores, and Rosillo made it a base of operations to strike at shipping passing through the Windward Passage. The British Navy sent a force to secure the bay from the Spanish in 1741. The Army contingent, led by General Wentworth, landed at the bay (called Walthenham Harbor on British maps) and marched on to Santiago. They reached the small town of Guantánamo, but became bogged down in the drive to Santiago, only 16 miles away. Malaria and the oppressive climate ground the British advance inland to a halt. The British eventually withdrew and consolidated their holdings at the entrance to the bay, where the arid climate was more hospitable. After several months, even this toehold was abandoned.

By 1898, Guantánamo Bay had become a major Spanish port for shipping sugar supplies out of cane fields and molasses from plants in the Cuban interior. A small rail line had been built between Guantánamo City and Calmanera. While the bay prospered, the turmoil in Cuba was growing between the Spanish rulers and the Cuban people. Insurrection by Cuban rebels, bent on driving the Spanish off-island, was centered in the Oriente Province, where the bay was located. The United States was drawn into the conflict when the USS *Maine* exploded and sank in Havana Harbor. The initial investigation into the act pointed to a Spanish mine. Fanned by the American press, the US Government declared war on Spain, and Cuba, the closest of her colonies to the US, became the focal point of operations.

America's first invasion of Cuba took place on 6 June 1898 when the cruiser USS *Marblehead* and the auxiliary ship *St Louis* arrived at Guantánamo Bay to reconnoiter its potential use as a naval base. The *St Louis* had the additional duty of severing the telegraph cables at Fisherman's Point.

The USS *Marblehead* opened fire on a Spanish Army blockhouse, destroying it. Other Spanish guns opened fire on the cruiser, with no effect. After their cable-cutting mission, the two American vessels left. Their report indicated that Guantánamo Bay would make an excellent naval base. The American ship the *Panther* was sent to debark the first four of six companies of US Marines. Their would-be adversaries fled, most leaving behind their personal gear and even some weapons. Near the Well of Cuzco, the Spanish managed to rally. They had 400 troops, and the well was the only fresh water source other than Guantánamo City. Holding it, they could eventually wear down the Marines, who would be tied to their ship for water supplies.

Colonel Huntington, the Marine Commander, led his troops to within 300 yards of the Spanish position, and lost all of his troops; the first US casualties after the war with Spain had been declared.

The Marines were exhausted, having been on the march and in fighting for nearly 100 hours. They were reinforced by 50 Cuban insurgents who welcomed the Americans. The Spanish probed at their defenses and sniped at their lines.

The plan devised for defeating the Spanish at Cuzco was tricky. The Cubans, along with the bulk of the Marines, would approach Cuzco along the seaside cliffs. A smaller force of Marines would advance through an inland valley to keep the Spanish infantry's attention. The cliff-assault force was discovered at the last moments and a race ensued between the Marines and the Spanish for the high-crested hill overlooking the Spanish positions. The Americans and Cubans won, eventually driving out the Spanish forces. Over 7,000 Spanish troops remained in Guantánamo City, but were too far to represent any immediate threat to the control of the bay.[14]

This victory at Guantánamo Bay not only secured the base for the Americans, but laid the foundation for the rest of the American operations on Cuba. The American expeditionary force under General W. R. Shafter landed east of Guantánamo City at the Port of Daiquiri and Siboney on 22-25 June 1898. Their march inland was slow, as the Americans struggled against the heat and humidity of the Cuban summer. At week later came the fighting at El Caney and San Juan Hill, which opened up the approaches to the site of Santiago itself. These victories spelled the end of Spanish rule of Cuba.

Five years later, the US still had troops in the bay and cemented the control of the bay from the Cubans in 1903 under a treaty agreement. The US leased the bay for a naval and coaling station. The property consisted of 7,940 acres of land on both sides (leeward (west) and windward (east) of the entrance to the bay). The area was only 5 x 9 miles, and could only be returned to Cuba if the US abandoned the base, or by mutual agreement of the US and Cuban Governments. The base grew in terms of size and complexity after the First World War with the addition of airfields to support scouting aircraft. With the digging of the Panama Canal, the position of Guantánamo Bay gave the US Navy a perfect outpost for protecting and defending the strategically vital canal.

1962 Guantánamo Bay

The presence of the base, until Castro's rise to power, was seen as a boon by the Cuban people. Many locals worked on the base providing support services. The naval personnel taking leave on the island spurred businesses, albeit bars and clubs, bringing much needed dollars into the area. That all changed with Castro's rise to power. He made several speeches calling for the ouster of the Americans from the bay and demanding its return. In one radio speech, he claimed that the base officers were establishing 'counter-revolutionary elements' opposed to his administration.[15] Castro sympathizers handed out inflammatory handbills to the Cubans that worked on the base. Rallies were held in Santiago calling for the United States to leave Cuban waters. Raul Castro called Guantánamo Bay, 'A cancer and a permanent focus of provocation.'[16]

Prior to the missile crisis, Guantánamo Bay was a major command of the 10th Naval District, and was considered a medium-sized base used primarily for training operations. There were several component activities tied to the base: the naval station, naval air station, marine barracks, hospital, dental clinic, supply clinic, public works, two fleet commands, the Fleet Training Group, and Utility Squadron Ten. The personnel stationed there were 4,000 military personnel and 280 civilians. In addition to these were 2,700 dependants and 2,500 local Cubans who came into the post every day, working to provide support services.[17]

The marine barracks were augmented by a tank platoon, an artillery battery, a self-propelled artillery platoon from Camp Lejeune, and a rifle company from the Caribbean contingency battalion. These forces were present primarily for training purposes, undertaking exercises that ran 12 hours, almost always in daylight.[18]

Preparing for the Storm

The Guantánamo Bay naval base fell under the command of the Naval Antilles Defense Command under the CINCLANT. In early 1962, as Castro's rhetoric increased regarding the base, a study was undertaken about improving the base's defense.

The problems were numerous. The naval base relied on electricity and fresh water from the Cubans. While Castro had not yet cut it off, that threat existed, and although the base personnel could be supplied by the sea, that was not a long-term solution.

The American base was not situated well. It was poised in a bowl of sorts, holding the low-lands at the water's edge. Even the hills and ridges that the Americans did have under their patrol were overlooked by higher hills. The perimeter was fenced and barb wire was strung, but it was far from impressive. The security system in some parts of the perimeter consisted of empty beer cans tied to the barbed wire to make a sound if someone attempted to come through.

The base lacked air search radar. Its only means of anti-air defense came from the F8U aircraft of Utility Squadron Ten and any ships that were in port at the time.[19] After the Bay of Pigs, it was recognized that the Cuban Air Force was still a potential risk should military operations start, but there was no early warning system. Prior to October 1962, Utility Squadron Ten would run the risk that, in any surprise attack, they would be caught on the tarmac and destroyed before they could get into action.

The base defenses were thin at best. Up until 1959, Cuba had been friendly to the base, so it was not necessary to defend it. While some trenches and sandbagged bunkers did exist, they were inadequate to defend against a large-scale attack.

Perhaps the most glaring weakness of the base was the lack of conventional fire power. Prior to October 1962, the base had only two 155-mm self-propelled artillery pieces, six 155-mm howitzers, and four 105-mm howitzers as their artillery defense. There were a number of 4.2-mm mortars also available for defense. The base commander on intelligence analysis at Guantánamo in October, at the start of the missile crisis, showed that the Cubans had at least forty-three artillery pieces poised over his base. These consisted of:

Guns	Range
122-mm M-1938 howitzers	12,904 yards
122-mm gun M-1931-1937	24,000 yards
152-mm gun-howitzer M-1937	18,880 yards
37-mm gun M-6	5,486 yards
130-mm field gun	30,000 yards
Assault gun, SU-100	15,316 yards
FROG (FKR missile)	40-50,000 yards
Snapper anti-tank missile	2,675 yards[20]

The range of the Soviet and Cuban artillery alone put them in striking distance of the airfields at the naval air station where Utility Squadron Ten was based. That facility did not have bomb-proof hangers or protection. If an attack was launched, the Cubans would have been able to destroy the aircraft, or at least damage the airstrip quickly, leaving the base vulnerable. It was not just that the Cubans and their Soviet allies had superior fire power and better (higher) terrain to work from, they also were employing movement at night to change their positions.

This meant that daily, the US forces would not know where the potential enemies were.

The naval base relied not on ground artillery to support their troops, but on naval gunfire. At almost any point in time, there was a destroyer or cruiser in port at Guantánamo Bay that could lend its fire power to any potential ground assault. The range of the 5-inch guns of the destroyers were 2,900 yards, and the 3-inch guns of those ships could reach 13,000 yards. The 8-inch guns common on the cruisers had a range of 31,000 yards. Even with these ranges, the ship-based guns could not reach targets from the sea north of the naval base's boundaries unless the cruisers entered the Cuban-controlled waters.[21] There was no way to know if mines were planted, which would have made such a move even more dangerous.

Castro seemed to be preparing for conflict over the base himself. He had declared a 6-mile radius around the base a 'militarized zone'. Farms and families were evacuated, and travel restrictions were placed on the roads entering the zone. Work was undertaken to prepare field fortifications and clear potential fields of fire. He ordered a deep band of the territory to be planted with Opuntia cactus, designed to impede the movement of troops. The US dubbed it the 'Cactus Curtain', paying homage to the Iron Curtain in Europe. Both sides planted tens of thousands of land mines in the area. For all intents and purposes, Castro kept a firm gaze on Guantánamo and saw it as a potential risk that had to be dealt with.[22] Daily radio broadcasts from Cuba claimed on a daily basis that the base was being used for espionage, and complained of over 180 alleged US aircraft violations of Cuban territorial limits.[23]

To control and monitor the base in September, Cuban militiamen built a cattle-chute, a parallel set of fencing, and buildings next to the perimeter entrance to the post. Here, workers coming in and out of the base would have to pass for identification. They were searched thoroughly for contraband, both going in and coming out, in the hope of finding documentation that proved the base was attempting to contact counter-revolutionary teams. This process slowed down the passage of Cuban civilians entering and leaving the base by hours, and served to heighten the tension between the two nations.[24]

Both the Cubans and the United States saw Guantánamo Bay and its naval base as a focal point for any conflict between them. And that conflict was coming only a few weeks away.

CHAPTER FOUR

The Crisis Emerges

But at a moment when the United States is taking measures to mobilize its Armed Forces and preparing for aggression against Cuba and other peace-loving states, the Soviet Government would like to draw attention to the fact that no one can now attack Cuba and expect that the aggressor will be free from punishment for this attack. If this attack is made, this will be the beginning of the unleashing of war.[1]

A Change in the Balance of Power

The 7,000-mile movement of over 40,000 Soviet troops and a massive amount of equipment was not something that happened without attracting some attention from intelligence services. The NSA (National Security Agency) initially detected indications that something was amiss with the large number of transport ships shuttling between the USSR and Cuba. Electronic surveillance of the vessels was done, but revealed little. Cuban refugees were reporting 'an unusual number of ships' unloading foreign passengers and cargo that was being handled with high security in the ports of Mariel and Havana.[2]

In July 1962, while Operation Anadyr was fully underway, the CIA (Central Intelligence Agency) was convinced that the Soviets were sending something to Cuba, although they were unsure as to what. The Director of Central Intelligence John McCone ordered an increase in U2 photographic reconnaissance flights over Cuba. The U2 was a marvel when it was first introduced. The sleek, glider-like, 103-foot wingspan aircraft was created to fly at the edge of the atmosphere (over 70,000 feet) taking state of the art photographs. In an age when satellite photography was only starting to appear on the drawing board, the U2 provided the best means of surveillance coverage.

That is not to say there were not weaknesses. The Soviets were aware of the American over-flights of their airspace and developed their own technological solution to the problem of the stealthy, high-flying aircraft – the SA-2 SAM missile. U2 pilot Francis Gary Powers was shot down by a SA-2 over the Soviet Union in 1960. His downing and subsequent capture (and show trial) had given the

Eisenhower administration a black eye. While the U2 had enjoyed several years of superiority in terms of spy aircraft, its time was coming to an end by 1962.

The initial flight over Cuba on 5 August 1962 failed to show any of the significant Soviet build-up. Tropical storms and cloud cover prevented another U2 flight until 29 August. The results of this mission were dramatically different. Eight SA-2 SAM launch sites were identified as being either under construction or nearing completion. Also, sites were being prepared for the coastal-based Sopka cruise missiles. There was more; the presence of KOMAR missile-launching patrol craft were confirmed. Cuba, it seemed, was being transformed militarily. Two days later, Director McCone filled in President Kennedy. What no one could answer at the time was, what were the SAMs there to protect?

Naval intelligence began charting the shipping to Cuba. Fifteen arrived in June, thirty ships in July, fifty-five in August, and another sixty-six were expected by the end of September. Passenger ships should have given them a clue as to the size of the force being deployed as well. Only one passenger ship arrived in Cuba from the USSR in the first five months of 1962. Eleven vessels arrived in July and August.[3]

John McCone was the first to raise the flag at the senior levels of the US Government that Cuba was undergoing a military metamorphosis. He saw the arrival of new MIG fighters detected earlier, the KOMAR patrol boats, the cruise missile launch sites, and the SA-2 SAM sites as evidence that Cuba was being turned into a major Soviet military base. McCone voiced this concern at the National Security Council meeting on 23 August, but Secretary of State Rusk and Secretary of Defense McNamara disagreed with McCone.

McCone was not alone in voicing concerns about Cuba. Republican Senator Kenneth Keating of New York made a statement in the US Senate on 31 August: 'There are Soviet rocket installations in Cuba.' Keating refused to reveal his sources, but it was clear that the word of the Soviet build-up in Cuba was no longer a secret.

The Soviet Union, for its part, claimed (via Ambassador Anatoly Dobrynin) that the hardware going into Cuba was defensive in nature – it did not represent an offensive threat to the United States. What no one knew at the time was that the Soviet ambassador was in the dark as much as the US as to what was really happening on the island.

The U2 flights were increased, with missions on 26 and 29 September, and 5 and 7 October. These missions were restricted because of the fear that the SA-2 missiles might be used on the U2, as had happened with Francis Gary Powers. None of these over-flights spotted any offensive missions, but they did locate a large number of SAM sites either under construction or being completed. The NSA was reporting that, based on radar emissions detected by ships off of the coast of Cuba, the missile-tracking radar of the SAM sites were active.

The first inkling of the scale and nature of the Soviet build-up emerged in September. Several Soviet IL-28 bomber fuselages were spotted being moved by truck to the San Julian Airfield for assembly. While the IL-28 was nearing the end of its life, it was still considered an offensive weapon. A number of IL-28s were spotted on the airfield in various stages of assembly. A detailed photograph of the Holquin Airfield near the navy base at Guantánamo Bay had nine, which were identified by their crates.[4]

On 19 September, the National Board of Estimates released a report entitled, 'The Military Build-up in Cuba.' While usually considered a source for US policy decisions, this time they made a blunder, assuming that there was no reasonable chance that the Soviets were putting offensive weapons into Cuba. Given that much of Cuba had not been photographed, and the overwhelming number of shipments from the USSR to Cuba, this report is seen as a horrible mistake that lulled some US officials into a sense of complacency.

Only the US military seemed to maintain its guard against the rise of Soviet actions. Electronic surveillance of Cuba increased off-shore in hopes of gleaning information about Soviet intentions. The Navy stepped up photographic flights over Soviet transport shipping. These images could be searched for clues as to what the ships were carrying. The 55th Strategic Reconnaissance Wing of SAC was relocated from Forbes Air Force Base outside of Topeka, Kansas, to MacDill Air Force Base in Florida. This unit consisted of RB-47H aircraft equipped for electronic intelligence gathering, specifically emissions from Cuban/Soviet radars, etc.[5] The American military machine seemed to recognize the change in the air and was preparing to counter those threats.

'Rock Pile' OP Plan 312-62

The US Air Force, led by the bombastic and opinionated General Curtis LeMay, began to draw up a new plan regarding air strikes on Cuba. This plan, started in early September, built off of the plan (OP Plan 312-61) that had been drawn up in 1961. This version called for a more extensive air campaign, and presented a broad range of options, given the changing military landscape in Cuba. On 27 September, General LeMay approved the plan, code named, 'Rock Pile', which was sent to Admiral Dennison. Dennison and his staff adopted this plan as a replacement to the existing air war campaign, re-designating it as OP Plan 312-62.

Rock Pile differed from previous air war plans against Cuba in several respects. Firstly, it took into account the SAM missile sites known to be in Cuba – the supposed impetus for drawing up the plan in the first place. Secondly, it provided a broad range of options to Admiral Dennison, depending on the kind of operation being undertaken. Its 1961 version had simply been a plan for an all-out attack on Cuban airfields, command centers, and concentrations of troops and armor.

When Rock Pile was devised, it was done with an almost prophetic view of the coming weeks.

The outlook is for the Soviets to continue with the arms build-up in Cuba with the objective of setting the price of US intervention at an unacceptably high level, and denying the US surveillance of the Soviet offensive build-up. We believe that the offensive weapons will include ballistic missiles, jet bombers, missile and submarine bases, and airfields for the recovery of Soviet long-range bombers.[6]

While some policy makers in Washington DC tried to deny what was happening in Cuba, the US Air Force appeared to fully understand the future direction of events. Even their drafting of Rock Pile to deal with these contingencies is an acknowledgement of their comprehension of what the SAM sites represented long-term.

Rock Pile offered a number of different options to the CINCLANT. The contingencies in OP Plan 312-62 each had a code name and a designated set of targets, although the targeting lists were separate and could be modified as the CINCLANT saw fit. These variants were:

Fire Hose: The selective destruction of specific surface-to-air missile sites (SAMs.) This would likely be employed as a retaliatory strike if a reconnaissance aircraft were shot down prior to the start of hostilities, or in the event of crippling part of the Cuban air defense network to support landings of unconventional warfare teams, for example. Fire Hose was the most restricted option available under the air war plan in that it was against specific SAM sites to blind the Cubans in a portion of the island.

Black Shoe: This was a broader air campaign targeting all Cuban airfields capable of supporting jet aircraft, SAM sites, and enemy combat air patrols, all hangers and aircraft on the ground, and specific ground targets related to command and control of aviation assets. Black Shoe was seen as an air-only campaign against Cuba, where invasion was not necessary and the destruction of potential Cuban threats were to be suppressed solely by bombing efforts. This operation worked off a highly flexible list of targets. If invasion was not an option being considered, Black Shoe would be the option that would be employed, relying entirely on the US Air Force to suppress Cuba's air capabilities.

Full House: Destruction of all SAMs on the island of Cuba. The option would leave the airfields and aircraft of the Revolutionary Air Force intact, but would wipe out the SAMs being installed by the Soviet.

Royal Flush: This variant called for the destruction of all Cuban/Soviet air defenses, including anti-aircraft gun emplacements. Unlike Black Shoe, this option was not seen as only an air war campaign. The assumption is that some sort of invasion would be part of this operation, albeit on a limited basis.

Scabbards 312: Scabbards was envisioned as a long large-scale air campaign as a precursor to a full invasion of Cuba. The objective of Scabbards was to destroy the Cuban Air Force, Navy, and ground forces. Missions would include an extensive campaign to be tied to the invasion landing zones and beaches, as well to attempt to wipe out any defenders there.[7]

None of these options assumed the presence of offensive strategic weapons in the form of missiles and IL-28 bombers. Rock Pile's options were all envisioned to be performed by Tactical Air Command (TAC) and the US Navy, although the resource commitments on the part of the Navy were not defined. General LeMay's vision was that this would be, as much as possible, an Air Force controlled operation. Admiral Dennison and his staff recognized that there would be a substantial role to be played by naval aviators based on carriers. Rather than immediately redrafting the plan, the CINCLANT accepted it with the provision that it would be updated and changed as conditions would merit. Few realized just how quickly that time was approaching.

'Blue Water' and 'Three Pairs'

Oftentimes, the missile crisis is portrayed as having caught the Kennedy administration off-guard. In reality, military options and planning were very much on the forefront of thinking. On 2 October 1962, the Secretary of Defense Robert McNamara sent a message to the Joint Chiefs of Staff detailing the circumstances that might require military action against Cuba. These were:

- a. Soviet action against western rights of access to Berlin.
- b. Evidence that the Castro regime has obtained and positioned Soviet block offensive weapons on Cuban soil or Cuban waters.
- c. An attack against Guantánamo Naval Base or against US planes and vessels.
- d. A substantial popular uprising in Cuba, which compelled the need for American assistance to remove Castro from power.
- e. Cuba providing armed assistance and subversion in other parts of the hemisphere.
- f. A decision by the President that the situation/affairs in Cuba had reached a point 'inconsistent with US national security'.

McNamara emphasizes that any contingency planning needed to put emphasis on the basis that Fidel Castro be removed from power.[8]

Even without prompting from the Secretary of Defense, Admiral Dennison and his staff had been far from idle in their preparations for any possible contingency. Even before the Soviet SAM sites had been identified, he had begun a series of exercises to test coordinating the vast array of military assets that would need to come into play if an invasion of Cuba was called for. On 7 May 1962, an exercise called 'Quick Kick' ran to test coordinating the Air Force, the Navy, and the Marine Corps in a simulated assault involving thousands of troops.[9] Quick Kick was considered a success, although for Admiral Dennison, it pointed out the complexities of the various commands that would need to be pulled together for any invasion or air strike on Cuba. October was slated to be a training period for the Atlantic and Caribbean, designed to prepare forces for some of the contingencies presented in OP Plan 314-61, as well as the other invasion plans being contemplated.

The first was a plan called 'Blue Water', which was an exercise conducted by the US Navy to practice setting up of a blockade line to seal off Cuba. It is clear that Admiral Dennison and his staff were keeping all military options open. Blue Water was not an encirclement of Cuba by the Navy, but a screen of ships to block traffic from Africa and the North Atlantic.

Another exercise known as PHIBRIGLEX-62 (Amphibious Brigade Landing Exercise), more commonly referred to as operation 'Three Pairs', was planned for early October, designed to provide marine and navy personnel with experience of an amphibious assault. Three Pairs was planned to take place on the island of Vieques Island part of Puerto Rico. Vieques Island had been used since the Second World War as a navy and marine training facility and target range.

Three Pairs was designed to be a three-week operation. The scenario called for the marines to be landing as part of an operation to topple a mythical dictator named 'Ortsac'; Castro spelled backwards. The operations were to be conducted using an amphibious task force organized as the 4th Marine Expeditionary Brigade, which consisted of a RLT (Regimental Landing Team) headquarters, three battalion landing teams, an anti-submarine hunter-killer group, and a logistics support force. The man placed in command of Three Pairs was Vice Admiral Rivero.

In total, 20,000 naval personnel and 4,000 marines were slated to take part in Three Pairs and the toppling of the Ortsac regime. It was not only going to be an amphibious exercise, but was also going to involve an airborne assault by the marines in seventy-four helicopters.[10] The use of helicopters to bring in assault troops was a relatively new concept in warfare, and Three Pairs was going to be a rehearsal for this kind of attack.

The only thing holding off on Three Pairs was the weather. Hurricane Ella formed over the Caribbean the first week of October and moved along east coast. While it remained out at sea, there were some forecasts that showed it making landfall in North Carolina. With the ships to be used for the operation being based out of Norfolk, Virginia, most of the ships put to sea to skirt Ella – delaying the operation. Norfolk and Continental Army Command at Fort Monroe, Virginia, were preoccupied with filling sandbags and preparing to weather the storm, rather than the delay in the exercise.

The name of the fictitious dictator Ortsac caught the attention of the press. No attempt to was made to conceal the true intent of Three Pairs or of its precursor Quick Kick. It was designed to train troops and to make sure that Fidel Castro received a clear message as to the United States resolve when it came to Cuba.

A Step Closer to Conflict

Invasion OP Plans 314 and 316 were considered off during this period, and updates were made somewhat on the fly as events unfolded. The first of these changes took place on 4 October when the targeting list for the air strikes was updated to include 'KOMAR PGM' boats, which were now known to be in place in Cuba.[11] In this case, the navy was taking no risks for any of its amphibious forces, and wanted these missile patrol boats dealt with in the first few waves of air strikes. All of these OP Plans were given the suffix of '-62' at this time. Their refinement would continue up until the time of the invasion.

Secretary of Defense Robert McNamara must have sensed some of the risks that General LeMay had raised with his creation of Operation Rock Pile. On 6 October 1962, he ordered Admiral Dennison to increase their readiness to execute OP Plans 314, 316, and 312. The CINCLANT called for the repositioning of troops, ships, aircraft, equipment, and supplies.

There were some restrictions to this; there was to be no formal announcement of this increased readiness. CINCLANT was instructed to keep this low key. Furthermore, it was to be done under the auspices of the current budget – but Admiral Dennison was given leeway to go beyond his budget if it was required. CINCLANT was also told to execute this increased readiness without disruption to current deployment and training exercises.

Given that this order came at roughly the same time that Hurricane Ella was bearing down on the East Coast, Admiral Dennison and his staff opted to keep Operation Three Pairs on the calendar. If an invasion of Cuba was called for on short notice, he would already have the heart and core of his amphibious forces in the Caribbean and within rapid striking range of Cuba. CINCLANT was given until 15 October to prepare its plans to meet this heightened state of readiness.[12]

Mission 3101

The finicky Caribbean weather caused a delay in U2 flights in early October. President Kennedy approved the fights, but switched the control of the flights from the CIA to Strategic Air Command. The CIA's older U2s operated at a lower altitude. Given the CIA had control over Francis Gary Power's doomed flight, the thought was to turn over the reconnaissance flights to SAC, whose U2s were a newer model that could fly 5,000 feet higher. The formal reason for the change was that the increase in altitude might be beyond the range of the Soviet SAMs in Cuba. Another factor most likely was that the President and his cabinet were still stinging from the CIA's perceived failures at the Bay of Pigs.

Mission 3101 was stated to be flown by Major Richard Heyser of the 4080th Strategic Reconnaissance Wing (SRW) on 14 October 1962. He took off flying a U2F from Edwards AFB (Air Force Base) at 0731 Eastern time. His flight was to take him on a pass over the western end of Cuba, from south to north, with recovery at McCoy AFB in Florida. The western portion of the island had not been filmed in any detail at this point. The entire time given to Heyser to investigate and take photographs of the areas was a mere 12 minutes. Major Heyser called the flight, 'A piece of cake; a milk run.'[13]

The images were sent to the Naval Photographic Intelligence Center, (NAVPIC) in Suitland, Maryland. They processed the film and forwarded it onto NPIC, the National Photographic Interpretation Center in south-east Washington DC on 15 October. Under the leadership of Art Lundahl, this unit had the painstaking task of reviewing every image taken, attempting to analyze and spot any signs of the Soviet build-up. The skilled professionals looked at the shape of images, their size (relative to other objects and known military hardware), the tone or brilliance of reflection of the object, the texture of the photographed object, its shadows and patterns, scale, and association with other objects in the image.[14] In 1962, this was not an automated process, but a slow and careful visual check of each and every image by a team of professionals.

On one image, six long, canvas-covered objects were spotted. Their length and proximity to other support vehicles seemed to indicate that they might be some sort of missile. Turning to intelligence photographs of Soviet missiles, a check was made to attempt to identify them by their approximate size; 75 feet. This ruled out the SA-2 SAMs. The team came to the conclusion after review and analysis was that these were SS-4s – MRBMs – medium-range ballistic missiles, although there was thought by some of the analysts that they may be SS-3s.[15] These were Soviet nuclear weapon delivery systems, and they were in range of a significant portion of the United States.

Another image uncovered what at first appeared like boats, but far from the Cuban coast. As these images were checked, it was determined that these too were SS-4 missiles, along with supporting tents, trailers, and construction equipment. The searching continued and revealed a third site in a valley approximately 10 miles from the other two. While the Soviets had made use of the trees and covering their equipment with tarps, it was becoming quite clear that this too was a medium-range missile site.[16]

In total, the sites were identified by the largest town near them – San Cristóbal, and labeled as San Cristóbal MRBM 1, 2, and 3.

Military Options Front and Center

On the morning of 16 October, President Kennedy and members of his National Security Council were briefed on the findings. Dubbed 'ExComm', the Executive Committee of the National Security Council was as smaller group with informal membership that changed throughout the crisis. For the President, it was an advisory group designed to work through the plausible scenarios.

There have been many books on the Cuban Missile Crisis where the transcripts of these meetings have been analyzed and interpreted over the years. Insomuch as this book is written with a focus on the military actions and the planned invasion of Cuba, the specific political and diplomatic actions will only be covered as they pertain to the military plans and operations, or to provide context for the reader. The bibliography of this book provides a number of excellent sources where the politics, decision making, and diplomatic maneuvering are better represented.

The initial response by the Kennedy administration was to step up U2 flights to obtain further evidence of the Soviet efforts and to fully cover all of Cuba. By the time this was announced, additional flights had already been flown, but the development and analysis of images from those flights took days to be ready for conclusions to be drawn. While low-level reconnaissance missions over the sites would provide much clearer photographs, these were ruled out at the onset of the crisis. The use of jets at low altitude would tip the American's hands to the Cuban and Soviets before the Americans were prepared to take a formal course of action.[17]

A series of meetings unfolded with the Kennedy administration in an attempt to wrap their proverbial heads around the seemingly sudden presence of Soviet medium-range missiles in Cuba. The President was shown the photographic evidence from the U2 flights and the interpretation of the images. Kennedy contacted John McCloy, a highly respected statesman who rose to prominence in America for successfully getting Germany to pay reparations for damages caused in the Great War. McCloy, despite being a Republican, was a trusted advisor to President Kennedy. The senior McCloy recommended that Kennedy take forceful action to remove the missiles – even if that warranted air strikes, followed by an invasion.[18]

The Excomm group reviewed the known intelligence and began heated discussion and debate on what the Soviet motivations might be in undertaking this kind and scale of military placement. They further defined the initial options they believed were available. These included:

1. A single 'surgical' air strike on the missile bases, and them alone, to remove them as a threat.
2. Attacks on a range of Cuban facilities, including the missile complexes. These air strikes could include the SAM sites and Cuban airfields.
3. A combined series of air strikes with a follow-on invasion of Cuba to ensure that the missile threat has indeed been removed.
4. A blockade of Cuba.[19]

On the first day of the crisis, the emphasis was on military actions to be taken against Cuba. The concern raised on options one and two was that they could not guarantee that the missiles would all be destroyed. Intelligence could only confirm the missiles and launch equipment that had been identified. The location of the nuclear warheads was not yet discovered. No one could qualify just what hardware and potential missiles existed that they had *not* yet seen. Air strikes alone could inflict incredible damage to known targets, but was that everything? The recommendation from the Joints Chiefs of Staff was that air strikes alone would never be enough alone to ensure American security.

As the Chairman of the Joint Chiefs said, 'Our recommendation would be to get complete intelligence, get all the photography we need over the next two or three days, no, no hurry in our book. Then look at this target system. If it really threatens the United States, then take it right out with one hard crack.'[20] Not every one of the Excomm members agreed with this thinking; there was just too much unresolved.

Secretary of Defense McNamara qualified the risks of military action for the members:

> The third course of action is one of these variants of military action directed against Cuba, starting with an air attack against the missiles. The Chiefs are strongly opposed to so limited an air attack. But even so limited an air attack is a very very extensive air attack. It's not 20 sorties, or 50 sorties or a 100 sorties, but probably several hundred sorties. Uh, we haven't worked out the details. It's difficult to do so when we lack certain intelligence that we hope to have tomorrow or the next day. But it's a substantial air attack.[21]

A few minutes later, the Secretary of Defense addressed the invasion alternative directly:

> Almost certainly, we should accompany the initial air strike with at least a partial mobilization. We should accompany an invasion following an air strike with a large-scale mobilization, a very large-scale mobilization, certainly exceeding the limits of the authority we have from Congress requiring a declaration therefore of a national emergency.[22]

The recommendation was made to alert the Strategic Air Command and put them on airborne alert.

The military options floated served multiple purposes. First and foremost, they provided a potential solution to the threat perceived by the Soviet missiles. Secondly, almost lost in the debate, was that the threat of military action was a powerful diplomatic incentive and leverage against both the Cubans and the USSR.

General Taylor walked a tightrope with the members of Excomm. After the Bay of Pigs fiasco, members of the Kennedy administration set the blame on the shoulders of the CIA and the Joint Chiefs of the Staff for misleading the President in the probability of success of the operation. General Taylor represented the JCS in many of their eyes. But Taylor had been brought in out of retirement by

President Kennedy to be a trusted advisor and to help clean-up after the Bay of Pigs. His stepping in as the Chairman of the Joint Chiefs of Staff cut off several of the sitting chiefs who saw themselves in line for that job. Max Taylor was a voice of reason, but at the same time, he had to represent the Pentagon's thinking.

The Excomm members did not just discuss air strikes, blockade, or invasion; General Taylor also warned them of the dangers Americans faced in Cuba:

> We think Mr. President, that under any of these plans we will probably get an attack on, on Guantánamo, at least by, by fire. They have artillery and mortars in the area, easily within range, and, uh, any of these actions we take we'll have to give our support to Guantánamo and probably reinforce the garrison.[23]

Taylor's assessment matched that of the naval base commander who recognized the difficulty in defending the base surrounded by hills dotted with Cuban artillery.

Excomm's military discussions were not limited to the Caribbean. There was a genuine concern that any pressure exerted on the Soviets would result in responses that could occur anywhere in the world. Berlin was the most logical spot. Surrounded by Communist East Germany and armed Soviet troops, Berlin had been a political and diplomatic hot spot only a year before. The assumption was that Chairman Khrushchev was playing a complex diplomatic game and would use Cuba to again exert pressure on Berlin.

The other military topic that reared its ugly head was that of the crisis escalating to all-out nuclear war with the Soviets. Secretary of Defense McNamara summed it up:

> And then an ul-, I call it an ultimatum associated with these two actions is a statement to the world, particularly to Khrushchev that we have located these offensive weapons [and] we're maintaining constant surveillance over them; if there is ever any indication that they're about to be launched against this country, we will respond not only against Cuba, but we will respond directly against the Soviet Union, with, with a full nuclear strike.[24]

With the full weight of military options on the table, Robert Kennedy, the brother and trusted advisor to the President, slid him a note: 'I now know how Tojo felt when he was planning Pearl Harbor.'[25]

Option Afloat

While Excomm debated a course of action, Admiral Dennison proceeded with the Three Pairs exercise. The core of the invasion fleet that would lead any amphibious assault put to sea on 16 October. Putting the fleet out to sea gave the Pentagon troops in the immediate vicinity of Cuba, which could be used for any rapid response to a change in the situation. Additionally, the highly publicized exercise would provide excellent cover for any additional troop build-ups that were going to be required in the event of a full-blown invasion.[26]

The use of Three Pairs to cover a broader military mobilization would only hold water for a few days. Beyond that, the concern was that press would start to suspect that the operation was more than an exercise. For the time being, the troops on ships would represent not only America's sword, but diplomatic leverage if/when the details of the USSR's activities in Cuba were exposed. The officers and men aboard the task force vessels thought they were heading down to Puerto Rico for maneuvers. They had no idea that they were being pre-positioned to invade Cuba.

The Situation Becomes Worse

The U2 flights underway had their film developed and analyzed while Excomm met on 16 October. On 17 October, the results of those flights was revealed to the President and his advisers. Construction on the SS-4 missiles seemed to be moving along at a brisk pace. The GMAIC (Guided Missile and Astronautics Intelligence Committee) who analyzed the images, felt that, according to the pace of construction demonstrated in the new photographs, the Soviets and Cubans would have as many as thirty-two of the missiles ready for launch within a week's time.

There was more; based on some of the new photographs, the Soviets were constructing a launch site for their R-14 (NATO designation SS-5 Skean) intermediate-range missiles (IRMs). There was no indication that the missiles were present, but the distinctive patterns of the launch facilities left little doubt. The GMAIC felt that the intermediate-range nuclear missiles would not be ready for launch prior to December.[27]

It was these missiles that were the most disturbing to the members of Excomm. While the SS-4 medium-range missiles could reach as far as Washington DC and possibly New York, the intermediate-range SS-4 missiles could strike all of the Continental United States with the exception of Seattle, Washington. The perception of the Excomm members was that the introduction of these longer range missiles into Cuba represented a fundamental shift in Soviet policy towards these weapons and the United States. From Cuba, a first strike could be launched with only a few minutes' notice, with the capability to decimate America's strategic weapons before they could even clear their silos.

Excomm's view of the situation was one though a filter. The Soviet Union had been facing a similar threat from NATO for some time. There were US-made Thor missiles positioned in Great Britain, and Jupiter missiles in Italy and Turkey – all aimed at the USSR. Likewise, France had its own nuclear arsenal that would be directed at the Soviet Union in the event of an attack on NATO as well. The Soviets had lived under the shadow of a quick-strike nuclear attack for several years already. But for the members of Excomm, this sudden appearance of the missiles (combined with the IL-28 bombers that were also on the island) presented a shift in Soviet doctrine and represented an immediate threat that had to be eradicated. The USSR's interference in the affairs of the western hemisphere was a violation of the American Monroe Doctrine too, which only seemed to be more flagrant and daring on the part of the Soviets.

Excomm went over a broad range of scenarios, weighing their pros and cons. Ultimately, there were four tracks of action that were being considered. These were:

Track A: Political action, pressure, and warning, followed by a military strike if satisfaction is not received.

Track B: A military strike without prior warning, pressure, or action, accompanied by messages making clear the limited nature of this action.

Track C: Political actions, pressure, and warnings, followed by a total naval blockade, under the authority of the Rio-Pact, and either a congressional declaration of war on Cuba or the Cuban resolution of the 87th Congress.

Track D: Full-scale invasion, to 'take Cuba way from Castro'.[28]

Tracks A, B, and D all involved exercising a military solution to the Cuban situation. Excomm was demonstrating a wide range of flexibility in their thinking – flexibility that the current military plans, with the exception of OP Plan 312-62 'Rock Pile', lacked. Admiral Dennison and the JCS were going to have adjust a great deal of their thinking if any of the choices were employed.

> Within Tracks A, and B, the most likely military alternatives aside from blockade and invasion included the following:
>
> a: A 50 sortie, 1 swoop air strike limited to the missile complex, followed by surveillance and announcement that future missile sites would be similarly struck.
>
> b: Broadened air strikes to eliminate all Cuban air power or other retaliatory capacity, up to 200 sortie [sic] (one day's activities).
>
> c: Not yet considered: Commando raid, under air cover, by helicopter or otherwise, to take out missiles with bullets, destroy launchers, and leave.
>
> d: Note: It is generally agreed that we must be prepared to take further action to protect Guantánamo, from which dependants will have to be evacuated in advance.[29]

The risks to the military personnel was very much in the minds of Excomm in these debates. The two complicating factors that they identified were centered on two points. Firstly, it was impossible to know what weapons might be concealed on the island. Secondly, if the missiles were made fully operational, it would severely complicate military operations. The fear or risk of the Soviets launching a missile before it could be destroyed – a 'use it or lose it,' mentality – might cost the lives of millions and jeopardize military operations in Cuba.

The thinking of the President's advisers was that the best option for success was to strike before the missiles all became operational. This would have a direct impact on which of the invasion plans, if exercised, would be used – especially if the missiles were expected to be operational in the next week.

Option C was a new scenario that had not even remotely been planned by the JCS or the CINCLANT – sending special operations forces into Cuba to destroy the missiles and launch sites on the ground. Earlier in the year, President Kennedy had authorized the creation of the Navy SEALS. The Army Special Forces had been formed in 1952, and while both organizations had been in existence for some time, both lacked any real-world experience in undertaking such a complicated mission, for a prolonged period of time, on a hostile, enemy-controlled island.

Sending in some form of special forces in a commando-style raid would have been a high-risk operation. First and foremost, there was a marked lack of intelligence about what was actually in Cuba from a Soviet perspective, as well as the make-up and nature of the USSR's rearming of the Revolutionary Army. The fact that the Soviet missile sites were so far along before their discovery was an indication of just how lacking intelligence on the island was. There were over 40,000 Soviet troops, heavily armed and armored, in Cuba, but the CIA only estimated their numbers to be no more than 17,000 – proof of the lack of credible eyes and ears on the ground. Any raid of this type would be hampered by this lack of practical and usable intelligence even if the option was seriously considered.

Such a set of missions most likely would have been destined to failure, at least as outlined at this stage of the crisis. With the SAM sites being completed rapidly around the island, the insertion of a team by helicopter may have wiped out a team even before their penetration of the island. The Cuban Army had demonstrated a capability to rapidly mobilize, as had happened at the Bay of Pigs, which would have worked against any sort of special forces – especially once missile sites started to explode. The sheer size of the Soviet mechanized forces would have been brought to bear to protect any sites not taken out in the initial raid. Using special forces troops or SEALs might result in Americans being taken prisoner, and once more, hand Fidel Castro a political/military victory.

The US Navy's monitoring of Soviet shipping spotted a navy replenishment ship, the *Terek*, in the North Atlantic on 17 October. It was seen in the vicinity of the Azores, refueling a Zulu class USSR submarine. The fact that that sub was taking on fuel was an indication that it had been at sea for a long period of time. The discovery of this submarine introduced the specter of the USSR sending navy assets to Cuba to reinforce their obviously large air and ground presence. Using Cuba as a naval base for submarines would suddenly place shipping through the

Panama Canal at risk in the event of war, and could upset the balance of naval power along the American East Coast.[30]

The Joint Chiefs of Staff were leaning strongly for decisive military action. In reality, the Joint Chiefs' arguments were based on the missiles becoming operational and the risks of attempting to remove them once they were. For all intents and purposes, Cuba was being turned into a dangerously armed fortress. A blockade alone might stop supplies and more missiles from coming into the island, but it would not prevent the weapons there from being made operational, or even fired. Charged with the defense of the United States, the missiles represented a Sword of Damocles being raised above America's head. Recommending quick and strong military action was not the act of mad-men attempting to drive the United States into war. It was the recommendation of men tasked with protecting the country and offering the best, most effective alternative to removing that sword.

The time had come to dust off OP Plans 312, 314, and 316, and turn these contingency plans into actionable military operations.

CHAPTER FIVE

Refining the Invasion Plan

Bundy: 'What's our military plan?'
McNamara: 'Well, the military plan now is very clear. A limited strike is out. We can't go on a limited strike without the reconnaissance aircraft. So the military plan is now basically invasion, because we've set a large strike to lead to invasion. We might try a large strike without starting the invasion, or without any plan to get started with the invasion at the time of the strike, because we can't carry it out anyhow for a period of x days. So we have time to cancel invasion plans. But they should be put on. We should start the strike; call up the reserves. We need the air units for the invasion in any case. We need the army units in reserve and our strategic reserve in relation to actions elsewhere in the world.'[1]

Views of a Coming Battle

The Joint Chiefs of Staffs' war room in the Pentagon had been renamed the National Military Command Center, and it was where the OP Plans were brought to the table, along with the most current intelligence about the emerging picture coming from Cuba. From this new command centre, the Joint Chiefs provided the Secretary of Defense with their best, up-to-date, recommendations.

But which to use – OP Plan 314 or OP Plan 316? That was the dominant question facing the Joint Chiefs and Admiral Dennison. OP Plan 314 had a longer time to implement; the longer time allowed for more troops. By all accounts, OP Plan 314 was designed for a non-crisis situation where speed and expediency were not the dominating factors.

Counterbalance to this was OP Plan 316, which employed a smaller force, but did so much more quickly. This plan had been drawn up for those situations where a rapid response was required in Cuba.

After the 17 October Excomm meetings, two things became clear. Firstly, the size and scope of threat in Cuba was larger than had previously been anticipated. Secondly, time was going to be a determining factor in events. Estimates were that the Soviets would have at least sixteen, possibly as many as thirty-two, medium-range missiles in a launch-ready state by 24 October, with the latest date for the entire medium-range missile force being ready by 28 October.[2] The intermediate-range missile complex was not very far along, but even having the medium-range missiles poised would drastically limit military options.

Time, in the form of a closing window, was the drive that would determine which invasion plan was chosen. First and foremost, the JCS recommended OP Plan 312-62 (Rock Pile) as the core set of plans for the Cuban air war. Operations under this plan could completed within a 24-hour period, beginning 12 hours after the order to execute. While Rock Pile had a number of contingency options, the JCS stated that full air superiority would be a requirement for any invasion, if warranted, to be launched.[3] Tactical Air Command had not only been aware of the plan, but their training exercises since mid-September had concentrated on the type of bombing and reconnaissance missions that would be required as part of Rock Pile. The JCS felt they could be ready to execute OP Plan 312-62 by 20 October, depending on the option chosen.

On 17 October, OP Plan 314-61 was still on the table as an option. This plan called for simultaneous amphibious and airborne assaults. In Eastern Cuba, the marine force would land on the beaches of Tarará, east of Havana. The Army forces, designed as Task Force 125, would be led initially by the two airborne divisions, the 82nd and the 101st. The airborne forces would strike at four major airfields surrounding Havana – José Marti International Airport, Baracoa Airfield, the Mariel Naval Air Station, and the San Antonio de los Baños (formally 'Batista') Airport. Once they secured the airfields, additional equipment would be transported in to reinforce them.

The marines would swing around Havana, in the process linking up with the airborne forces. The only airfield not planned to be taken by airborne assault was that the Port of Mariel and the Mariel Naval Air Station. These needed to be secured by the airborne forces by ground assault. If they could not do it alone, the reinforcing marines would secure it. Once the port of Mariel was secured, the 2nd Armored Division would be landed there, as well as at Tarará beach. OP Plan 314-61 required eighteen days to fully implement. This was based on the assumption that none of the divisions would be prepositions and have to be moved across the US to ports and airfields in order to be fully deployed. The fact that exercise Three Pairs was already being loaded, with some of the advance forces already aboard ships for the training mission, meant that some forces were actually ahead of the schedule required under OP Plan 314-61.

OP Plan 316-61 had one major variation to it. In using a smaller overall force in order to get engaged more quickly, the plan did *not* call for a simultaneous assault by airborne and amphibious forces. The airborne elements would make their assaults between one and three days *before* the marine invasion at Tarará. For at least a day, if not longer, the airborne forces would be alone on the island, surrounded by the enemy and dependant on transports and air drops for supplies until the marine link-up could take place.

The trade-off in this plan was simple. The reaction time for the plan was not eighteen days as in OP Plan 314-61, but instead was a little as five days. The build-up of American forces on the island would be slower under OP Plan 316-61, but the target objectives remained the same. Two chief factors would determine which plan might be employed. First was the speed that the invasion might be required by events still unfolding in Cuba. Second was the amount of potential opposition expected to the invasion force. On 14 October, when the first details of the presence of offensive missiles were uncovered, the JCS favored OP Plan 314. OP Plan 316-62 had been conceived as a potential American response to a popular uprising in Cuba, where the isolation of the airborne forces might not be such a risky factor.[4] By 17 October, however, the view of the situation was changing. The Soviets on the island were moving rapidly to get their medium-range missiles operational. Suddenly, OP Plan 316-61 was starting to look more appealing, although it would have to be modified to fit the situation.

Analyzing the Battle Plans

Both of the plans had similar sets of objectives. OP Plan 314-61 called for simultaneous amphibious and airborne assaults, while OP Plan 316-61 called for a gap between the two of upwards of three days. In both plans, the airborne troops would be isolated and at risk of a concentrated counter-attack, the difference being that the risks were much greater under OP Plan 316-61, when the Cubans and Soviets might have days to mount such counter-attacks.

Another risk that both plans had was getting the surface echelon, namely in the form of the 2nd Armored Division, ashore before the full brunt of any counter-attack might be launched. This would not be the only force that would be brought ashore. Elements of the 1st and 2nd infantry divisions would also need to be landed, either at the beach at Tarará or the port. While the infantry support would be critical, the key to either operation was the landing of the armored division whose M-48 tanks would be needed to fend off any armored units that survived OP Plan 312's air campaign.

To land the bulk of the armored division, the Port of Mariel had to be secured, relatively intact. Under OP Plan 314, the landing of the 2nd Armored Division and the rest of the surface echelon of Task Force 125 was delayed in order to allow for a greater initial 'punch' in the simultaneous airborne and amphibious assaults. Under OP Plan 316-61, a smaller force would be landed a day after the port was secured, perhaps two depending on the resistance.[5] As such, the JCS favored the operational elements of the simultaneous assaults in OP Plan 314-61, but as intelligence showed the missile-readiness increasing, they desired the speed of OP Plan 316-61.

Prepositioning would be the key. Moving the 64 units, with a total strength of 25,674, to the ports of departure and airfields, along with the 258,000 tons of equipment and supplies just to support OP Plan 316-61, would be staggering and expensive – $5,611,000 for the movement alone, and another $2,460,000 for costs of support at the staging areas.[6] The costs were less for OP Plan 314-61, but were spread out over a longer period of time.

Since OP Plan 314-61 required a larger force overall, it introduced another risk. It would limit the capability of the United States to respond somewhere else in the world if the Soviets chose to respond, for example, in Berlin. The Soviets were not the only Communists that the United States had to keep a watchful eye on. China, in the middle of this emerging crisis, launched an attack on India. The forces slotted for use in OP Plan 314-61 might dramatically restrict the ability of the United States to react if North Korea broke the armistice there, or of China decided to strike at Formosa or in Indochina. If the Soviets or Chinese wanted to apply pressure anywhere else in the world, the attack on Cuba would be the perfect time.

During the assault phase of the OP Plan 314-61, the JCS felt that the US would be unable to cope with any other contingency. The aircraft alone required for supplies, reinforcements, and transports would strip America's ability to react elsewhere. If the Soviets put another Stalin-era blockade of Berlin in place, the transport aircraft needed to supply Berlin would be tied down in Cuba for at least a week, and that is if the plans were executed on the projected timelines.[7] A greater challenge lay ahead. While both plans relied on the 2nd Armored Division, the unit was not going to be available for the invasion. A change was made to swap it for the 1st Armored Division.

A Decision is Reached

17 October 1962 was a milestone date for the Joint Chiefs of Staff when it came to Cuba. The new intelligence about missile readiness in Cuba and their own analysis of the contingency plans forced a decision. The options were twofold: modify OP Plan 314-61 to accelerate the time to deploy forces, or modify OP Plan 316-61 to compress the time between the airborne and amphibious assaults.

The final choice was to modify OP Plan 316-61. The CINCLANT received new orders as a result of this decision. 'Under utmost security precautions', bring all units designated in OP Plan 316 to 'the highest state of readiness for possible execution' of the plan.[8]

The next day, 18 October, Admiral Dennison and his staff received this message, along with the plan's changes. The 'potentially hazardous gap' between the landing of the airborne forces and the amphibious assault was to be changed to mirror that of OP Plan 314-61 – a simultaneous assault. The second change to the plan was to postpone the assaults from the fifth to the seventh day after the opening of hostilities. This would provide more time to assemble and embark the surface echelon, while giving the Air Force and Navy two more days to complete the air attacks outlined in Rock Pile. The airborne assault on Mariel was discarded so as to simplify the operation.

The new plan was designated as OP Plan 316-62.

OP Plan 314-61 proved to be a difficult operation to simply set aside. Since some preliminary work had begun to accelerate the timing, some of Admiral Dennison's staff were still keeping their hands on this plan, hoping to leverage some of the work they had done on movement and loading schedules. The tinkering with 314-61 would continue until the JCS and CINCLANT issued orders on 26 October to permanently shelve 314-61 to concentrate planning resources on OP Plan 316-62.[9]

Rock Pile

As outlined previously, OP Plan 312 provided for an extensive air campaign for a week prior to the invasion. The targeting list was highly flexible, but there were some guidelines tied to the airborne and amphibious assaults that were put in place.

The strikes against Cuba were designed to come in three attack waves each day – at dawn, early afternoon, and evening. The first day's worth of operations called for 1,190 sorties from the targeting list.[10]

The only targets to not be bombed directly were the airfields where the airborne troops would be assaulting. These could be strafed, and defending units around the airfields attacked, but the airfields themselves were generally spared until 3 hours prior to the landing of troops. At that time, the target airfields would become the focal point of the air campaign – a last minute softening up of defenders surrounding these fields.[11]

In stark opposition to this was the targeting of the invasion beaches. These would be attacked starting on D-Day, along with other potential beaches. This would be done so as to confuse the Cuban defenders as to which beaches might bear the brunt of an amphibious assault. Leaving the beaches intact was simply not a concern as was the airfields, which were required for additional reinforcements.

The Invasion Coordination

The invasion of Cuba was to be a complicated and complex operation even under optimal circumstances. The Army had four contingents that were part of the plan. There was the airborne/air-landing force, a surface echelon, a reserve force to be kept off-shore of Cuba, and an on-call reserve in staging areas in the United States if needed.

The invasion required coordination between the varied services. A standard timetable was established for the assault:

E-Day: CINCLANT orders plan executed
D-Day: Assault operations commence

P-Hour: Airborne assaults commence
H-Hour: Surface assault commences – 4 hours prior to P-Hour
L-Hour: Helicopter assault commences[12]
G-Hour: Divisional reserve heliborne force lands[13]

This timetable, as generic as it is, is one of the few common threads in the invasion plan – along with the coding for calling for air support missions. Each branch of the military, along with the units involved themselves, had variations on the structure of the plan. On the surface, OP Plan 316-62 appears very much like a conglomeration of independent missions and operations stitched together with vague objectives. Despite this initial appearance, Admiral Dennison and his staff managed to create a truly unified plan of operations, albeit one that lacked uniformity and details beyond D-Day +5.

OP Plan 316-62 called for a more gradual build-up of forces as opposed to its predecessors. The build-up is reflected in Table 5-1 below:

Table 5-1: Build-up of Rifle Companies, Artillery Batteries, and Tank Companies – OP Plan 316-62 (cumulative totals)[14]

Units	Deployment Zones	D-Day	D-Day+1	D-Day+2	D-Day+3	D-Day+4	D-Day+5
Rifle Companies		70	80	95			95
	Jose Marti and Los Banos	25		35			35
	Mariel – Baracoa	25		30			30
	Tarará	20	30				30
Artillery Batteries		30	34	43	46	55	55
	Jose Marti and Los Banos	8		12			12
	Mariel – Baracoa	8		13			13
	Tarará	14	18		21	30	30
Tank Companies		10		15	16		16
	Jose Marti and Los Banos	1					1
	Mariel – Baracoa	1		6	7		7
	Tarará	8					8

Note: *Tarará numbers reflect US Marine numbers.*

Armor and artillery could easily tip the scales one way or another in terms of facing Cuban and Soviet counter-attacks. The amphibious landing force had a greater ability to land this type of unit on D-Day, but the airborne divisions were limited by their ability to get their airfields/airports secured and operational; and by the successful seizure of Mariel's port. To fully appreciate the limited resources the invasion force faced, the following table outlines the projected arrival of heavy weapons to the island:

Table 5-2: Summary of Heavy Weapons Arrival in Cuba – OP Plan 316-62 (cumulative totals)[15]

Units	Deployment Zones	D-Day	D-Day+1	D-Day+2	D-Day+3	D-Day+4	D-Day+5
105-mm Howitzer		104	116	150	168	186	186
	Jose Marti and Los Banos	37		47			47
	Mariel – Baracoa	25		49			49
	Tarará	42	54		75	90	90
155-mm Howitzer		72	84	102		138	138
	Jose Marti and Los Banos	30		42			42
	Mariel – Baracoa	18		24			24
	Tarará	24	36			72	72
76-mm Guns (M 41 Tank)		39			41		41
	Jose Marti and Los Banos	17					17
	Mariel – Baracoa	22			24		24
90-mm Guns (M48 Tank)		101		157	174		174
	Mariel – Baracoa			56	73		73
	Tarará	101*					101

Note: The tank forces listed as landing at Mariel were contingent on the Port of Mariel not being available. The actual scheduled landing force at Tarará was 17-20, with the rest being slated for Mariel

The Army Elements of OP Plan 316-62 – Task Force 125 and Task Force Charlie

The Army element Task Force 125 bore some of the riskiest elements of the operation. The two airborne divisions would be arriving first on D-Day. The 82nd Airborne Division, augmented by a brigade task force, built around two battle groups from the 1st Infantry Division and a company of light tanks, would capture the airports at Jose Marti and San Antonio de los Banos (also known as Batista Airport in American plans). The 82nd would land first to secure the airfield, and were expected to have any damage repaired within 3 hours to allow transports to land the 1st Infantry Division and light tanks. The initial landing forces would have an engineering company (sans heavy equipment) to effect these repairs.[16] Each airfield would be attacked by paratroopers from two landing zones.

The Screaming Eagles of the 101st Airborne Division would be augmented by a single battle group from the 1st Infantry Division and would be landing at Baracoa Airport.[17] Once Baracoa was secured and the infantry joined their airborne colleagues, they would drive on to Mariel, complete the securing of the Naval Air Station (if not done already), and secure the Mariel's port.

Courtesy of the Earth Sciences and Map Library, University of California, Berkeley

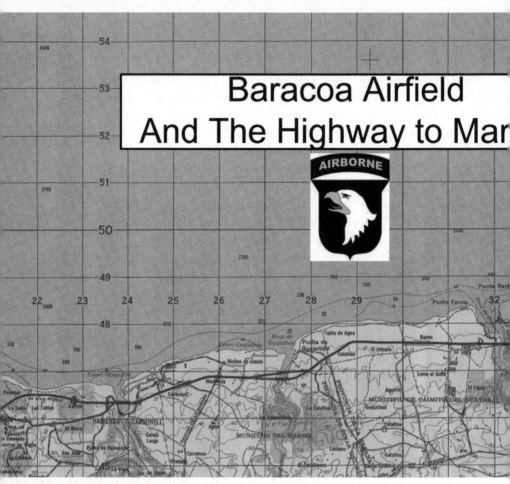

Courtesy of the Earth Sciences and Map Library, University of California, Berkeley

Both of the airborne divisions would be augmented with a battalion of air-landed artillery 155-mm howitzers. Planners struggled with this aspect of the plan. The artillery support, which would have been so critical D-Day, lacked enough transport aircraft. Chances were fairly certain that both divisions would not have their full contingency of artillery, logistical support units, etc., until D Day +3. By that time, their total strength would number 35,000.[18]

Following the marine's amphibious landing at Tarará, two brigades of the 2nd Infantry Division were to be landed on the same beaches. This landing was intended to take place on D-Day or no later than D-Day +1. They would then execute a passage of the lines in the vicinity of La Gellega and Bayurayabo. From there, along with marine elements, they would drive to the south where the 82nd Airborne's airfields were presumably being secured. This force would be reinforced by troops from the 1st Armored Division, including a medium tank battalion, an artillery group of four battalions, and a target acquisition battery. The mission of the 2nd Infantry Division was simple – effect a link-up with the airborne elements, and along with the

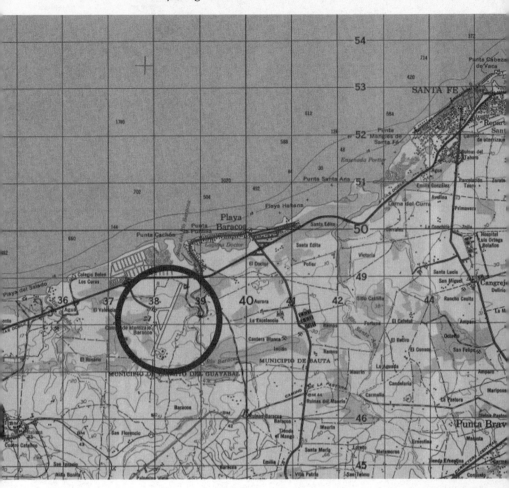

marines, execute a swing south and west of Havana. The intent was that they would link up with the 101st Airborne Division and the soon-advancing elements of the 1st Armored Division – but that presumed that the 101st successfully secured Mariel.[19]

The full Army force slated for the invasion was as follows:

<u>Air Echelon</u>
101st Airborne Division*
82nd Airborne Division*
1st Infantry Division
66th Armor, Company D Light Tank
92nd Field Artillery, First Battalion
11th Field Artillery, 2nd Battalion

<u>Surface Echelon</u>
One brigade of the 2nd Infantry Division, (Two battle groups of the 2nd Infantry

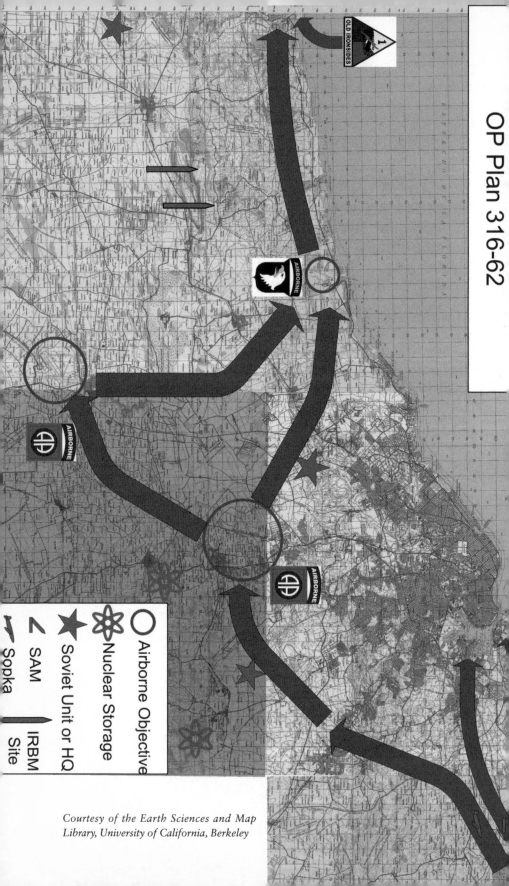

OP Plan 316-62

OLD IRONSIDES
1

ESTRECHO DE LA FLORIDA

AIRBORNE

AIRBORNE

AIRBORNE

○ Airborne Objective
☢ Nuclear Storage
★ Soviet Unit or HQ
⟋ SAM
⬦ IRBM
➤ Sopka | Site

Courtesy of the Earth Sciences and Map Library, University of California, Berkeley

Division – includes 2nd Battalion of the 69th Armored)
To be landed at Red Beach 2 at D-Day +1

Special Forces
Four teams – to be inserted at the start of Scabbards 312

Task Force Charlie
1st Armored Division
11th Field Artillery, 2nd Battalion
32nd Field Artillery, 1st Battalion
54th Artillery Group

Floating Reserve
Headquarters, 1st Armored Division
One brigade of the 1st Armored Division
2nd Infantry Division (two brigades)

Potential Additional Reserves
4th Infantry Division
5th Infantry Division
2nd Armored Division

Note: None of these units were to be fully poised for immediate deployment, limiting their use until at least eight days after D-Day

On-Call Echelon
Brigade, 1st Armored Division
34th Armor, 8th Battalion
16th Field Artillery, 3rd Battalion
Headquarters, 2nd Infantry Division and supporting forces if required
52nd Artillery Group

* Units involved with D-Day landings[20]

Armor was going to be the key in executing OP Plan 316-62. Until the landing of American armored forces, in number, there was a chance for the Cubans/Soviets to leverage their superior number of tanks to counter-attack. CININCLANT assumed that the number of the Cuban and Soviet tanks and armored vehicles would be significantly reduced as a result of the air campaign. That assumption would be of little use to the surrounded and potentially besieged men of the two airborne divisions.

The revised plan called for the 1st Armored Division, designed as Task Force Charlie, to be anticipated to land at Mariel and Tarará on D-Day, the latest being

D-Day +1. At Mariel, the armored element was brigade-size in strength. It consisted of a medium tank battalion, an armored cavalry squadron, a mechanized infantry battalion, and a direct-support artillery battalion. All of these units would be at reinforced strength at the time of landing. Additional forces would accompany the armored landing at Mariel, which included administrative and supporting logistical units to keep the task-force self-sustaining. A great deal of this was the tanker trucks and pumping materials for the fuel that the 1st Armored Division was likely to consume. The remaining elements, which included two non-divisional field artillery battalions, would have to be landed at Mariel as well, due to a lack of air transport the first few days of the invasion.

The landings of the 1st Infantry Division, the 66th Armor, Company D Light Tank, the 92nd Field Artillery, 1st Battalion, and the 11th Field Artillery, 2nd Battalion was to be done post D-Day – brought in by airlift transport to the airfields that the airborne troops were to liberate. There were issues with this effort, since it was dependant on all of the airfields being secured and operational. If they were not, units designed for one airfield could, at the discretion of the ground commander, be brought into one of the other secured airports. On paper or to a layman, this does not seem to be a problem. In practical application, it meant that some units might be broken up from their commands – landing where they had not planned on doing so. It also meant that the vital reinforcements were being landed where they were not needed; where the airports/airfields were already secured, as opposed to those facilities that were still being contested.

The Marine Forces of OP Plan 316-62

The marine forces were organized under the 2nd Marine Expeditionary Force and the 5th Marine Expeditionary Brigade. The 2nd Marine Expeditionary Force was already committed to the Caribbean as part of the Three Pairs exercise, although it would be highly augmented during the mobilization and plan refinement.

The 2nd Marine Expeditionary Force (II MEF) was made up following:

Headquarters FMFLANT (Fleet Marine Force Atlantic)
2nd Marine Division
  RLT (Regimental Landing Team) 8
  BLT (Battalion Landing Team) 3/8
    BLT 2/8
    BLT 3/6
    BLT 2/2
    BLT 2/6
    BLT 1/2

RLT 2
    BLT 2/2
    BLT 1/6
    BLT 3/2
    3rd Battalion, 10th Marine

MAG (Marine Air Group)
    VMA (Marine Attack Squadron) 331
    VMF (Marine Fighter Squadron) 333

4th MEB (Marine Expeditionary Brigade)
Headquarters of RLT 6
One battalion of the 22nd Marine

HMM (Helicopter Marine Medium squadron) 261
HMM 264

2nd MAW (Marine Air Wing)
    VMA 331
    VMF 333

Headquarters FMFLANT

Sub Unit of HMM 262
MAG 26
Force Troops of FMFLANT

5th MEB (Task Force 128)21

Note: Marine unit designations can be difficult to interpret for the uninitiated. A RLT is a regimental landing team. These consist of three battalion landing teams (BLTs). The number following RLT is the number assigned to the regiment. BLTs consist of a headquarters company, a service company, four rifle companies and support troops. The BLTs can be augmented with a amphibious tracked vehicle, an anti-armor platoon, or an attached artillery battery of howitzers. The numbering on BLTs represents their regiment, followed by the BLT designation. Thus BLT 2/8 is the Second Marines Regiment, 8th Battalion Landing Team.

Aviation squadrons have the prefix of 'V' ,which designates fixed-wing aircraft.[22] The differences between a VMF (Marine Fighter Squadron) and a VMA (Marine Attack Squadron) is that a Marine Fighter Squadron's primary mission is combat air patrols and the engagement of enemy aircraft where a Marine Attack Squadron would be primarily tasks with ground support tactical bombing operations.

At the start of the crisis, the US Marine Corps was poised on both the East and West coasts of the Continental United States. On the West Coast was the 1st Marine Division, stationed at Camp Pendleton, California, and the 3rd Marine Air Wing at El Toro, California. The 2nd Marine Division was stationed at Camp Lejeune, North Carolina, and the 2nd Marine Air Wing at the Marine Corps Air Station, New River, North Carolina. Various other marine air and garrison forces to be used in the operation were stationed at other bases around the world.

As the crisis emerged, the Marine Corps was tied up in the Three Pairs exercise, which used units from the East Coast-based FMFLANT, or Fleet Marine Force Atlantic Command out of Norfolk, Virginia. As it became clear that the Three Pairs exercise was not likely, but that the option of a full-blown invasion of Cuba was unfolding, the FMFLANT took the preparatory steps of moving the 2nd MAW to Roosevelt Roads, Puerto Rico, and the Naval Air Station in Key West, Florida.

This was not the only shift in forces. On 18 October, a battalion of the 2nd Marine Division was flown in by the 2nd MAW to Guantánamo Naval Base. Additional BLT from the Three Pairs exercise was diverted to Guantánamo and debarked by ship. A reinforced battalion form the 1st Marine Division was airlifted to Guantánamo Bay by the Military Air Transit Services (MATS). No one was sure if this was enough to protect the naval base, but it was going to make taking it much more difficult and costly.

The 2nd Marine Expeditionary Force would be the amphibious force tasked with the initial landing on Cuba. Their target was east of Havana, the infamous tourist beaches of Tarará. The ground where this landing was to take place was a long slope back nearly 1 mile from the beach, where the hills emerged. Tarará itself was a beach resort community, covered with rental villas and huts lining the sloping hills off the beach. Even Fidel Castro had a villa there. The resort was a leftover relic of Havana's tourist trade, now all but crushed by the American embargo.

The beach was divided into three zones; Red Beach one and two, and Blue Beach. At a strategic level, the marines were to assault the beaches with ten battalions of force and drive inland. A helicopter assault would begin at the time of the landings, dropping off marines inland to secure strategic hills and roads to allow a breakout. This helicopter assault would be the first test of the air-mobile landing in combat operations for the Americans, and presumed that the Cuban forces in the area would have been all but wiped out by the air assaults of Rock Pile. The marines needed to secure the 2-36 highway, which would provide them, along with support from the Army forces, with the ability to swing south of Havana to link up with the 82nd Airborne. From the San Antonio de los Baños and Jose Marti airports, they would continue their swing around Havana, linking up with the 101st Airborne Division at Baracoa Airfield, then link up with the 1st Armored Division, which should be debarking at Mariel. If Mariel was not taken, the marines would provide the additional punch to complete that seizure.[23]

The Wild Card: the 5th MEB

The other major marine element was the 5th MEB. This force was not in the Caribbean, but was embarking on the West Coast of the United States to be rushed into the vicinity for use. Out of all of the aspects of OP Plan 316-62, the mission of the 5th MEB was adaptable, depending on the circumstances. It would provide Admiral Dennison with a significant military asset that could be employed in four potential areas of conflict: the naval base at Guantánamo Bay; Playa Vista Del Mar and Boca Dominica, west of the Bay of Mariel; near Matanzas in Western Cuba; conduct helicopter assaults in Western Cuba.[24] The choice of where to use the 5th MEB fell upon the CINCLANT.

If employed at Guantánamo, it would be either to defend the naval base or to prepare to conduct breakout operations. Assigned to the 5th MEB was a helicopter assault BLT, which would be debarked as well, giving the forces the capability to exercise this asset in the event of breakout operations. The hope was that the landings would take place at the piers of the windward side of the base. For the marines, it should have been a simple debarkation from ships, then movement to the base perimeter for defense. The marines listed one specific target objective that they were to move and secure once debarked – the vital Yateras Water Plant, which provided fresh water to the base, but was located outside of Guantanamo's defense perimeter.

There was an option in the OP Plan that assumed Guantánamo Bay was under attack. In this scenario, the landing would be impossible at the piers, most likely due to incoming enemy fire or they having already fallen to Cuban/Soviet troops. If this was the situation unfolding, the 5th MEB would be deployed on the narrower leeward (western) side of the base, landing at a narrow strip of beach code named 'Brown'. There, they would move out to secure a series of five hills that dominated the base. To supplement this, the helicopter BLT would move in and secure LZ (Landing Zone) Owl on a hilltop in the middle of the 5th MEB's objectives. It was from this position, overlooking the naval air station, that the counter-attack to retake Guantánamo Bay could commence.[25]

The other potential use for the 5th MEB was at the other end of Cuba, west of the Port of Mariel. Under this contingency, something had prevented the 101st Airborne Division and/or the ground forces from successfully securing Mariel in order to land the 1st Armored Division. This landing group, designated as Task Group 129.2, would land at beaches at Playa Vista Del Mar and Boca Dominica. These landings would be proceeded by naval gunfire and aerial bombardment. Naval support determined: 'A cruiser, if assigned will be placed in general support of RLT-1. One destroyer is assigned in direct support of each surface landed BLT, and one in direct support of the helicopter-borne BLT.'[26]

The plans were deliberately vague:

The location of the landing beaches and the penetration of the bay into the operating area dictate the seizure of the western portion of the bay complex initially. Once this is accomplished, the western portion is rendered untenable by enemy forces facilitating its seizure by means of amphibious vehicle and helicopter-borne forces. Early liaison must be affected with the remaining elements of the previous positioned friendly forces in order to pinpoint the location of their forces and effective the necessary fire support coordination.[27]

The reality of this option is the failure to take Mariel keeps the bulk of the 1st Armored Division at sea. With the number of tanks, both those turned over the Cubans and those attached to the four mechanized Soviet units, the need for the 1st Armored Division to be ashore was critical. Clearly, this option would only be employed if the Cuban Naval Air Station at Mariel did not fall – putting the entire invasion force at risk.

The third place where the 5th MEB could be utilized was in Western Cuba, in the vicinity of Matanzas. This plan provided for:

a. Seizure of a limited beachhead to facilitate landing of other forces, as required, or from which to continue the attack and gain control of the city of Matanzas and its port facilities.

b. Rapid exploitation of enemy forces should they collapse as a result of other friendly forces in the Havana area.

c. A diversionary action to apply pressure to the enemies rear or flank in support of landings in the Havana area.[28]

This particular operation leveraged the debarkation schedule from the Playa Vista Del Mar and Boca Dominica missions (above). In reviewing this plan, there is a marked lack of detail about the landing, including any inland objectives. This seems to indicate that this option only would have been employed under options b or c above – where resistance was expected to be low.

Option a would only be employed if the Port of Mariel and/or Havana could not be secured. Matanzas was not as robust a facility as Mariel, but if the Cubans and their Soviet allies rendered Mariel unusable, and Havana could not be secured – or had been rendered unusable – Matanzas would have to do.

The final potential use of the 5th MEB was to not use the ground forces, but rather the helicopter assets of the force, on an ad hoc basis as defined by the CINCLANT. These missions, as outlined in the plan, called for the use of these helicopters for:

• Providing close air support and landings as deemed appropriate. While not stated in the orders directly, this seems to imply the use of this force to be dropped near the missile complexes.

• Providing observation to operate from amphibious shipping during any initial assault phases.

• Be prepared to employ helicopter nuclear, biological, and chemical monitoring teams beginning H-Hour.

- Be prepared to conduct radiological and chemical decontamination beginning at H-Hour.
- Provide search and rescue (SAR) in accordance with an event requiring an SAR event.
- Be prepared to exercise coordination and control of close air support operations as responsibilities are passed ashore.
- Provide liaison officers to the (HDC) Helicopter Direction Center to direct air support.[29]

The Primary Landing Beaches – Red One, Red Two, and Blue Beach

Like so many battlefields, the beaches at Tarará had seen happier times when Batista was in power, and tourists, ironically most from the United States, enjoyed the warm Caribbean sun and surf. By October and November 1962, the Americans and Cubans both planned for these vacation spots to be turned into bloody scenes of carnage.

The beaches were situated 20-km east of Havana. There were closer beaches to Havana, but OP Plan 316 did not call for the capture of the capital city, only isolating it from the rest of Cuba. The right flank of the landing beaches was 700-m east of a flashing beacon used to warn ships of the coast. The west flank was to be 985-m west of the mouth of the Rio Itabo River.

The Red Two Beach was 800-m long; Red one was 985 m; Blue Beach was 1,525 m. The three beaches were side by side, running from east to west in the order of Red Two, Red One, and Blue Beach. The beaches themselves were 45-m deep and were made of light sand.[30] US Navy analysis of the beaches indicated that the surf was usually light with a tidal range of 1 foot. There were off-shore counter-currents following from east to west at 0.5 knots.

The area immediately behind beaches Red One and Red Two was mostly sandy with a few scattered trees and scrub brush. A little further inland there were several resort hotels and private residences in the area. Continuing back to the main coastal highway, the ground rose gently and the area had been developed into a beach-front subdivision.

It was Blue Beach, the largest of the landing beaches, that was the most confining. Most of the area behind Blue Beach was composed of brush covered marsh.[31] This marshy area was determined to be difficult to maneuver in, and the terrain ill-suited even for tanks or other tracked vehicles.

While the characteristics of a landing beach itself are important, the ability to get off the beaches was important too – otherwise, the assaulting marines might find themselves forced to fight with the ocean at their backs. Getting off the beaches and moving inland was critical to provide the amphibious landing forces with the flexibility to defend themselves while allowing them to reach their broader strategic objectives of reaching the airborne troops.

There were numerous exists available from the Red One and Red Two beaches. That was not the case however with Blue Beach. The marshland would act as a funnel at Blue Beach, channeling the landing forces towards the Red Beaches to move inland, or if they were under heavy fire, shift laterally along the beach of Boca Ciega further to the east.[32] Near Boca Ciega, the beach ended with older resort houses, huts, and villas, and allowed inland access to the coastal highway, although it would leave a significant gap in the lines.

Another terrain factor that came into play were the rivers that cut into the landing sites. Three rivers ran north and south, perpendicular to the coast. They were the Rio Condesa (Tarará), Rio Bacuranao, and Rio Cojimar. While relatively shallow, they were subject to flash flooding during thunderstorms.[33] These rivers would serve to further channel troops as they attempted to move inland.

The Sweep Around Havana: the Terrain

OP Plan 316-62 called for the amphibious force, along with their Army colleagues landed at the beaches, to drive around Havana to link up with the airborne forces. The terrain they would be fighting across would be wide and varied, ranging from bare rolling hills to urban venues. The Army's intelligence on the terrain was limited to what one might be able to glean from topographic maps of the period, rather than solid intelligence. Much if this is due to the nature of contingency plans such as OP Plan 316; they were designed to be utilized only in extreme conditions and added to or modified as the date for invasion approached. In this case, however, the intelligence was not getting better, and so the information was somewhat limited.

The ground south and east of Havana is rather hilly, with hill tops ranging from 90-120 m in the Cotorro area, and up to 150 m in the western approaches to Matanzas. Many of these hills were barren, and based on photographs and maps, quite steep. The further south you went from Havana, the more you moved into sugar plantations and fields – especially in the valleys of the hills. Depending on the harvest for a particular field, they could be deadly, almost impassable obstructions, clear, or filled with potential kindling. After a harvest, the unprocessed cane was often burned off. If left in the fields, it tended to dry and become a fire hazard.

Parts of the marine mission included seizing the access to the Havana Port of Regla and the port itself. To do this, the marines would have to enter Havana from the east. Getting there meant moving through the hilly Cotorro area, where steep hills rose as much as 111 m, many dotted with copses of trees and undergrowth; perfect cover. The area encompassed by Cojimir, Tarará, La Gallega, and residential Guanabaco was generally urban with scattered vegetation, small family farms, and winding secondary streets. The land is made up of small rolling hills with ridges of 70 m found in the Loma San Pedro and Rio Tarará section. This area is cut through by the rivers Cojimar, Tarará, and Bacuranao. The section along the coast between Tarará and Santa Maria Del Mar was generally urban in 1962. East of Santa Maria Del Mar was the mangrove swamp, beyond the Blue Beach, which extended to the city limits of Boca Ciega and the Itaro River.[34]

Havana's eastern approaches were heavily populated, with narrow winding streets in the poorer suburbs. Movement into the city by any path other than a major highway was going to mean fire fights in close quarters, evening the odds for any defending Cubans. Moving through the city to secure the Port of Regla would be treacherous.

The Amphibious Landings at Tarará

The landings at Tarará was to be proceeded by days of aerial bombardment and a massive navy bombardment of the beaches and rear areas. When H-Hour came, the thinking was that Cuban defenses would have been shattered, broken, or destroyed.

On a more strategic level, the goals for the Tarará landings were summarized as follows:

> The 2nd Marine Division as landing group WEST conducts amphibious and helicopter borne assault to seize the BACURANO–BAJURAYABO area of north-west CUBA in order to permit the rapid landing and initiation of further operation by the 2nd Infantry Division Brigade, then seizes the COJIMAR Penninsula [sic] to secure the eastern approaches to HAVANA Harbor; upon completion of the amphibious operation prepares to report to the Commander Army Task forces for OPCON or re-embark to conduct further operations as directed.[35]

This overview does not relay the overall complexity of the operation.

The 2nd Marine Division had a fairly broad number of objectives that needed to be secured as part of their assault on Cuba. These objectives were broken down as division and regimental objectives. The lettering and numbering scheme used in the OP Plan had gaps in it, presumably to allow some flexibility to add objectives at the last minute. These objectives are not listed in the order that they were to be performed; simply by the objectives themselves.

Division Objectives

F: Morro Castle
This sixteenth-century fort was located at the entrance to the Havana/Regla harbor. The opening to the harbor narrows at Morro Castle, giving the fort command of the entrance to the port. Taking it meant driving across the coastal Cojimar peninsula nearly 20 km from the landing beaches. Any force moving on

Morro Castle ran the risk of being isolated on the Cojimar peninsula in the event of a counter-attack.

G: Port access of Regla
To reach this objective, the marines would have to drive through the eastern outskirts of Havana itself. This objective was marked as either an alternative to the Port of Mariel for landing the 1st Armored Division, or for supplies. Simply securing Morro Castle and the Port of Regla did not guarantee access to the port by American ships, but would necessitate removal of the any Cuban units that could potentially shell the port once it was needed.

I: Seizure of intact bridges over the Rio Condesa and Rio Bacuramo
These four-lane highway bridges would permit the use of the coastal highway by the marines. If the Cubans were able to affect the destruction of these bridges, the marines would be forced to circumvent this area, adding long hours of cross country travel.

Regimental Objectives

AA: Tarará
This coastal village was destined to be the first objective that the marines would secure a few minutes after H-Hour. Little Tarará had to be secured to protect the beachhead, but in reality, after the bombing and shore bombardment, there was not destined to be too much left to capture, except any defenders that survived.

BB: Bajurayabo
This village was south and west of the landing beaches and along a large highway. Holding this would prevent counter-attack by Cuban forces that would be moving directly on the landing beachhead.

CC: Barreras
This village sat astride the highway leading from coastal highway, south and west. Securing it would give a vital road link into Havana. At the same time, it was vital to hold this to protect the forces that were assaulting Morro Castle. Any Cuban or Soviet counter-attack would need this road to cut off the Cojimar peninsula.

DD: Cojimar
This urban beach community was critical for two reasons. Firstly, control of Cojimar controlled access west across the Cojimar peninsula and to Morro Castle. Secondly, control of Cojimar allowed access to a network of roads heading south and west into Guanabaco.

EE: Minas
South of Bajurayabo, this tiny crossroads village links up the highway running south and west with a large highway running south. Holding this crossroads would protect the beachhead.

GG: Pealver
This village is the start (or end) of a road that leads west into Havana. For the marines, it would provide an alternate way of heading towards Guanabaco/Havana.

KK: Guanabaco
A large urban area that was astride of the Port of Regla. This town was substantial in size and represented the largest of the urban objective that the marines would have. South of Morro Castle, this was the doorway to Regla's port facilities. The traffic circle just north of Guanabaco controlled a key access point to the highway 2-53, which held the key bridge's points from the Tarará beachhead.[36]

JJ: Road intersection; two major highways at La Gallega
On the map, La Gallega is little more than a dozen homes and small businesses. What made this village critical was that it was the intersection for roads that connected Minas and Bajurayabo. Holding it was crucial for the force that would be sent against Guanabaco and Regla.[37]

The central highway (La Carretera Central) in Cuba, while not spelled out as a specific objective per se, was clearly a broader strategic target. Running 713-miles long from Pinar Del Rio to Santiago De Cuba in the east, this road served as a central spine for road travel through the heart of Cuba. The road passed south-east of Havana. This four-lane road was flanked in most areas by 100-foot easements on both sides, fenced with barbed wire. Since its bridges covered all of the major streams and rivers crossing the island, the possession of the highway was of long-term importance. While not listed specifically in the invasion as a target, post the initial landings, the securing of this road was vital to expanding out to the missile launch sites.[38]

The landing calls for the landing of two BLTs abreast over beaches Red One and Red Two.[39] The Blue Beach landings would consist of one BLT coming ashore at a time. Each wave of landing craft would be ten each, except for the landing of recon and armored forces, which would come in five landing craft tanks (LCTs).

On Red Beach Two, the second wave would follow the first by 3 minutes, and 2 minutes later, the third wave would come ashore – bringing with it the First Platoon Company B, 2nd Tank Battalion. This wave would be the bulk of the armored forces landing that day in Cuba. Ten minute later would be wave four – then in 5 minute increments, the final two waves of landing craft would hit the sands at Tarará. Both of the other beaches had similar landing plans, minus the armored vehicles.

The plan of attack was for the landing forces of beaches Red One and Red Two to sweep to the west, taking Tarará. The landing forces on Blue Beach would then be channeled to the west, since the swamps prevented a direct thrust to the south. From Tarará, the marines could start moving south and west towards their objectives.

Specific missions were designed for each of the BLTs. BLT 3/6 seemed to bear the brunt of the work of the invasion force. Landing on Red Beach Two, it was to move swiftly ashore to take part in the assault and capture of Tarará. Once this mission was completed, it was to observe the Tarará population's reaction to loudspeaker broadcast and leaflet drops instructions, and provide spot report as soon as possible as to the population's compliance. They were also supposed to report on the flow of refugee traffic into or out of the zone of operations.

As soon as BLT 3/6 took part in securing Tarará, at the direction of the field commander, they were assigned to provide reconnaissance of Rio Bacuranao and determine all possible fording points. The concern was that the road brides might be rigged for demolition by the Cuban defenders, or be damaged/destroyed, either during the shore bombardment or during the proceeding air campaign.

BLT 3/6's work was far from done. They were to effect the seizure of the coastal highway bridges over the Rio Bacuranao and Rio Codesa. These bridges were designated as Division Objectives I. Once these had been secured, BLT 3/6 was to proceed to move westward and establish observation over the Cojimar Regla and Guanaboca area.[40] In addition to this, this BLT was to secure the flank and provide communications and air support coordination. Given the broad range of missions and objectives assigned to BLT 3/6, the CINCLANT planners provided Battery A and Battery C with a mortar battery attachment that would provide direct fire support to BLT 3/6.[41]

BLT 2/8 was designated to arrive at Red Beach One. While they would be involved in the initial assault on Tarará, this BLT was to breakout from the beaches to secure two of the key objectives: (BB) Bajurayabo and (CC) Barreras. Once these objectives had been secured, they were to move forward to seize (EE) Minas and (GG) Pealver. This path of objectives would allow roadways to be secured to allow for the drive on the Port of Regla and the roads necessary to swing around Havana.

Once BLT 2/8 was able, they were to establish contact via radio with BLT 3/8 (the heliborne force) on the hills outside of Guanabaco. If the heliborne forces had not secured Guanabaco, BLT 2/8 was designed to link up with them and effect a junction to jointly move on the city. BLT's final mission was to extend southward to extend an angle of attack along the road network to allow for the link-up with the 82nd Airborne Division.[42] This movement was important, allowing for a push-off to help relieve the airborne forces.

On top of all of these mission objectives, BLT 2/8 was supposed to watch over and manage any refugee traffic in and out of the zone of operations. The shore bombardment and days of aerial attacks were bound to have displaced a number of civilians. Refugees fleeing on the narrow Cuban road network would impede the movement of the American landing forces. Finally, BLT 2/8 would be tasked with inspecting and reporting on an airstrip between Bacuranao and La Gallega. They were to attempt to determine its suitability for use by helicopter and observation-type aircraft operations.[43]

The landing of the 2nd Reconnaissance on Red Beach Two was designed for establishing a perimeter to the landings and recon of potential enemy positions. This unit was tasked with maintaining surveillance over 2nd Marine Division on the south and east flanks as their primary mission. In addition, they were to provide support in the drive towards Guanabaco in a scouting role for the advancing marines.[44]

The ground component BLT 3/8 was to watch refugee traffic upon landing, while the remainder of the unit was to be used during the heliborne assaults. Once Tarará was secured, they were then to move to secure the city Guanabaco, conducting reconnaissance to the south along Highway 2-19 to a distance of 5,000 m. As soon as practical, they were to submit a report on the road conditions and the capability to support heavy military traffic. These efforts were to be coordinated with BLT 2/8.[45] This BLT was being kept out of the majority of the fighting so that it could help in the final push on the port facilities at Regla. Planners also recognized that the assault on Morro Castle might require reinforcement, and the road intersection of two major highways at La Gallega. BLT 3/8 drew the assignment of seizing the entrance of Havana Harbor at Morro Castle – perhaps one of the toughest nuts to crack on D-Day. The land-forces of BLT 3/8 were to link up with BLT 2/8 and work in conjunction on their target objectives.[46]

The flexibility of OP Plan 316-62 was such that many of the BLTs in the initial landing force had not yet been assigned specific assignments. These literally could be penciled in on the drafts of the plans in the space provided. This gave the planners and the officers involved with the ability to make last minute changes to the plans. It also served to reduce the amount of time that units would have to prepare and plan their part of the operation.

One undesignated BLT would be landed at Blue Beach and ordered to go east along the beach to engage and destroy the enemy forces in the Santa Maria Delmar. This unit would then perform an anchoring function, protecting the left flank of the invasion beach (buffered by the swampland flanking the inland approaches of the Blue Beach), before moving to seize the bridge at Santa Cruz de Acosta. This bridge was critical because it was both a highway bridge and a rail-line bridge over the river of Rio Itabo. Securing this bridge helped defend the flank of the invasion zone.[47]

Another designated BLT would be landed on the right flank of the Blue Beach. Their role would be to be prepared to assist the 2nd Infantry Division in the passage of lines in the vicinity of Bayuranabo from the assembly areas at La Torre Bacuranao.

It is clear from the mission objectives for these landing forces that only light resistance was expected given the number of objectives tasked to each BLT. The marines landing at Tarará had a dizzying list of targets and were going to be marching considerable distances, presumably mopping up a battered and blasted enemy along the way. These assumptions would play havoc if indeed the Cubans and Soviets proved to be more resilient in their defenses.

Fire Support for the Landing Marines

The 10th Marines were in charge of coordinating all fire support and gun support missiles for the landing force.[48] Landing on Blue Beach, they were to secure a position just inland from the beach, and from there direct fire support. Fire support came in three different varieties for the marines hitting the beaches: aerial attack, naval fire missions, and coordinating/directing on-shore landed artillery. The artillery elements that would be coming ashore on D-Day were:

- Battery 'A', 1st Bn, 10th Marines, RLT 8 – attached to BLT 2/8
- Battery 'C', RLT 8 (independent)
- 4th Bn, 10th Marines, 2nd Marine Division (reinforcements)
- 2nd Field Artillery Group GS
- Mortar Bn 1/10, attached to BLT 3/8[49]

Pre-landing bombardment consisted of 5-inch impact bursts kept at least 400 yards in advance of the leading elements, and 6-inch and 8-inch bursts 500 yards in advance. No air bursts (VT or timed) were scheduled where the line of fire passed within 300 yards of friendly troops or craft.[50]

Targeting for the shore bombardment was set as follows:

a. Guided missile sites
b. Coast defense guns
c. Heavy artillery sites
d. Heavy AA guns
e. Light AA guns
f. Block houses
g. Pill boxes[51]

When naval gunfire was called for, it would come in pre-designated salvos. The following were the standard salvos for call fire:

A. Adjustment
    5"/54:   One gun – one salvo
    All others: Two guns – one salvo

B. Fire for Effect
    5"/54:   Two guns – eight salvos (sixteen rounds)
    5"/39:   Four guns – four salvos (sixteen rounds)
    6"/47:   Two or three guns – six or four salvos (twelve rounds)
    8"/55:   Three guns – three salvos (nine rounds)[52]

In support of any anti-mechanized naval, gunfire would not be measured in rounds, but more in terms of minutes. 'Against major attacks (at least five vehicles), ammunition expenditures will not exceed the rapid rate of 2 minutes and sustained rate for 3 minutes, except that 5"/54, rapid fire 6"/47, and 8"/55 will not exceed 50 percent rapid rate for 1 minute and 50 percent sustained rate for 1 minute.'[53]

Table 5-3: Air Support Code Phrases and Armaments[54]

Reno	20-mm cannon
Dallas	One Sidewinder
Austin	One Sparrow
Portland	One 2.75 FEAR (Pkg of 7)
Seattle	One 2.75 FEAR (Pkg of 19)
Burbank	One HVAR (High Velocity Aircraft Rocket) General Purpose
Miami	One HVAR (Armor Piercing)
Oynard [sic]	One HVAR (Shaped Charged Head)
Wichita	One HVAR (Anti-Submarine Head)
San Juan	One ZVN: Pack (General Purpose)
Fresno	One ZVN: Pack (Armor Piercing)
White Sands	One ZVN: Pack HEAT (High Explosive Anti-Tank)
St Louis	One Smoke Rocket
Beeville	One Bullpup
Vegas	One Napalm
Norfolk	One 100-lb General Purpose
Joplin	One 250-lb General Purpose
Dayton	One 250-lb Fragmentary
Eerie	One 500-lb Frag Cluster
Frisco	One 500-lb General Purpose
Richmond	One 500-lb Semi-Armor Piercing
Chicago	One 750-lb General Purpose
Boston	One 1000-lb General Purpose
Denver	One 1000-lb General Purpose
San Diego	One 2000-lb General Purpose
Los Angeles	One Smoke Tank

The planner's thinking was that the air controllers would be able to draw upon a vast array of aircraft and arms based in Florida and in the US aircraft carriers in the task force. While the Navy forces would be first on-call due to their proximity, the flight time from Florida to the invasion beaches or landing zones, including approximate time to re-arm, etc., could be as much as 40 minutes. As such, the fastest response would come from the Navy fighters off-shore.

Anti-Mechanized Operations

The influx of Soviet armor and artillery did not escape the planners of the invasion of Cuba. Their operating assumption was that the air campaign would destroy the majority of these forces, while at the same time, their own intelligence dramatically underestimated the Soviet military presence on the island. As such, anti-mechanized operations were destined to play a critical role on D-Day through D-Day +5.

The 2nd Anti-Tank Battalion has been directed to be prepared to conduct anti-mechanized defense of the 2nd Marine Division.[55] This unit would be landed on Blue Beach in the second wave of the assault. There were three alert conditions that would call for this unit to move forward and engage the enemy and what elements they would bring into action.

Table 5-4: Anti-Mechanized Response[56]

Alert Condition	Nature of Alert	Response Assets
III	Hostile mechanized force has been detected but contact is not imminent.	Tanks, Ontos (self-propelled, six 105-mm recoilless rifles) Pioneer, 106-mm recoilless rifle platform.
II	Hostile mechanized force contact is imminent.	• Air, artillery, and all firepower support ships carry out the mission as ordered. • Tanks and Ontos occupy positions as alerted. • Naval Gunfire Coordination teams and Air Coordination teams, when directed, will control all available aircraft and naval gunfire support. • Artillery displaces if necessary to bring all available fire on enemy forces.
I	Friendly units are under enemy mechanized attack.	• All tanks and Ontos and other anti-tank weapons move to the area to support the unit under attack. • Naval Gunfire Coordination teams and Air Coordination teams, when directed, will control all available aircraft and naval gunfire support with coordination of unit under fire.

Counter-intelligence Operations

All of the OP Plan 316-62 forces had strict procedures regarding counter-intelligence as part of their landings or assaults. Captured enemy personnel were to be broken into small groups and passed to the nearest regimental stockade for G-2 interrogation. Emphasis on counter-intelligence was to be concentrated in eight key areas. These were as follows:

- Sino-Soviet Bloc personnel – be they military or civilians advisers.
- Personnel whose names appeared on the final Cuban Personalities List (to be issued at the time of the invasion).
- Personnel with electronic warfare expertise, including radio and radar operators, and ECM (electronic countermeasures) operators.
- Personnel at the rank of captain or above. Emphasis would be made to capture aviators Of special interest were those officers that might possess strategic information or importance regarding Soviet or Cuban defense.
- Individuals believed to possess special intelligence information.
- Personnel claiming to be anti-Communist movement operators, paramilitary or otherwise. 'Where practical, such personnel or units professing to be friendly will be formed into units in close order formation under Cuban leaders. Weapons will be unloaded and explosive ordinance taken from them. They will be placed under adequate guard and circumstances reported to S-2.'[57]
- High ranking deserters of the Castro Government (civilian) professing a desire to cooperate with the invading American force.
- Wounded personnel in all of the above categories were to be immediately treated, but under the supervision of the appropriate S-2 personnel.[58]

Escapees and evaders were to be treated carefully as well. Publicity of the recovery of friendly personnel was strictly forbidden. Even transmitting their names to S-2 was not allowed; the messages were to be delivered by safe-hand messengers. Apparently, there was concern that the Soviets might have defectors or impersonators that might infiltrate friendly ranks.[59]

Personnel was not the only area of interest to military intelligence. Captured documents and material were considered of vital importance as well. Any code books or cryptographic materials were to be turned over immediately for analysis. Any battle plans or reports of tactical interest could be examined before passing them up to higher authority for detailed analysis. This could give local field commanders useful information on defenses or potential counter-attacks that could be acted on quickly.

Priority material and documents included 'Sino-Soviet Bloc plans for aggression in the western hemisphere other than Cuba'.[60] American intelligence and military planners were obviously concerned that Cuba was the proverbial tip of the iceberg in terms of Soviet incursions.

Specific targets for counter-intelligence also included suspected or known enemy agents listed in the personality lists, suspected or known members of the Communist Party, other non-Cuban nationals, especially those from Central or South America, and finally, persons who are apprehended after curfew.[61]

Heliborne Assaults

OP Plan 316 called for RLT-8 to land with two BLTs abreast over beaches Red One and Red Two. These were not the only marine forces slated to land during D-Day. The marines also would be conducting the first air mobile (heliborne or helicopter ferried) troop assault in the history of the United States.[62] Flying in Sikorsky HUS-1 helicopters, the heliborne forces were slated to secure a number of landing zones and strategic objectives tied to the ground assault forces.[63] The largest of these would be the landing of a BLT in the final push for Guanabaco – of the key objectives.

The landings were scheduled to begin at L-Hour, which would be designated by the ground force commander. The use of the helicopter to bring troops into a battlefield was not a new idea, but it was one that had not been tested at this time. The Vietnam War would redefine the employment of such forces in combat, but in 1962, this was still a new concept that seemed to work on paper. Specific criteria as to when L-Hour could be declared were not part of the plans, leaving this to the broad discretion of the field commander.

The following table covers the intended landing zones and targets:

Table 5-5: Marine Heliborne Assaults – D-Day[64]

(LZ) Landing Zone	Target/Objective	Notes
Sparrow	Landing zone is a golf course (Campo de Golfo). This set of hills is bounded to the south and east by the Bacuranao River and to the north and west by Highway 2-53.	This set of hills provided good observation of the highway leading to Castle Morro.
Robin	Located to the west of Tarará. It is bounded to the west by the river Rio Condesa and by Tarará to the north and east.	
Quail	This LZ is north-east of the town of Barreras	There is an area of thick scrub brush to the northern end of the LZ.

Eagle	LZ is 3.5 miles south-east of Cojimar and two miles east of Guanabaco.	This LZ was astride a highway flanked by two large hills with good visibility into Guanabaco.
Hawk	The LZ is a single strip airfield located one mile west of the town of La Gallega. This LZ is bounded to the south by Highway 2-13 and to the west by a small stream.	This is the same airfield that BLT 2/8 was tasked with investigating for use by helicopters.
Finch	Located west of Tarará and 1.8 miles north-north-west from the town of Barreras.	This LZ is actually on a stretch of paved roadway. This is part of an unfinished and abandoned housing project.
Lark	This LZ is 4,000 meters from Havana's harbor (Regla), 1,000 meters south of Guanabaco.	There are two mines located to the south-west and south-east of the landing zone. This LZ is primarily a farming area. There is a hill adjacent to the LZ that would provide observation to the area south of Guanabaco.

Marine Air Group 26 was tasked with performing the landing operations. Each of the heliborne assaults were to be escorted in by at least two fighters to provide any cover that might be necessary. Four helicopters were to run a circuit over the landing zone in a pattern referred to as a 'race track', so as to confuse any enemy on the ground as to which helicopters were indeed those that would be landing. Additionally, four aircraft would be placed on standby for all heliborne assaults to provide ground support fire for the landing forces.[65] Complicated flight corridors were designed to ensure that the marine helicopters did not drift into Tactical Air Command's or the US Navy's designated flight paths for combat air patrols. The airspace over the invasion beaches and the TAOR (Tactical Area of Operations) was carefully designed so as to minimise the risk of aircraft colliding.[66]

In addition to heliborne landings, MAG 26 was also tasked with using its helicopters for rescuing downed aviators or the evacuation of ground personnel – if the situation was deemed necessary. Otherwise, they were to undertake a recon role, 'Determining the strength, disposition, and armament of all enemy forces, including militia and police, within the amphibious operation area.'[67]

The broad variety of landing zones indicates that the choice of LZs would be governed by the needs or discretion of the ground commanders. A single BLT would be used for these assaults, although the composition and size of the landing force was not specified in the OP Plan. Ultimately, the overarching target was the seizure of Guanabaco and the opening of the Port of Regla.

Special Forces

In 1962, the concept of special forces, or as they are often referred to, 'unconventional warfare units', was still in its early stages. While Army Special Forces units had been in existence since the late 1950s, they had not been employed extensively. The Navy SEALs (Sea Air and Land Teams) had been established at the beginning of 1962 – morphing out of the Navy's UDT teams (Underwater Demolition Teams). It had been thought that such units would have led to a general uprising, as conceived in the Bay of Pigs, which never materialized. This failure at the Bay of Pigs, even though US forces were not to be directly involved, soured some planners to the idea of employing such units. Yet despite this, there was a recognition on the part of the CINCLANT planning team that unconventional warfare forces were going to be a component of OP Plan 316-62.

There were hurdles to any such plans. The military's estimate was that 30-35 percent of the population would be actively opposed to the American military intervention. Only 5-10 percent would actively support the presence of American troops in their country. The remainder would be initially undecided. As such, the lesson of the Bay of Pigs sunk in; there would not be a groundswell of support for the American troops. At best, only a handful of men and women would consider the US forces as friendly.[68]

On 25 October, the CINCLANT activated the headquarters of the Joint Unconventional Warfare Task Force Atlantic (JUWTFA), under Major General William P. Yarborough, to have them prepare a plan for their integration into OP Plan 316-62. Their planning focused on reducing the military and political effectives of the Castro Government by using American Special Forces to encourage and assist insurrection acts by the Cuban people. The two areas they concentrated on were:

- Infiltrate into Cuba prior to D-Day and accompany and operate in conjunction with the Army and Marine Corps units involved with the invasion. This would involve the establishment of guerilla camps, and providing recon and intelligence information to the invasion forces.
- Special Forces A-Detachments would land with the airborne landing forces to establish camps to recruit and train Cuban dissidents to form units willing and able to fight the Castro regime.[69]

As part of the pre-D-Day invasion, the Army established eight Army Special Forces A-Detachments, each made up of two officers, ten enlisted men, and a number of

Cuban nationals. These units would be deployed in the mountain regions across Cuba during the execution of OP Plan 312 – using the air campaign as cover for their infiltrations. Given they would only have a few days with which to operate prior to D-Day, it was believed that these teams would be most useful if attempting to monitor and track Cuban and Soviet armored forces and their movements, and potentially interdict some of the vital communications lines. No bridges or roads were to be destroyed, since it was felt that the invasion forces would need these as they moved inland.[70]

The second set of units was to consist of four Special Forces A-Detachments and would be landed with the 101st and 82nd Airborne Divisions. They were to establish two camps, one at Cayo La Rosa and the other at Pilar. From there, they planned on recruiting and training anti-Castro Cubans to be used for refugee control and as guards for the rear areas after the American invasion had established itself. The A-Detachments would operate independently until they came in contact with the American conventional forces on the island, at which point they would fall under the command and control of a B-Detachment. The B-Detachment consisted of six officers and seventeen enlisted men who would maintain an active liaison with the JUWTFA.[71]

The final element of the unconventional warfare units slated to be deployed to Cuba was a force of 360 Cuban exiles who volunteered for service in the US Army. This ad hoc small battalion was dubbed 'Task Force Bucko', and was trained in secrecy at Fort Knox, Kentucky. This ghost of the Bay of Pigs unit was intended to play an active combat role in the invasion. The first forty of these men would be landed in the 82nd Airborne Division's zone of operations on D-Day +1. The remainder would come ashore with the 2nd Infantry Division and would follow that unit until it linked up with their comrades in arms in the sweep around Havana.[72]

Even military planners had justifiable doubts about the eventual effectiveness of these units in swaying the course of the invasion. The Bay of Pigs had taught them one thing; there were not masses of population waiting to rise up against Castro. For such forces to be effective, they would need to be in place much more than a few days prior to the invasion. How would dissidents know where the Special Forces teams were and how to contact them? Could these teams operate isolated and behind enemy lines without detection? The Army was plagued with a shortage of Spanish-speaking officers, meaning that some of these units had to rely entirely on their embedded Cuban associates in order to be able to communicate with the local population. The topic of the use of Navy SEALs is covered in detail in Appendix Two. The SEALs were not planned to be utilized during OP Plan 316-62. Not because they would not be of use, but because the two existing teams were on assignments elsewhere in the world (Vietnam and Europe), and could not be brought back with planning put in place fast enough to utilize them.

The Navy's UDTs would play a role in the invasion. The planning called for the use of the UDTs 24-hours prior to the invasion. Navy frogmen would swim to the Tarará beaches in the darkness to check and remove any naval mines. If necessary, they could post marker buoys the night before the landings to indicate the perimeter of the beaches as well.[73]

Stealing a SAM

On 20 October, CINCLANT considered another modification of the invasion plans. This one was based on the US military's desire to capture a complete Soviet SA-2 SAM. These missiles had been an innovation when they downed Francis Gary Powers' U2 flight, and intelligence experts wanted a chance to examine a complete system.

The scheme, as devised, called for two of the SA-2 sites to be isolated from the standard attacks. At one of the sites, the bomb targeting would go after the SA-2 missile launcher only, leaving the fire control systems intact. At the other site, only the fire control systems would be attacked, leaving the launcher intact. When the follow-on invasion took place, the two sites would be secured, and between the two of them, would provide a complete SA-2 system for study.

While the plan was considered feasible, it was deemed to be impractical in terms of execution. The limitations of 1962 bombing accuracy factored into the decision. AFLANT argued that such surgical strikes might place additional personnel at risk, and the idea was shelved, at least as of late October.[74]

Managing Civil Affairs

Assuming that the US invasion of Cuba was successful, an occupation by military forces would be necessary. In the military assessment, 'If the Castro regime collapsed abruptly, the prospects for a coherent program for the direction of civil affairs in Cuba were not promising.'[75] The rapid evolution of OP Plan 316-62 and the increasing urgency in the timing – with the threat of the missile sites becoming fully operational – put pressures on time and personnel that were only going to hinder any attempts to plan a military occupation correctly.

The solution that the Joint Chiefs of Staff came to was to effectively punt the issue over to the Department of State, claiming that they should accept responsibility for the ongoing governance of Cuba. The State Department had, 'Primary or collateral interest in determination, among others, of policies concerning the Government of a particular country with which the US Armed Forces will deal, and to the extent to which the commander of US forces will intervene in the Government of that country.'[76]

The reality of OP Plan 316-62 was that it presumed that, after Havana had been completely cut off from the rest of the island, resistance would collapse. Meaning that on D-Day +5, it was conceivable that the Cuban military would surrender.

While grossly optimistic, it presented a real problem in terms of establishing a new form of Cuban Government to replace Fidel Castro. The US State Department was not prepared to accept the responsibility that the JCS attempted to pawn off to it. Rather than respond, they simply said nothing – leaving no official policy or procedures for the military commanders on the ground should the Cuban Government actually collapse. Admiral Dennison realized that not having anyone in charge of the civilian affairs was unacceptable. As such, he directed the ground commander, the commanding general of the XVIII Airborne Corps, to assume responsibly for planning and directing civil affairs operation. Admiral Dennison noted, 'Concern that guidance in this area will be most difficult to obtain until such time as operations commence and the political situation jells.'[77]

Planning outside of OP Plan 316-62 began for a number of contingencies that the ground commander might face during the first year of a Cuban occupation. These included but were not limited to:

- Establishment of a Cuban Government-in-exile in the United States, and bringing that body back to Havana once the proper timing could be established.
- Dealing with a Junta Government of 'acceptable Cuban figures' to rule in the interim.
- Establishment of security protocols and approaches should outside influences attempt to sway the creation of a Government on the island.
- Basic procedures for dealing with captured Soviets civilians and military personnel, equipment, and cargo.
- The release of Cuban political prisoners, including the prisoners taken during the Bay of Pigs invasion.
- The handling of returning exiles desiring to return to Cuba after Castro's removal.[78]

No matter how it was viewed, the long-term future of Cuba and the Cuban people was far from certain. In such uncertainty, only problems would surface; problems that the American Government was ill-equipped for. The old adage of 'winning the war and losing the peace' seemed appropriate when looking at the post-invasion political environment in Cuba.

Counter-Guerilla Warfare

Another area where OP Plan 316-62 seemed to be lacking was in the area of Cuban guerilla activities. Only one page of the plan was dedicated to such operations, and the guidelines provided were thin at best.

The planning was more in the form of 'guidelines' for dealing with guerilla operations. 'Due to the great emphasis placed on the use of low-level clandestine agents by the enemy, all units will ensure that supply and equipment storage areas are guarded at all times against sabotage.' 'All units will be alert to the discovery and confiscation of cached arms and equipment, the identification and apprehension of those civilians who actively support guerilla activities and the discovery and neutralisation of clandestine communications media.'[79]

To counter guerilla operations, the following were established:

1. Strict camouflage discipline will be adhered to in order to achieve maximum concealment from air and ground observation.
2. An active systems of counter-reconnaissance [sic] patrolling will be instituted by units.
3. All command posts, bivouac areas, and other installation will be policed before abandonment to insure that no classified material or matter of intelligence value to the enemy is left behind.
4. Displacement of command posts shall be conducted during period of reduce
5. Local security of rear area installations, must be emphasized to prevent capture of staff and command personnel during operations.[80]

When one looks at how Castro came to power – by waging a successful guerilla war against the Batista regime – it initially strikes one as odd that this area of planning is so weak. America's last real experience in a major guerilla war was when the US Army engaged in the American-Philippine War (1899-1902). In the Second World War, the Army dealt with some guerilla operations against German hold-out units (Werewolves), but in general, did not have to mount any major anti-guerilla operations. Even with the knowledge that such a style of warfare was how Castro rose to power, the 1962 doctrine, in these pre-Vietnam days, was weak at best.

In order for OP-Plan 316-62 to be implemented, a massive mobilization of forces was required. There would also be a number of command changes and logistical challenges that had to be overcome before there was any hope of successfully seizing control of the missiles and Cuba.

CHAPTER SIX

The Shakedown

Regardless of how persistent our diplomacy might be in activities stretching around the world, in the final analysis, it rests upon the power of the United States.[1]

President John F. Kennedy

Challenges and Politics of Command

The period between 15 and 22 October was one of the more stressful times for the US military. They were being asked to do something that had not been done since the Second World War; prepare for the defense of the United States from foreign attack, while at the same time, prepare to launch a massive invasion of another country. Moreover, the preparations for this attack and defense had to be conducted in relative secrecy. President Kennedy and the members of Excomm felt strongly that they needed to use the time before the presence of missiles was made public in order to have a course of action in hand. Still included in those options were air strikes against Cuba, and potentially the execution of OP Plan 316-62.

While the Three Pairs exercise had US Navy and Marine Corps troops conveniently in place for the crisis – almost unheard of in the annals of military planning – such was not the case with the US Army. The US military was facing a crisis both domestically and organizationally. Domestically, October 1962 was a pivotal time in the emerging race crisis in the United States. On 1 October, the University of Mississippi had granted admission to James H. Meredith as its first black student. His admission had become a rallying point for white separatists who converged on the city of Oxford; a race riot ensued. The man sent in to command the Army and Mississippi National Guard forces to restore order was General Hamilton H. Howze. The military mission there was designed as Operation Rapid Road.

General Howze graduated the US Military Academy at West Point in 1930. He had served with distinction in the 1st Armored Division in Italy during the Second World War. Howze was a visionary, seeing a role for the helicopter in the Army beyond rear-area transports. He realized that with the proper equipment and tactics, the helicopter could become an air-mobile means of assault – an aviation cavalry force. His vision was so clearly articulated to the Army that he was named the first director of Army aviation and went on to command the 82nd Airborne Division, then the XVIII Airborne Corps – comprised on the 101st and 82nd Airborne Divisions.

The issue with him being in Oxford, Mississippi, is that under OP Plan 316-62, the command of the ground forces in Cuba was to fall to the Army Commander, which under the command structure was the CO of the XVIII Corps. Given the emerging situation in Cuba, the CINCLANT need to extract General Howze from the domestic security of Oxford and have him shift into his new role. This had to be done without tipping off the press. Given the massive movement of troops and equipment that was already unfolding in relative secrecy, such a swapping of commanders in such a media hot-spot might give the media a clue as to what was happening.[2]

This issue was resolved by a change to the command structure of the Army. General Herbert Powell, Commanding General of US Continental Army Command, was directed to assume responsibility for the Army's role in the possible invasion of Cuba. This action had the ripple effect of reliving General Howze from his role as Commanding Officer of the XVIII Airborne Corps. While the press only saw this as a shuffling of top officers, this action freed up General Howze to assume command of the Joint Task Force as the ground commander, under the title as Commander of the Army Task Force.[3]

While General Howze was apprised of the unfolding affairs in Cuba and his intended role, he still had the difficult task of extracting elements of two airborne divisions from their anti-riot civil duties, replacing them with National Guard and other army units, and doing so discreetly to avoiding any media suspicion.

The riots in Oxford presented yet another challenge. When the CINCLANT and the Joint Chiefs went to activate the 'war room' for managing the situation on 18 October, they had to share the room with the Army, who were already using the room to manage the situation in Oxford. The war room, as a command post, was not designed for handling multiple hot-spots around the globe at the same time, and for a short few days, the staffs managed to work around each other.[4]

The other issue facing the US military was around organizational issues. Cuba represented a threat very different than any faced in the lifetimes of the men in command. Not only did they have to plan an invasion of a nation technically only 90 miles from the US, they had other issues. Firstly, there was a risk that Cuba and their Soviet allies would get the missiles operational. This meant that there was a potential risk of an attack against American soil. The defense of the United States resided in several parts of the military infrastructure. First was the Air Force, specifically NORAD (North American Aerospace Defense Command), which had the responsibility to track and coordinate defense of missile and bomber attacks. If the Cubans or the Soviets escalated the conflict and struck at the US, NORAD would be the first to know that the attack was coming.

There was also CONARC (Continental Army Command) out of Fort Monroe, Virginia. Technically, they had the responsibility for the Army units in the Continental United States. They also had, at least on paper, technical responsibility for part of the Caribbean theatre of operations, which included Cuba. Also, the movement of troops across the United States to their staging areas for the invasion would fall under their overall jurisdiction, as well as military transport command. When the Joint Chiefs of Staff engaged CINCLANT to coordinate the invasion, which relieved Continental Army Command of that aspect of responsibility, it still required a great deal of coordination between the two entities.

Admiral Dennison also had the 19th Air Force, which had responsibility for Florida, which would bear the brunt of coordinating any of the OP Plan 312 air strike plans. This unit fell under the command of AFLANT (Air Force Atlantic) TAC (Tactical Air Command). On top of this, Admiral Dennison had to attempt to coordinate his own Naval Task Forces and Marine Corps troops.

Other military entities that had some input, authority, jurisdiction, or control over the events unfolding in the Caribbean included the Joint Unconventional Warfare Task Force Atlantic (JUWTFA), which was supported by the Army Special Forces Operating Base (SFOB), the Commanding General, Army Air Defense Command (CGARADCOM), the Commander in Chief, Continental Air Defense Command (CINCCONAD), Strike Command (STRICOM), Commander in Chief, United States Strike Forces (CINCSTRIKE), and the Army Component, Atlantic (ARLANT).[5] Simply keeping track of the acronyms alone was a tricky job.

Matters were even more complex given that the Joint Chiefs of Staff were taking a very hands-on approach with changes to OP Plan 316-62, and the ever-changing targeting lists for OP Plan 312. Excomm was still weighing a variety of options, including a blockade, which would fall under the CINCLANT's command too. The Kennedy administration, via the Secretary of Defense, was also involved with a great deal of micro-managing the Joint Chiefs of Staff – most likely a result of the stinging wounds of the Bay of Pigs. Keeping all of the options in play, while having senior officials and officers poking into constantly changing plans, presented Admiral Dennison with challenges that few other military commanders had been forced to juggle since the Second World War.

In terms of the command structure that Admiral Dennison had in place at the start of the crisis, it had all of the hallmarks of being cumbersome. The amphibious fleet and naval assets were organized as Joint Task Force 122. This had been the designation of the task force as part of the Three Pairs exercise, which was still acting as cover for the movement of troops. Once the amphibious force lanced in Cuba, Joint Task Force 122 would fall under command of the headquarters of the XVIII Airborne Corps. This had been the designed structure as part of OP Plan 312-62 and the training exercise.

One decision that hampered Admiral Dennison was that the Joint Chiefs had declared that the actual prepositioning of major units would not commence until 22 October at 1900 hours, when President Kennedy would announce to the world that there were Soviet missiles in Cuba.[6] This did not limit the Admiral in terms of moving material, advanced headquarters units, and logistical support, but it did mean that any large-scale troop and equipment maneuvers would be on hold until 22 October.

On 19 October, Admiral Dennison announced a changed to the command structure. Rather than have Joint Task Force 122 operate as a combined group, the Admiral disbanded the task force structure. Direct command of the various forces (Navy, Air Force, Marine, and Army) would report directly up to CINCLANT.[7]

On paper to a layman, this seems prudent. It removed the task force command element, flattening the structure to give the CINCLANT greater control over the component organizations that would be invading Cuba. Military structures are not like corporate ones; they exist for specific purposes. The Joint Task Force commanders on the scene would not be orchestrating the fighting forces, but instead, they would be directed by the CINCLANT from Norfolk. This change could have potentially been disastrous, with the need for highly coordinated, concerted action being directed from someone hundreds of miles away.[8]

Why would Admiral Dennison undertake such a change in the command structure so close to the launch of an invasion? The Cuban Missile Crisis was unprecedented in the way that the Kennedy administration, via the Secretary of Defense, was involving itself 'hands-on' with the military operations. While Admiral Dennison never voiced why the change was necessary in his eyes, it could very well be a response to pressure by the administration to be closer to the action.[9]

As a result of Admiral Dennison's decision, Continental Army Command quickly improvised the establishment of two headquarters in Florida to fill the gap left by removing the Joint Task Force Commander. The belief was that Norfolk, Virginia, was too far from the theatre of battle to do direct management of the assets. As such, temporary headquarters were put in place to help facilitate the coordination. One was for operations (ARLANT), while the other supported he logistics for the assault (designated as Peninsular Base Command).

These two commands created more problems than they solved. Both were staffed with men with only scant understanding of the OP Plan 316-62 and the myriad of changes that were being made to the plans. The two command posts required extensive communications access both with the invasion fleet, the ground force's commander (once the landings took place), and with CINCLANT.[10] In 1962, quickly putting in secured telecommunication lines took weeks, and the US military did not have that long.

The deficiency in the way that OP-Plan 316-62 evolved over time proved to be a problem as well. The original plans were an Army contingency plan that morphed into a joint task force. This was merged with an Air Force bombing campaign, OP Plan 312-62. The problem was that the plans combined to make the invasion plan had never been reconciled against each other. As a result, the Army portion of the planning required the use of key Tactical Air Command bases in Florida for transport aircraft to bring in the paratroopers of the airborne forces as well as their follow-on infantry and artillery. The Air Force, without knowledge of the Army's needs, needed the same air bases for fighter-bombers, armaments, etc., and so the Air Force bases were hopelessly overloaded with equipment, all with conflicting priorities.

Also, the flight routes into and out of Cuba needed to be merged into a comprehensive plan, otherwise flight corridors for transports and ferrying aircraft would collide with those used for reconnaissance and bombing missions. These two issues forced changes to the airborne drop timetables and a massive amount of replanning as it became clear that the contingency plan was about to become a reality.[11]

On 20 October, the Joint Chiefs of Staff ordered that the units in the Three Pairs exercise, which was still running as a diversion and excuse for American military forces to be in the region, to be transferred under CINCLANT's authority. Command of Three Pairs was under CINCSTRIKE's authority, General Paul D. Hood, given it had begun as nothing more than a military exercise. The chairman of the Joint Chiefs Maxwell Taylor still felt that Three Pairs served a purpose in providing deception and cover for the massive troop build-up in the south. General Hood felt differently, and despite the chairman's desires, canceled Three Pairs as a result of organizational change.[12]

This transfer of authority and control was far from smooth. On 21 October, a day after the decision was made, no transfer had taken place. This was due to the fact that the other changes to the command structure made it difficult to know who (and where) to transfer to the units to. New command posts were being established in Florida, but coastal Virginia (Norfolk, Langley AFB, and Fort Monroe) was still the epicenter of command for the operation. It was not until late in the afternoon on 22 October that the first units of Task Force Charlie were transferred to CINCLANT and orders were sent out to move the bulk of the 1st Armored Division from Fort Hood and Fort Benning to the ports of Savannah, Georgia, and Everglades, Florida.[13]

On 27 October, General Powell (ARLANT) asked Admiral Dennison to subordinate the Joint Unconventional Warfare Task Force Atlantic (JUWTFA) under his command. He felt that the commander of the conventional invasion forces had to control unconventional troops operating in the area – a sound premise. Admiral Dennison declined and kept the JUWTFA under CINCLANT control. His thinking was that if unconventional forces were working in an area near conventional forces, coordination would be done on a incident-by-incident basis. In reality, this premise could have resulted in friendly fire incidents, or worse, with conventional forces potentially calling in air strikes on friendly unconventional forces, not aware they were in the area.[14]

Once a foothold was established on Cuba, Admiral Dennison planned on establishing a Joint Task Force Cuba, which would report directly to him and assume control over all operations on the island. Given the OP Plan 316-62 initially

Chain of Command – US Forces

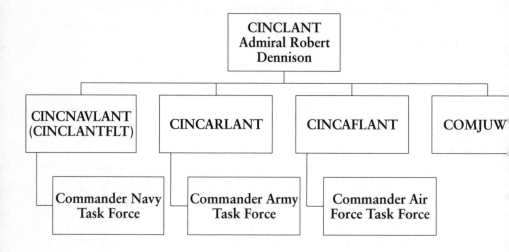

planned for the landings and subsequent isolation of Havana, this would mean
that this individual would assume the next unplanned phase of the operation; the
overland advance to the missile sites to ensure that they had been deactivated.
No specific timing was provided as to when the Joint Task Force Cuba would be
established, but the guidelines indicated that it would happen only after Havana
had been cut off.

The OP Plan called the Joint Task Force Cuba to be headed up by the Army
Task Force Commander, in this case, General Howze. On 20 October however,
CINCLANT announced that the position would be filled by General Powell, the
Commanding General of Continental Army Command (CONARC). This caused
consternation in the ranks; not from General Howze, but from General Powell.
His responsibilities in terms of moving troops and equipment into position for
the invasion were massive given the time crunch. Suddenly, he was being asked
to step in and run a tactical or theatre operational on an island off-shore. On
paper, the Army troops in Cuba would report to General Powell, regardless of his
heading up the task force – it was simply inconceivable that he would assume a
field command at that juncture of the operation. General Powell pushed back on
Admiral Dennison, who acquiesced on 23 October, naming General Howze as the
Commanding Officer of Joint Task Force Cuba.[15]

It became clear to General Powell that he was going to be expected to be
more hands-on in the Cuban operation. As such, on 22 October, he created his
own command arrangement as CINCARLANT. Two new Army headquarters
would be opened as a result: USARLANT Main at Fort Monroe, Virginia, where
General Powell was based, and a new base of operations USARLANT Forward at
Homestead Air Force Base near Miami. While General Powell would remain at Fort
Monroe, he wanted a base closer to Cuba to be established to coordinate tactical

operations as necessary. It was also supposed to be located on the Homestead AFB to liaison with the forward headquarters of the Air Force component of the landings. His intention was to establish the USARLANT Forward base as soon as the airborne landings commenced, and sent Major General George Duncan to Homestead AFB on 25 October to activate this headquarters in preparations for the landings.[16]

Within a matter of a few days, this headquarters' staff was over 200 officers and enlisted men. At the same time, the Air Force component 'Battle Staff', which it was supposed to coordinate with, was twelve to fifteen offices in size. General Charles Sweeney, who commanded the Air Force components of the invasion, had deliberately set up his command structure to be closer to General Powell, operating out of Langley Air Force Base. It was his thinking that given the proximity to Norfolk VA and CINCLANT, coordinating the operations out of Florida did not make sense.[17] General Powell's actions in establishing this base could only lead to confusion in command during operations.

The Army struggled with the invasion of Cuba. As CINCARLANT, General Powell wore two hats in terms of command responsibilities. One was Commanding General of the Continental Army Command, the other was that of the coordinating authority of the Department of the Army. As such, in his role of commanding Continental Army Command, he would have overall direction/responsibility and should control whatever support activities might be required by troops assembling in, or deploying from, his jurisdiction. At first, General Powell followed this per the existing Army command structure. The 3rd US Army had command of the United States east of the Mississippi River and south of the Virginia Kentucky borders. This is where the invasion of Cuba would originate from – so it would be the hub of staging, launching, and sustaining operations. On 23 October, General Powell directed the new commanding officer of the 3rd Army, Lieutenant General Trapnell, to activate and prepare to move an Army Staging Area Command to each of the staging bases in OP Plan 316-62. He also asked him to establish a headquarters, Army Staging Command, at the recently re-opened Opa Locka Airfield.[18]

General Trapnell responded swiftly, and by the end of the next day, the headquarters and eight commands were set up in Florida. These were created at Elgin, MacDill, Opa Locka, Homestead McCoy, Patrick, and Tyndall Air Force bases. One was also created as Stanford Naval Air Station. A ninth was planned to open at Key West International Airport, but would not be activated until 5 November.

While General Trapnell had moved swiftly to fulfill this set of orders, he was unaware that before he completed the task, General Powell had begun to undermine him and remove these bases from 3rd Army control. On 23 October, the same day he had ordered General Trapnell to establish the bases, General Powell alerted the 2nd Logistical Command for movement from Fort Lee, Virginia, to Opa Locka Airfield. Its Commanding Officer Brigadier General Horace Davisson established a new command post – Peninsula Base Command, reporting directly to General Powell with jurisdiction of all logistical and administrative support for the Army task force within the state of Florida. This was directly in contradiction with the already-established area of control that fell under the 3rd Army.

Admiral Dennison assumed that this was merely a forward advanced party of the 2nd Logistical Command. In reality, the authority given General Davisson was of the Transportation Terminal Command, along with a transportation group (movement control), and a medical group with four field hospitals and a large support staff. The formal activation of the Peninsula Base Command was not scheduled until 30 October.[19] Once it became operational, it formally stripped away the authority of 3rd Army in terms of movement and logistics. In the meantime, there were two command groups issuing orders and commands to Army units.

The creation of the Peninsula Base Command shared many of the same issues that the creation of the USARLANT Forward Command had. One, it was duplicative of existing command structures already established either by the Army or by OP Plan 316-62. Peninsula Base Command did not even have a working knowledge of OP Plan 316-62, so their capability to execute their mission was compromised.[20]

General Powell had full authority to create these headquarters. What he failed to do was delineate the lines of authority in creating these posts with existing Army commands. The new headquarters' functions were not sure of their responsibilities, and in the case of Peninsula Base Command, those of 3rd Army.

The activities of General Powell seem to have gone unnoticed by Admiral Dennison and CINCLANT. There was no way for the Admiral to understand the intricate and often confusing lines of authority and command within the US Army, even more blurred with the arriving crisis. At the same time, General Powell was making decisions that would complicate and even potentially compromise troops involved with the invasion. This lack of control and authority planted the seeds for issues that might surface at inopportune times for the assaulting troops.

Another complicating command structure with the new United States Strike Command (USSTRICOM). This command was created on 19 September 1961, and became operational on 9 October 1961 at MacDill Air Force Base, under the command of General Paul D. Adams. The mission was to be a general reserve of ready forces to reinforce other unified commands and to plan for, and if directed, conduct, military operations in remote areas, such as Central Africa, which were outside the boundaries of existing commands.[21] It was conceived as a highly mobile command; a flexible contingency force. The Berlin Crisis of 1961 emphasized the need for such a mobile force. While it was envisioned to be comprised of a land-fighting force (Strategic Army Corps – STRAC) of six divisions, by the time of the Berlin Crisis, it consisted of three stripped-down divisions.[22]

By January 1962, the Joint Chiefs of Staff had directed Generals Powell and Sweeney to put their forces dedicated to USSTRICOM under operational control of CINCSTRIKE (Commander in Chief Strike Command) for any joint training and contingency operations that fell outside the scope of their responsibilities. The creation of this new command structure so close to the invasion of Cuba added an additional layer of confusion. General Powell had forces in the Continental United States that he could not assign to support CINCLANT because of the authority of CINCSTRIKE. General Howze was told that his role in the invasion was to be an Army *component* commander, as opposed to a *task force* commander, as defined by the CINCLANT. The result of this was:

> General Howze was not entirely sure if he had, or was expected to have, any authority or any role beyond that of a task force commander. And despite all impressions to the contrary, the result of the misunderstanding seems to be that there was no legally-appointed Army component commander from 4 April until 16 October, when General Powell was directed to assume that role himself.[23]

Even more complex was that the Three Pairs exercise fell under the command of CINCSTRIKE. While the amphibious forces were at sea, part of the operation was to take place as land exercises at Fort Hood. On 17 October, the Joint Chiefs directed General Powell to bring the units tied to OP Plan 316-62 to the highest state of readiness. He could not technically do that to those that were in the Three Pairs exercise; he had to negotiate the release of those units, while at the same time, maintaining the integrity of the exercise itself.

Worse yet, General Adams was tasked with keeping a flexible fighting force for contingencies, and he became concerned that if he dedicated the resources to the Cuban operation, he would be stripping out his flexibility if the US needed war forces elsewhere, such as Berlin. This set Generals Powell and Adams into conflict as both men attempted to fulfill their orders. Finally, the Joint Chiefs intervened: 'In the event a decision is made to take military action against Cuba, the JCS will direct the changes of operational control to CINCLANT of Army and Air Force units currently included under CINCLANT operational plans.'[24]

This did not end the tug of war between generals Powell and Adams. General Powell asked General Adams to relieve eight technical service units and four field hospitals of their ARSTIKE designation to his command to allow him to use them in the defense of the Florida Keys and in support of the 3rd Army. Powell did not wait for a response; he simply issued orders for the units to begin deployment – especially those elements of the 3rd Missile Command, an air-deployable unit for air defense. General Powell's request would have split the unit apart – something General Adams advised against. Finally, the Department of the Army intervened, stating that General Powell was to take this and whatever actions were necessary to insure his readiness to defend the Continental United States.[25]

General Powell's head-butting within the chain of command was far from over. His gaze seemed to shift in the middle of the crisis of the headquarters of the Antilles Command (ANTCOM). Headquartered at Fort Brooke in Puerto Rico, it was also a planning command for the Department of the Army, and managed to reserve forces in the region. ANTCOM was under the US Army Caribbean – outside the scope of responsibility of General Powell. Given the proximity of this command over the Caribbean and the Panama Canal, General Powell, with the blessing of Admiral Dennison, was promoted to suggest moving ANTCOM under his authority for the duration of the crisis. The Department of the Army had suggested that this was not necessary until the air strikes under OP Plan 312 began, but Powell felt differently. The Joint Chiefs responded on 4 November, agreeing that ANTCOM would fall under General Powell's authority as long as the state of emergency existed.[26]

While ANTCOM did not factor greatly into the execution of OP Plan 316-62, it would have if the invasion had gone ahead. Several Latin American countries offered ships to take part in the eventual blockade/quarantine of Cuba, and many indicated that they would be sending land forces if the planned invasion took place. If that had occurred, General Powell's move to put ANTCOM under his command would have proven to be a greater stretch of his authority; the commanding of a multi-national fighting force on Cuba.[27]

General Powell attempted to leverage this new base, suggesting that ANTCOM in Puerto Rico should serve as a staging base for other Latin American countries that might be called upon to invade Cuba. He cited the fact that ANTCOM had a language training centre and an abundance of multilingual officers. His logic was lacking any practical experience with this new command. ANTCOM simply did not have the size of base large enough to support such a massive invasion. General Howze and Lieutenant General Andrew P. O'Meara, commander in chief of the Caribbean Command, both felt that this was the wrong solution. For General Howze, he saw a political impact of having these countries stage and train in Puerto Rico before landing in Cuba. It would have a greater impact if they sailed from their own countries under the escorts of their own ships, and moved in to provide supporting roles until their combat effectiveness could be ascertained. General O'Meara indicated that the inhabitants of Puerto Rico had a high degree of apathy to the other Latin American countries, and having their forces stage there would not provide anything other than additional headaches and problems. He suggested that if training was needed, the best facilities and country for it was in the Panama Canal zone. Eventually, General Powell conceded the point.[28]

The War Room

During the 1958 crisis in the Middle East, then Army chief of staff General Maxwell Taylor realized that the Army lacked a centre to collect and disseminate timely information to the decision makers. As such, the concept of a war room was created. While formally named the National Military Command Center, it was referred to as the 'war room.' The deputy chief of staff for military operations

(DCSOPS) was directed to create a facility of a single room where the Army could manage a crisis, having all pertinent and up-to-date information on hand as real-time as possible.

The war room was created in the Pentagon under maximum security. The room was a communications hub with field commands, allowing the plotting and mapping of any and all troop movements, as well as the tracking for combat situations. When the missile crisis broke out, the war room was already being used for monitoring three situations. Two were command training exercises: Spade Fork and High Heels. The third was referred to as the 'Oxford Augmentation,' also known as Operation Rapid Road; the posting of federal troops to Oxford, Mississippi, to help quell the tensions there.[29]

The physical space allotted for the war room was limited – even for tracking a minor crisis. It became clear early on that the facility was going to be cramped and confined for managing something as large as the invasion of Cuba. Prior to 18 October, the tracking of what was happening in Cuba was done through the DCSOPS 'Cuban Desk'. With the detection and confirmation of the strategic missiles in Cuba, the 'Cuban Desk' relocated to the war room officially as the 'Cuban Augmentation'.[30]

The war room during the missile crisis was staffed by three four-man teams, each one commanded by a colonel from the DCSOPS staff sections. Each 8-hour shift prepared situation reports, maintained the special operations journal, maintained all charts and maps, recorded and interpreted all incoming messages, and ensured that the proper Army commands were kept informed of emerging developments. These men were augmented by the DCSOPS staff, the representatives from the deputy chief of staff for personnel, and the chief signal officer. Overall command of the war room required general officers' watch at all times. Four major generals were assigned, with one always present in the room. These generals were Creighton Abrams Jr, William Rosson, Claire Hutchin Jr, and Edwin Carns.[31]

As the mobilization of the American military took place, this cramped room in the Pentagon provided the Joint Chiefs of Staff with the best up-to-date information on the planned invasion and air strikes that was possible with 1962 technologies.

The Challenges in Mobilizing Task Force 125

It is rare that contingency plans are ever put into motion; even rarer they are executed. In the conception of STRAC 55-61 (eventually OP Plan 314-61), the mix of units that were to be employed were different than those that made the final list (see the previous chapter). These changes, which were relatively significant, were driven by a number of different factors. Task Force 125 consisted of four basic elements: an air-landing echelon, a surface echelon, a floating reserve, and an on-call reserve that would remain in the United States unless needed.

One element that held true in OP Plan 316-62 from previous versions was the composition of the air echelon. The deployment plan for the 82nd and 101st Airborne Divisions was fairly straight-forward. These units would deploy from their home bases (the 82nd from Fort Bragg and the 101st from Fort Campbell) to intermediate staging bases – Air Force bases in Florida. They would be accompanied by two field artillery battalions of 155-mm howitzers, which were to be landed within the airhead seized by the divisions. The 82nd Airborne was to have the support of a company of M-41 light tanks once their airfield was secured and opened.

The remainder of the airborne forces would be air landed by transports on the captured airfields, consisting of an infantry brigade of two battle groups and a separate battle group from the task force – both from the 1st Infantry Division. The 1st Infantry Division would be deployed from their home base at Fort Riley, Kansas, to a staging base in Florida, before loading onto transport bound for the captured airfields.[32]

The biggest changes to the original plans was in the form of the surface assault forces, the reserve afloat, and the on-call reserves. OP Plan 314-61 had originally envisioned that the 4th Infantry Division from Fort Lewis, Washington, and the 2nd Armored Division at Fort Hood, Texas, would be the ground bulk of the these elements. The Berlin Crisis from the year before had inadvertently eliminated these two divisions from the invasion plan.

Following the Berlin Crisis, the Joint Chiefs of Staff felt it necessary to have divisions that could be rapidly deployed to Europe should another incident emerge there. This rapid reinforcement of Europe, dubbed US CONARC OPLAN 420, earmarked the 4th Infantry and 2nd Armored Divisions for this deployment.

This plan was audacious in scope. Both divisions had duplicates of their full equipment prepositioned in Europe. In the event of an emergency situation, both divisions' personnel could be airlifted, then married-up with their pre-deployed equipment. Normally, the Joint Chiefs would have simply reallocated these divisions to the invasion of Cuba, but the Kennedy administration felt that if the Soviets were pressured in Cuba, they might apply pressure elsewhere, specifically in Berlin. As such, if the JCS reallocated these divisions for OP Plan 316-62; they would not be able to respond to a potential crisis elsewhere, which they felt might be likely.

The choices were incredibly thin for replacing these units. The 1st and 2nd Infantry Divisions were already partially committed to the invasion of Cuba. The 1st Infantry Division had three battle groups assigned to the air echelon. Two battle groups from the 2nd Infantry Division were allocated to the surface echelon. The 1st Infantry Division was not complete due to a large air mobility exercise called Long Thrust in Europe, which tied up two of her battle groups. The 2nd Division was caught in the Army's European replacement system, ROTAPLAN, which had absorbed one of their four uncommitted battle groups, although still permitted three to be tasked for invading Cuba.[33]

From an infantry perspective, this left the Joint Chiefs of Staff with few options. The best choice was the 5th Infantry Division. A mechanized division, this unit was spread out to three different posts. One brigade was at Fort Devens, Massachusetts; two brigades and most of the division's artillery and division support elements were at Fort Carson in Colorado. The armored battalion was at Fort Irwin, California. Moving all of these forces across the country would be challenging, but not impossible. The only real problem with the 5th Infantry Division was that by 22 October 1962, it was at 85 percent equipped and staffed, but only 79 percent was considered qualified for overseas deployment. As such, the 5th Infantry Division was seen by the Joint Chiefs as potentially filling one of two roles: either as a reserve force for the airborne divisions, if needed; or to be deployed as an immediate ready force if the situation necessitated it in Europe, Korea, or any other part of the world.[34]

Old Ironsides'

Replacing the 2nd Armored Division with the 1st Armored Division initially looked simple to execute. OP Plan 316-62 was revised and updated to include the 1st Armored Division, per the decision by General Powell of CONARC. But declaring it and making it actually happen were two different things.

The 1st Armored Division, known as Old Ironsides' from her Second World War days, was essentially a new division. It had been reactivated in February 1962 at Fort Hood, Texas, to replace a federalized national guard division that had been brought to a ready state as a result of the crisis in Berlin.[35] Despite her namesakes illustrious history in the last world war, for all intents and purposes, the 1st Armored Division was a brand new division.

Also of importance was that it was the first of the Army divisions to be reorganized from a Pentomic to a ROAD structure. ROAD stood for Reorganization Objective Army Division, which was a new organization and training structure for a division. In March 1962, the division had undergone extensive training exercises to adapt to the new structure. Going into Cuba, Old Ironsides' would be the first division with this new structure.

The 1st Armored Division had been declared combat-ready in August of 1962, only a few months before the crisis. One of her brigades had been attached to the Three Pairs exercise for their first assault landing training. In swapping out the 1st for the 2nd Armored Division, it simplified the logistics of replacing the amphibious armored force. If the 2nd Armored Division went in, it might necessitate pulling back that brigade of the 1st Armored and repositioning the 2nd for deployment to Cuba. In many respects, it made things easier to have the 1st Armored Division to be the core of the armored forces landing in Cuba, while at the same time, it introduced a risk in that this unit was new and untested in battle.[36]

On 18 October, Major General Ralph E. Haines Jr, division commander, was called at his field command post by General Howze and told to report to Fort

Bragg for instructions. General Haines returned on 20 October with orders to commence mobilizing the division. Many of his men had just returned from preliminary assignment on Three Pairs.[37] Suddenly, these men, tired and weary from this recent deployment, faced another arduous task – redeploying to invade Cuba for real.

On 22 October, when the President prepared to make his first public announcement regarding the missile crisis, CINCLANT still did not know where the 1st Armored Division was going to have to be relocated to.

Air Force Preparations

Moving an armored or infantry division attracted a great deal of attention – it would mean diverting railroads, movement of convoys on the interstates, etc.. The Air Force was not so encumbered during the days leading up to 22 October. AFLANT General Walter Sweeney was not following the pattern that his Army counterpart was performing. The result was that the Air Force did not undergo the massive reorganizations and confusion that the Army was struggling with. With all of the changes implemented by Admiral Dennison, the result was that General Sweeney was reporting directly to the admiral as opposed to CINCSTRIKE.

AFLANT's role was larger than just tactical air command assets. General Sweeney was in control of all air assets – including those of the Marine Air Groups 26 and 14, and the naval carrier-based assets. AFLANT also had sole responsibility for controlling the master target list for Cuba.

Much like the Army, Navy and Marine Corps, the Air Force was uniquely prepared for the crisis. On 18 September 1962, Tactical Air Command had issued TAC Ops Order 173-62, which was an exercise to redeploy a large number of units to Florida. This drill in early October *already* had the key Air Force aircraft in place when the Cuban crisis began to emerge. As such, the Air Force simply took out TAC Ops Order 173-62 and supplemented it with Frag Order No. 2, which increased the scale and scope of the exercise – turning it from a training tool to an operational order.

In normal peacetime conditions, two TAC Wings, the 12th and 15th Tactical Fighter Wings (TFW), were normally stationed at MacDill AFB. The 31st TFW was located at Homestead AFB. TAC Ops Order 173-62 dramatically altered that. As part of TAC Ops Order 173-62 and Frag Order No. 2:

- The 474th Tactical Fighter Wing was moved to Homestead AFB on 18 October
- The 4th and 354th TFWs were moved to McCoy AFB on 19 October
- The 401st TFW relocated to Homestead AFB on 19 October
- The 479th TFW was moved to Key West on 20 October
- Support personnel and additional equipment was to be moved into place,

The USS *Comet* struggles to test-load a tank at New Orleans. (*Author's Private Collection*)

Two months prior to the missile crisis, the Cactus Curtain with an empty-beer-can security system. (*Author's Private Collection*)

A cigar-toting Fidel Castro.

Mariel – critical for the First Armored Division's landing – as it appeared in January of 1963. (*US National Archives*)

John Kennedy and Nikita Khrushchev met over lunch at the Vienna summit on June 3, 1961, prior to the crisis.

MISSILE HOLD AREA

SIGUANEA CRUISE MIS
21-37N 82-58W

MISSILE TRANSPORTERS

SUPPORT AREA

UNCOVERED LAUNCHER

CANVAS COVERED LAUNCHER

GUIDANCE AREA

PERSONNEL TRENCHES

Above: On the Isle of Pines – a Soviet cruise missile installation. (*US National Archives*)

Left: Robert Strange McNamara, (1916-2009). McNamara was eighth Secretary of State for Defense and served under Presidents John F. Kennedy and Lyndon B. Johnson from 1961 to 1968.

Opposite above: Intelligence briefing of Soviet missile sites and build-up on the island of Cuba, October 1962. (*US National Archives*)

Opposite below: US intelligence plot of Soviet SAM sites and their overlapping coverage. (*US National Archives*)

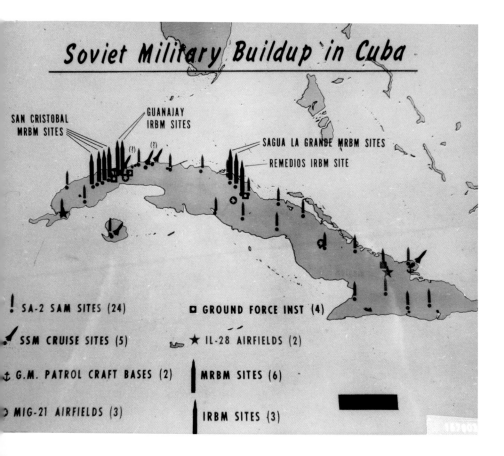

Soviet Military Buildup in Cuba

SAN CRISTOBAL
MRBM SITES

GUANAJAY
IRBM SITES

SAGUA LA GRANDE MRBM SITES

REMEDIOS IRBM SITE

- SA-2 SAM SITES (24)
- SSM CRUISE SITES (5)
- G.M. PATROL CRAFT BASES (2)
- MIG-21 AIRFIELDS (3)

- GROUND FORCE INST (4)
- ★ IL-28 AIRFIELDS (2)
- MRBM SITES (6)
- IRBM SITES (3)

SA-2 SAM DEPLOYMENT IN CUBA

Havana
Mariel
Bahai Honda
Santa Lucia
Matanzas
Beleite
Sagua la Granda
Caibarien
La Coloma
San Julián
Cienfuegos
Chambas
Sancti Spiritus
Esmeralda
Ciego de Avila
Siguanea
Camaguey
Manati
Holguin
Los Angeles
Jiguani
Manzanillo
Cabañas
Santiago de Cuba

24 - ● SA-2 SITE

167782 USAF

In this post-crisis military exercise the Army drives ashore much as they would have in Cuba. (*US National Archives*)

Marines assault a beach in Florida in an exercise that mimicked the assaults of OP Plan 316-62. (*US National Archives*)

Above: Airborne forces prepare for an assault that never happened. (*Author's Personal Collection*)

Right: Admiral Robert Lee Dennison, the man who would have commanded the invasion of Cuba. (*US Navy*)

The 101st Airborne Division in practice in January 1963, much as their landing would have happened at the Baracoa Airfield if the invasion had taken place. (*US National Archives*)

Guantanamo civilians and dependants evacuate prior to the President's announcement on 22 October. (*US Naval Historical Research Center*)

TWO NAVY DESTROYERS CONTINUE SURVEILLANCE OF RUSSIAN SUBMARI

One of the four Soviet subs detected by the US Navy during the crisis. (*US Naval Historical Research Center*)

The First Armored Division assaults Fort Lauderdale Florida in 1963, practicing the assault they would have executed in the invasion of Cuba. (*US National Archives*)

San Cristobal Missile Complex from a Blue Moon flight. (*National Security Archive*)

San Diego de Los Banos medium range missile complex. (*National Security Archive*)

CIA image of FKR cruise missile. (*National Security Archive*)

Antiaircraft emplacements surrounding the San Crisobal missile site taken from a Blue Moon mission. (*National Security Archive*)

Previously unpublished photographic composite of the invasion beaches. (*US National Archives*)

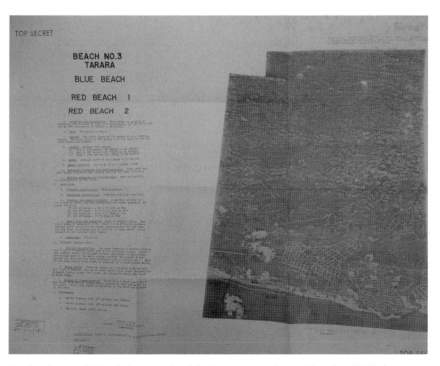

Previously unpublished photograph of the invasion beach corridors for OP Plan 316-62. (*US National Archives*)

The Baracoa airfield, target objective on D-Day of the 101st Airborne Division. (*US National Archives*)

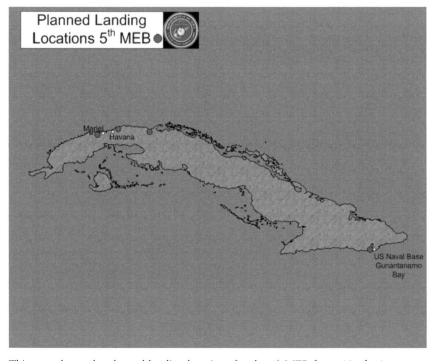

This map shows the planned landing locations for the 5th MEB force. (*Author*)

Army Staging Areas and Associated Bases

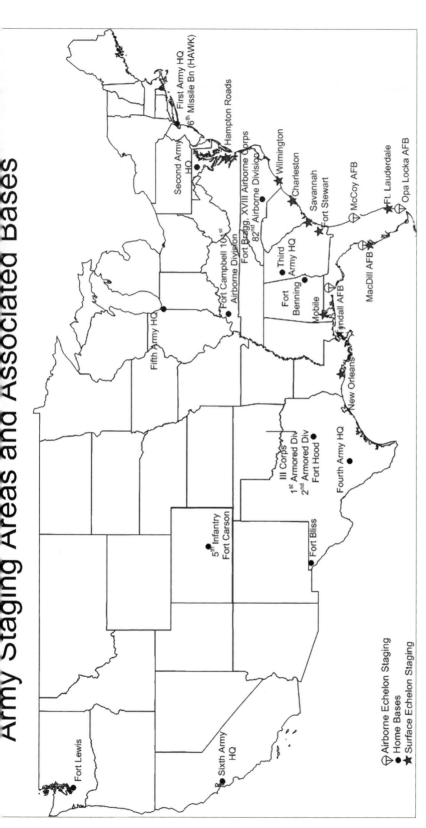

The mobilization of troops showing home fort locations and staging areas for the invasion. (*Author*)

Map of the US Naval Base at Guantanamo Bay in 1964. This map shows the roadways and defensive positions added during the Cuban Crisis. (*The History of Guantanamo Bay, US Navy, 1964*)

per Frag Order No. 2, by no later than 21 October
- The 31st TFW at Homestead AFB was joined by the 4150th Combat Crew Training Wing CCTW from Luke AFB
- Luke Air Force Base contributed aircraft (F-100s) to augment the 354th TFW at McCoy AFB and to Homestead AFB
- Nellis AFB's 4520th CCTW provided F-105s to the 4th TFW
- A squadron from the 4505th Air Force Refueling (AFR) tankers were sent to McCoy AFB
- A second squadron of tankers (KB-50's) were relocated to McDill AFB
- The 12th and 15th TFW's at MacDill consisted of F-84 aircraft. These were augmented by F100's from the 27th TFW from Cannon AFB, and RB-66's and RF-101's of the 363rd Tactical Reconnaissance Wing (TRW) from Shaw AFB[38]

The exercise-turned-mobilization had the Tactical Air Command flying over 428 training sorties up to the time of the crisis.[39]

By 22 October, the normal contingent of aircraft at the bases exploded. There was over 500 aircraft in Florida, with the closest strike contingent to Cuba being in Key West with 24 F-104's.

The airlift capability of the Air Force was brought to bear on the crisis as well. This mobilization by the Air Force was no just a simply ferrying task. Movement of aircraft was done over the Gulf of Mexico or the Atlantic with pre-computed arrival landfalls. Air-to-air refueling capabilities and ordnance were also moved down to Florida. Starting on 18 October, TAC's C-123's and C-130's began to shift the personnel needed to keep the jets operational. Over 6,966 passengers and 3,152 tons of cargo were airlifted into Florida during the crisis.[40] The total airlift capability poised for operations in Cuba were:

Table 6-1: Airlift Aircraft and Numbers [41]

Aircraft	Number Deployed by 3 November
C-130	107
C-123	82
C-119	378
Total Air Force Lift Aircraft	567

The placement of navy and marine units under AFLANT meant coordinating and directing with units that the Air Force traditionally was not accustomed to working with for prolonged operations. By 18 October, the navy and marine air elements were poised as the following:

Table 6-2: Status of Naval and Marine Air Units Designated for OP Plan 312[42]

Aircraft	Location	Type	Aircraft Available in 6 hours	Aircraft Available in 12 hours	Aircraft Available in 24 hours
VF-31	Cecil Naval Air Station (NAS)	F3H-2	6	8	9
VF-32	Cecil NAS	F8U-2N	3	4	4
VA-34	Cecil NAS	A4D-2N	4	7	7
VA36	Cecil NAS	A4D-2N	4	7	7
VAH-9	Sanford NAS	A3D-2	4	6	7
VAH-3	Sanford NAS	A3D-1	6	8	10
VF-62	Cecil NAS	F8U-1E	6	8	9
VA-46	Cecil NAS	A4D-2N	4	7	7
VA-106	Cecil NAS	A4D-2	4	7	7
VA-176	Jacksonville NAS	AD-6	7	10	10
VA-44	Jacksonville NAS	AD-6	7	10	10
VA-44	Jacksonville NAS	A4D-2N	6	8	8
VA-44	Jacksonville NAS	A4D-2	8	10	10
VAP-62	Jacksonville NAS	A3D-2P	3	5	6
VF-174	Cecil NAS	F8U-1	4	6	8
VF-174	Cecil NAS	F8U-2	6	8	9
VF-174	Cecil NAS	F8U-2N	6	8	8
VF-174	Cecil NAS	F8U-2N	2	4	4
VFP-62	Cecil NAS	F8U-1P	3	6	6
VMF-333	Roosevelt Roads NAS	F8U-2	12	16	16
VMA-324	Beaufort NAS	A4D-2	0	0	12
VMA-331*	Roosevelt NAS Roads	A4D-2	12	12	12
VF-13	USS *Independence* (2nd Fleet)	F3H-2	10	10	10
VF-84	USS *Independence* (2nd Fleet)	F8U-2	9	9	10
VA-72	USS *Independence* (2nd Fleet)	A4D-2N	10	12	12

VA-64	USS *Independence* (2ⁿᵈ Fleet)	A4D-2N	9	11	11
VA-75	USS *Independence* (2ⁿᵈ Fleet)	AD-6	9	11	11
VAH-11	USS *Independence* (2ⁿᵈ Fleet)	A3D-2	3	6	6

*Four A4Ds stationed at Guantánamo Bay Naval Air Station

VAH: Heavy Attack Squadron
VA: Attack Squadron
VF: Fighting Plane Squadron
VFP: Light Reconnaissance Squadron
VMF: Marine Fighter Squadron
VAP: Heavy Reconnaissance Squadron

The positioning of units at Key West NAS posed the greatest burden logistically. The base was not designed to be the front line airfield for a major military operation. Billeting space was very limited and Key West NAS had exploded overnight. Tents had be erected for the support personnel, but that did not help with a kitchen facility and food storage that was now pressed far beyond its limitations.[43]

AFLANT centered on Langley AFB, Virginia, as their primary command facility. As soon as the crisis was declared, the Air Force created a small Forward component in Florida, AFLANT ADVON, established at Homestead AFB.[44] The commander of AFLANT Advon was Major General Maurice Preston.[45] His role in the event of the execution of OP Plan 312 was direct coordination of a vast air armada – both to bomb Cuba and the Soviets into submission, destroy the missile launch sites, and direct the largest airborne parachuting and air landing mission since the Second World War.

The final change to the Air Force's plans was the inclusion of a psychological warfare program – Operation Bugle Call. On 26 October, President Kennedy approved the program, which would be included as part of the Rock Pile air strikes. In Bugle Call, two F 105 or container-capable aircraft would be flown over Havana and the major cities, starting on the first day of the air campaign. Two strikes were slated to take place, each dropping 1,500,000 leaflets on the cities with a message from President Kennedy and encouragement for citizens to resist the Castro Government and assist and Americans. There were concerns over potential losses of these aircraft, but the JCS determined they would be operating at the same amount of risk that low-level reconnaissance missions were destined to be exposed to.[46]

CHAPTER SEVEN

Policy and Mobilization

If we can't lick the Cubans with what we already have, we are in terrible shape.[1]

Chairman of the Joint Chiefs of Staff, General Maxwell Taylor

Policy

The period between 18 and 22 October 1962 was a period dominated by with the formulation of a strategy for dealing with the missiles in Cuba. More over-flights by U2 surveillance aircraft were ordered, each pass providing decision makers with a greater sense of the scale and pace of work on the island. Each passing day narrowed the window of undertaking actions before the missiles became operational.

U2 photography revealed for the first time that there were Soviet Luna (NATO: FROG – Free Rocket Over Ground) missile launchers. These mobile launch systems were almost glossed over initially, but they represented a new threat to invasion. Decision makers focused almost entirely on the strategic nuclear missiles, not realizing the threat that the tactical missiles might represent. Throughout Europe, these tactical battlefield missile systems had the capability of being armed with tactical nuclear warheads. Employed against an invasion beach or a captured airfield covered with American personnel could upset the balance of any coming conflict.

The courses of action being considered were:

- A surgical surprise air strike to attempt to take out the missiles and their launch facilities
- An extended air campaign to neutralize all strategic military threats, such as the IL-28 bombers being assembled in Cuba
- Following up the air campaign with an invasion to ensure that the threat has been neutralized
- A blockade of Cuba to prevent additional missiles, troops, or equipment being delivered from the USSR to Cuba

All of the President's advisers agreed with one aspect of the response; a decision about policy had to be made prior to making the US knowledge of the missile sites public. That way, the President could outline not only the threat to the United States, but how the country would be responding to it.

On 18 October, President Kennedy met with Soviet Foreign Minister Andrei Gromyko at the White House. Kennedy could have directly confronted the minister with the evidence that the Americans had already accumulated, but instead, he asked for clarification around the military assistance being sent to Cuba. Gromyko assured Kennedy that the assistance the USSR was rendering was defensive in nature. The President reiterated his stand from a policy speech on 4 September warning against the deployment of offensive weapons in Cuba.

Time was working against the administration. Two of the missile sites were believed to be operational – indicating they could launch within 18 hours. The construction of the launch facilities indicated that in a week, all of the medium-range missiles could become operational, and once they were, the risk of using military force against them might risk the Soviets being placed in a 'use or lose' situation with their missiles. The advisers agreed that once the missiles were all operational, the risks increased if military action was used against the island nation.

Regardless of the course of action taken, the use of America's military might was required to implement any one of the solutions. While the various members of Excomm struggled through the options, President Kennedy felt that meeting with the Joint Chiefs of Staff directly might help him in the decision-making process.

This was not going to be an easy meeting. There were distinct tensions between the President and the Joint Chiefs in the post-Bay of Pigs environment, where both sides blamed each other for the debacle.

Meeting with the Joint Chiefs of Staff

The meeting between President Kennedy and the Joint Chiefs was climatic in many respects.

At this stage of the crisis, the Joint Chiefs of Staff are often portrayed in slanted historical accounts as wanting to rush into war or a full-scale invasion. That representation is not entirely fair. As Robert Kennedy noted:

> The members of the Joint Chiefs of Staff were unanimous in calling for immediate military action. They forcefully presented their view that the blockade would not be effective. General Curtis LeMay, Air Force Chief of Staff, argued strongly with the President that that a military attack was essential. When the President questioned what the response of the Russians might be, General LeMay assured him that there would be no reaction. President Kennedy was skeptical: 'They, no more than we, can let these things go by without doing something. They can't, after all their statements, permit us to take out their missiles, kill a lot of Russians, and

they do nothing. If they don't take action in Cuba, they certainly will in Berlin.

The President went on to say that he recognized the validity of their arguments made by the Joint Chiefs, the danger that more and more missiles would be placed in Cuba, and the likelihood if we did nothing was that the Russians would move on Berlin and in other areas of the world, feeling the US was completely impotent. Then it would be too late to do anything in Cuba, for that time all their missiles would be operational.[2]

The Joint Chiefs did not see a blockade as resolving the issues with missiles in Cuba. A blockade did not remove the threat; it simply contained it. From a diplomatic stance, a blockade gave politicians time, but from the Chiefs' perspective, that time was only to allow the Soviets to get the missile launch sites completed and ensure that the island could not be invaded. Also, a blockade was considered by international law as an act of war. Even the politicians struggled with the use of the word 'blockade.' After Stalin's blockade of Berlin in 1948, there were worries that America would lose its

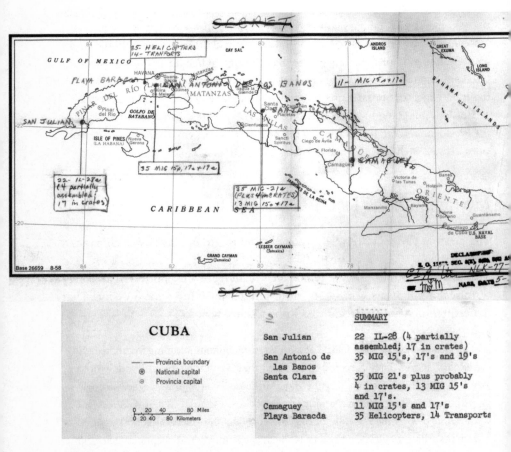

President Kennedy's map used for tracking the missile crisis. (*Courtesy of the US National Archives, John F. Kennedy Library*)

moral high ground and be seen as a bully, just what they had painted the Soviets as. General Taylor pointed out two risks from his perspective:

With regard to the blockade plan, Mr. President, I say we're studying it now to see all of the implications. One is the difficulty in maintaining surveillance. We just don't see how they can do that without taking losses and getting into some form of air warfare over the island. Second, there is the problem of Guantánamo, which is a curious obstacle to us to some degree.[3]

Admiral George Anderson, the chief of naval operations, expanded on the threat to Guantánamo Bay:

Well, our position in Guantánamo becomes increasingly vulnerable, because certainly the imposition of a blockade is going to infuriate the Cubans and they have got a mass of militia and they can come on around Guantánamo. And I don't know whether they would actually attack Guantánamo or not. Be we would certainly have to provide increased forces around there to defend Guantánamo, which we're in the process of reinforcing now. Also, they have these short-range cruise missiles. They have three groups of those primarily for coast defense. Their MIGs, their aircraft, all pose a threat to Guantánamo. So the threat is greatly increased and intensified during the course of a blockade.[4]

In the same meeting, the commandant of the Marine Corps General David Shoup chimed in: 'They have a considerable number of gun emplacements within range of Guantánamo. So unless something is done to also at the same point neutralize this ability to take on Guantánamo, well Guantánamo is in one hell of a fix.'[5] He further added:

It (the artillery) eliminates the airfield there, in a sense so we can't operate. They can bombard; then we can fit it, and we can operate. But it certainly terrifically reduces the potential value of the airfields there, the potential value of the shipping area, and what you have is just a hunk of dirty that you're hanging on to for pride, prestige, political reasons, or what have you.[6]

General Taylor summed it up succinctly: 'I think Guantánamo is going to cease to be a useful naval base and become more of a fortress, more or less in a permanent state of siege.'[7]

Kennedy pressed on the option for air strikes and General LeMay said that he could be ready to go, optimally on 23 October.

General of the Army Chief of Staff Earle Wheeler expressed his perspective:

Mr. President, in my judgment, from a military point of view, the lowest-risk course of action if we're thinking of protecting the people of the United States against a possible strike on us is to go ahead with a surprise air strike, the blockade, and an invasion, because these series of actions progressively will give us increasing assurance that we really have got the offensive capacity of the Cuban-Soviets cornered. Now admittedly, we can never be absolutely sure until and unless we actually occupy the island.[8]

In terms of the plans to invade, the Joint Chiefs of Staff said that seven to eleven days after the start of the bombing campaign, the plans called for the landing of troops. General Taylor pointed out that they still had the flexibility to not invade if political developments or the situation changed in some way.

The blockade option, as Admiral Anderson outlined, would be easier to implement if it was a partial blockade of Cuba, rather than a complete blockade. The concern that the Chiefs had at the time was that they were unsure of the nuclear warheads had been delivered to the island. There were structures being constructed that had the hallmarks of nuclear warhead storage bunkers. That seemed to imply that either the warheads were not on the island, or more chillingly, were stored somewhere where the United States could not see them.[9]

The President summed up the briefing:

I appreciate your views. As I said, I'm sure we all understand how rather unsatisfactory our alternatives are. The argument for the blockade was what we want to do is to avoid, if we can, nuclear war by escalation or imbalance. The Soviets increase, we use [force], they blockade Berlin. They blockade for military purposes. Then we take an initial action so that ... we've got to have some degree of control. Those people [the Soviets] last night were so away from reality that there's no telling what their response might be.[10]

General Curtis LeMay, chief of the Air Force, summed up everyone's feelings: 'You are in a pretty bad fix, Mr. President.' The President answered quickly: 'You are in it with me. Personally.' Everyone laughed, and with no final decision, the meeting adjourned.[11]

What the Joint Chiefs were unaware of was that the Secretary of Defense was severely undermining their position:

Later, Secretary McNamara, although he told the President he disagreed with the Joint Chiefs and favored a blockade rather than an attack, informed him that the necessary planes, men, and ammunition were being deployed, and that we could be ready to move with the necessary air bombardments on Tuesday 23 October, if that was to be the decision. The plans called for initial attack, consisting of 500 sorties, striking all military targets, including the missile sites, airfields, ports, and gun emplacements.[12]

Once the President, Secretary of Defense McNamara, and General Taylor left the room, the hidden audio recording system captured the discussion between some of the Chiefs, underlying the tension between the Pentagon and the Administration. General Shoup unleashed first: 'You, you pulled the rug right out from under him.' Lemay replied, 'Jesus Christ. What in the hell do you mean?'

Shoup responded:

> I agree with that answer, General. I just agree with you. I agree with you 100 percent. I just agree with you 100 percent. That's the only goddamn ... He [Kennedy] finally got the word 'escalation'. That's the only goddamn thing that's in the whole trick. It's been there in Laos; it's been there in every goddamn one [of these crises]. When he says *escalation*, that's it.
>
> If somebody could keep them from doing the goddamn thing piecemeal. That's our problem. You go in there and friggin' around with the missiles. You're screwed. You go in and frig around with anything else, you're screwed.

Lemay agreed, and Shoup continued: 'You're screwed, screwed, screwed. And if some goddamn thing, some way, he could say, "Either do this son of bitch and do it right and quit friggin' around." That was my conclusion. Don't frig around and go take a missile out.' A moment later he added, 'Goddamn it, if he wants to do it, you can't fiddle around with taking out missiles. You can't fiddle around with hitting the missile sites and then hitting the SAM sites. You got to go in and take out the goddamn thing that's going to stop you from doing your job.'[13]

Excomm, while leaning towards a blockade scenario, was still divided. The air strike/invasion options seemed to be the only way to remove the missile threat. The committee split into two groups; one focused on putting together plans for the blockade, the other dealing with the air strike options.

Blockade or Air Strike?

Excomm worked through its options while the President weighed both choices. On 20 October, a meeting was held of the National Security Council to explore both options. Secretary of Defense McNamara outlined the pros and cons of a naval blockade. These were as follows:

Advantages

- It would cause the least troubles with America's allies
- It avoids the connotation of a surprise air attack on Cuba – something seen as contrary to US tradition
- It is the only military action compatible with the United States position as leader in the free world
- It is the least provocative move, reducing the odds of a sudden military response that might escalate to a general war with the USSR

Disadvantages
- It would take a long time to achieve the goal of eliminating the missiles from Cuba
- It would result in series political trouble in the United States
- The world position might be that the US was weak in its response to such a threat[14]

The blockade proposed was strictly naval at this point. Implementing a full air blockade of Cuba required a larger number of naval air assets and planning.

McGeorge Bundy presented the case for air strikes. Given the lack of intelligence, the air strike option could only guarantee hitting two-thirds of the missiles themselves. There was no way to know how many missiles were concealed or otherwise hidden. The Soviet IL-28 bombers were being assembled, but were unprotected on the runway tarmac. These could be destroyed relatively easily. The fact, that they were not hidden seemed to indicate that the Cubans were at the time not worried about a US military strike.

The Secretary of Defense noted that the Joint Chiefs recommended approximately 800 sorties. Such a massive air attack would result in several thousands of Soviets killed. In his view, the probability was high and an air strike would lead inevitably to an invasion. The Soviets would feel obligated to respond somewhere in the world – which could lead to a general war. Robert Kennedy, the Attorney General, pointed out that if at any point a blockade was not proving to have the desired effect, an air strike could be called up.

Weighing all of the options, the decision was to implement a naval blockade. President Kennedy told General Taylor, 'I know you and your colleagues are unhappy with the decision, but I trust that you will support me in the decision.' Taylor responded they would. When he returned to the Pentagon, he told the Joint Chiefs, 'This was not one of our better days.' General Wheeler responded, 'I'd never thought I'd live to see the day when I would want to go to war.'[15]

The US Naval Response

The decision to implement a blockade of offensive weapons going into Cuba was to be timed with the President making an announcement to the public about the missiles in Cuba. The US Navy had implemented a number of steps even before the crisis emerged to plan for a naval blockade of Cuba. On 6 October, the Commander in Chief of the Atlantic Fleet (CINCLANTFLT) issued operation order 45-62, which designated the quarantine force commander as the 2nd Fleet commander, and directed the commander of Anti-Submarine Forces in the Atlantic to conduct air surveillance as requested. This was to be done in the event of a blockade. By 23 October, this had become a reality.

The naval response to the crisis was threefold. First was strategic in nature

– that is, the deployment of the Navy's missile launch-capable submarines. These strategic weapons would need to be deployed in the event that the Soviets sought to escalate the situation. The second response was in the form of the blockade force. The third was a task force that would need to be assembled south of Cuba to provide support to the invasion forces and Guantánamo Bay. The plan for the blockade of Cuba called for the formation of a task force, designated as Task Force 136, which would be responsible for manning the stations along a line to prevent the Soviet supply ships with military goods from reaching the island. This task force was broken into three task groups. These were composed as follows:

Task Force 136 Command Component: commander of the 2nd Fleet

Task Force 136.1 Command Cruiser-Destroyer Flotilla Six: two cruisers, two guided missile frigates, three guided missile destroyer, nine destroyers, two destroyers – radar picket, and one destroyer – self defense

Task Force 136.2 Command Carrier Division: one seaplane carrier and four destroyers

Task Force 136.3 Support Forces: commanded by USS *Elokomin* with two fleet oilers, one ammunition ship, and two destroyers[16]

The blockade response called for an arc of naval vessels in the Atlantic, 500 miles from Cape Maysi Cuba, from latitude 27-30N, longitude 70W to latitude 20N, longitude 65W. The reason for positioning the blockade force so far from Cuba was due to initial concerns that the Cuban Air Force, specifically the IL-28 bombers, might be able to reach the blockade force and attempt to engage it. This arc was dubbed 'The Walnut Line'. There were to be twelve stations along the arc, with 47 miles between each station. The Walnut Line was to be manned by Task Force 136.1 and 136.2, with 136.3 moving where needed to support the forces on station.[17]

The air support for the tentative air strikes and invasion of Cuba was a naval task force designated as 135. The core of this was to be centered around two aircraft carriers, the USS *Independence* and the USS *Enterprise*. The *Independence* set sail on 11 October accompanied by the USS *English*, USS *Hank*, USS *O'Hare*, and USS *Corry*. These vessels embarked to the Caribbean as part of normal operations – and to provide the US with a ready-reaction force should they be needed. This was done before the presence of the missiles in Cuba had been detected and was part of the general US build-up in the region given the rising tensions with Cuba.

The USS *Enterprise* had been assigned to European waters, and returned on 11 October to Norfolk. She got underway again on 19 October, allegedly to head south to avoid the approach of Hurricane Ella. The press was already noticing an increased amount of activity in Norfolk and was beginning to speculate that some sort of operation was going to be undertaken – so the hurricane provided a good cover to send the ship to join the *Independence*. CINCLANT issued OPORDER 43-62, which designed Task Force 135 officially to support OP Plan 312's air strikes and provide the necessary reinforcement and support of Guantánamo. The *Enterprise* was not destined to make the trip alone; the next day, the USS *Rush* and USS *Hawkins* departed Mayport, followed two days later by the USS *Fiske*, assigned to accompany the *Enterprise* on her cruise to join the *Independence*.[18]

On 21 October, the Task Force 135 made its way north of Cuba, staying within 150 miles of the island so as to be ready to strike on short notice. An additional set of orders were sent to the task force to order them to oversee the evacuation of the dependants and non-essential personnel from the Guantánamo Bay Naval Base. The Carrier USS *Essex* had just completed a 6-month overhaul and was already stationed off of Guantánamo Bay, but was not formally attached to Task Force 135.

The composition of Task Force 135 was as follows:

- USS *Independence* with CVG 7
- USS *Enterprise* with CVG 6
- Two destroyer squadrons
- One fleet oiler
- One ammunition ship
- One Marine air group (Two VMA, 1 VMF) at Roosevelt Roads[19]

Leading up to the President's announcement, the preoccupation of the Second Fleet commander Vice Admiral Alfred G. Ward was around the targeting list for OP Plan 312 and the establishment of Combat Air Patrols (CAPs) to protect Guantánamo, Roosevelt Roads, and other American naval air bases in the region. There were some points of confusion. At one point, the KOMAR missile boats were added to the strike list, but a contrary order came that did not include the KOMARs. This matter was clarified, but it took the better part of a day to do it, an example of the lag in communications and coordination that was common during this build-up phase.[20] In the event of orders to execute an air strike against Cuba, the first aircraft would be on target within 3 hours of the execution signal.[21]

The plan drawn up for the air defense of Guantánamo from Task Force 135 consisted of four Combat Air Patrols and eight Combat Air Strike (CAS) to support ground attacks during the daytime hours. Night time CAP coverage would be provided 'as the situation may require.'[22]

The Reinforcement of Guantánamo Bay

One of the many concerns facing the CINCLANT was the risk to Guantánamo Bay once the word of the missile crisis was made public. There was no way to know for sure how the Cubans would react, but the base had been a point of contention politically with them since Castro had come to power. The creation of the 'cactus curtain,' and the increased presence of Cuban forces in the hills surrounding the base might simply be the start of hostile actions. Matters would be even worse if the air strikes commenced, since Guantánamo represented the one location where American territory could be struck by the Cubans and Soviets on the island.

Some preparatory work was ordered to reinforce the base. The base lacked modern radar, and since the risk of air attack from Cuba was possible, a new air-search radar system was hurriedly installed by 22 October to at least give the base some notice before enemy aircraft attacked.[23]

Guantánamo Bay's commander was asked to provide a list of targets around the base facilities to be included in OP Plan 312. This was completed on 18 October, although intelligence beyond the 'cactus curtain' was sketchy at best.

As early as 12 October, days before the missiles were spotted, plans were in place that called for Guantánamo to be reinforced by a regimental headquarters and two marine battalion landing teams (BLTs) on the ground. For air support, plans called for a VMA squadron to be placed at Roosevelt Roads for air support and a VMF squadron to be kept on alert status at the same airfield. A destroyer division would be poised off-shore to provide close order bombardment support from the sea. Fresh water and electricity, always a risk at the base, would be provided by naval ships or through alternative plans if the Cubans cut them off.[24]

On 18 October, Joint Chiefs had ordered a reinforced infantry BLT to be moved by military air transit service (MATS) from the 5th MEB on the West Coast of the US to Guantánamo. Unfortunately, this was a move that had not been foreseen in any of the OP Plan 316-62 guidelines, so it was unanticipated and several key assets were out of place. The 2nd Battalion of the 1st Marines (BLT 2/1) under Lieutenant Colonel William Geftman was selected for the duty. They completed their transit by 22 October, with 1,797 men and 130,222 lb of equipment/cargo.[25]

The formal augmentation of the ground forces did not commence until 20 October. The orders issued then, OPORD 43-62, formally assigned Task Force 135 with the responsibility of providing combat air support to the base – much closer and faster than Roosevelt Roads in Puerto Rico. It also directed the amphibious force with BLT 2/2 to proceed to Guantánamo Bay at the best possible speed.

The next day, the changes actually started to unfold at the base. First was a change of command. Brigadier General William R. Collins of the Marine Corps was given overall command of the ground forces at the base, relieving Colonel George Killen. General Collins arrived on 20 October with a skeleton staff. Shortly after his arrival, Defense Condition Three (DEFCON 3) was set at the base – at the time, the only US forces brought to this state of readiness. The American DEFCON system was a five point scale. DEFCON 5 was peacetime operations, whereas DEFCON 1 was war. Guantánamo was moving to a war footing three days before the world knew of the presence of missiles in Cuba.

In response to this change in alert status, three marine rifle companies were placed on the perimeter of the base on the main-line of resistance – a series of trenches, bunkers, and sandbagged posts. Colonel Geftman's marines initially were put on the line on the leeward main line of resistance, but F, G, and H companies were ferried across the bay to the sea plan landing at Fisherman's Point, then up to the windward perimeter where they relieved a mobile construction company that had been armed and put on duty. General Collins put an observation aircraft in the form of a helicopter to monitor the perimeter as well. The USS *Essex* departed, moving to the west of the base at sea to provide air cover from that sector.

The Marine Corps in 1962 always retained one battalion in an advanced state of alert for emergency deployment situations. In the event of an urgent need, it could be airlifted to the crisis in a matter of hours. In this case, the 1st Battalion of the 8th Marines (BLT 1/8) under the command of Colonel James E. Wilson in Camp Lejeune were designated as the 'ready battalion'. On Saturday 20 October, they were moved to Cherry Point, and told that their deployment was not a drill, but a reinforcement for Guantánamo Bay. B Company was the first to arrive in Cuba and was placed under operational control of BLT 2/1 until the rest of the unit arrived. Within two days, BLT 1/8 assumed position on the windward main line of resistance.[26]

The final reinforcement came in the form of BLT 2/2. This unit had been loaded onto ships several days before as part of the Three Pairs exercise. The marines believed they were on their way to Vieques Island to topple the mythical dictator Ortsac. Instead, they were diverted to Guantánamo Bay, arriving the morning of 22 October. Their Commanding Officer, Colonel David Brewster Sr gave the order at 0915 hours to 'land the landing force', and they debarked on the leeward side of the bay, relieving some of the companies of BLT 1/8.[27]

With the landing of BLT 1/8, the next phase of preparing Guantánamo Bay began; the evacuation of the dependant families and non-military personnel. It is rare for the US to have to evacuate civilians from its bases, and while procedures were in place for years at the base, this would be their first ever real-world test. An hour after the landings, the announcement was made and families were given their packing orders. Each person was allowed once suitcase and needed to bring their pre-assigned evacuation cards and immunization cards with them, along with an emergency payment authorization. Pets were to be tied in their yards with promises that the military would see to them being fed. The keys to the house were to be place on the dining room tables and their homes were to remain unlocked. Buses were sent to the neighborhoods to bring the families to the ships at the dock – The USNS *Upshur*, the USS *Duxbury Bay*, the USS *Hyades*, and the USS *Desoto Country*. Hospital patients were to be flown out from the leeward airfield, with priority given to pregnant women who were hospitalised.[28]

On the morning of 22 October, to coincide with the day of President Kennedy's public announcement about the missiles and to provide air protection for the evacuating dependants, a dawn air demonstration was ordered for 1.5 hours. This was done to demonstrate to the Cubans surrounding the base that the US possessed overwhelming air assets and to ensure to the protection of the embarking civilians.[29]

The queue of buses at the docks determined what ship families were loaded on. The ships themselves were far from comfortable. While designed to transport troops, they were not designed for families with small children. Cramped, hot, and with limited amenities, the servicemen's families were remarkably calm and cooperative. The Navy made their best effort, setting up films on three of the ships and distributing books and games. Attempts were made to get all mothers with two or more children under the age of six, older women (over sixty years), and pregnant women with children into the limited number of cabins on each ship. The problem was that there was more demand than supply. By 5.00 p.m. local time, the ships pulled away from the wharfs, moving into convoy towards Little Creek, Virginia.

The weather in Virginia in October was markedly colder than the tropical warmth of Cuba, and as such, the families lacked the proper clothing. By the time the dependants and civilians arrived, the whole world would know the reason why they had to be evacuated. The citizens of the Norfolk and Tidewater area of Virginia were told of the arrival of the dependants and a massive outpouring of support in the form of donated clothing, food, and offers to put the families up in homes; the sense of military community was strong. The family members were allowed to write to their husbands and fathers, and over 2,000 such letters were drawn. No one knew how long they would be separated.[30]

With the families removed from harms' way, Guantánamo Bay transformed from idyllic tropical naval base and air station to a base preparing to be laid siege to. General Collins quickly ascertained the risk of an air attack on his airfields, an attack that could have quickly crippled the few aircraft there. While protection for the aircraft was being constructed immediately, he asked that a battery of surface-to-air missiles be placed in the base. CINCLANT concurred and ordered the 3rd Light Anti-Aircraft Missile Battalion (LAAM) at Twenty-Nine Palms be redeployed to Guantánamo. This unit was armed with HAWK missiles (Homing, All-The-Way Killer), a highly-mobile (trailer-mounted) missile battery, and supporting radar.[31] The 3rd LAAM was moved in its entirety from Twenty-Nine Palms to Cherry Hill, North Carolina. After studying the maps of Guantánamo Bay, it was decided that sending the entire unit to Cuba would be counterproductive given the small size of the base and the fact that once they were fired, the missiles had a greater range than the entire base (15 miles). Only Charlie Battery, along with forty-eight missiles, were sent via airlift to the base. Within a matter of hours, the battery was installed on John Paul Jones Hill by 26 October.

The Americans had only a limited amount of artillery at Guantánamo Bay. The leeward side of the base had the 105-mm howitzers of I Battery of the 3/10 and the 4.2-mm mortars of D Battery of the 1/11. The windward portion of the base was protected by K Battery of the 4/10 with six 155-mm howitzers and a platoon of 155-mm self-propelled guns. A fire control centre was established in an evacuated ammunition bunker in the Cuzco Valley. Artillery forces on both sides of the base began the task of registration of artillery fires in the event of attack.[32]

There were two Mobile Construction Battalions (4th and 7th) at Guantánamo Bay under normal conditions. General Collins had them move from a peacetime footing to turning the base into a small fortress. New access roads (20-miles worth) were cut, and the main line of resistance received new bunkers and trench systems. Communications lines were run to the headquarters bunker to provide quick battlefield information in the event of an attack.[33]

Marine Air Group 32, under Colonel T. L. Bronleewee Jr, moved its headquarters to Guantánamo on 23 October. MAG 32 was assigned detachments of VMF 333 and VMA 331. The presence of this headquarters unit allowed for direct air support control for the base. Its HQ was in a bomb shelter at McCalla Field.[34] Dawn patrols for 1 hour were ordered every day, utilizing six aircraft. This was to be prepared for any early morning attack by the Cubans.[35] In terms of heavy equipment, even with the reinforcement of the base, General Collins was still woefully short. Table 7-1 shows the full reinforced strength in terms of artillery that the base possessed:

Table 7-1: Guantánamo Bay Special Forces Equipment[36]

155-mm howitzers	6
105-mm howitzers	4
106-mm recoilless rifles	8
3.5" rocket launchers	11
81-mm mortars	16
50-cal. machine guns	12
30-cal. machine guns	14
7.62 machine guns	4
135-mm self-propelled gun	2
M48 tank (90-mm)	5
M67 tank (flame)	2
HRS 3	2
HAWK missile battery	1

The base facilities were pushed to their limits with the influx and activity of the rapid build-up. Marines were armed at all times, requiring new rules for using the PX, including a 'lay your pistol down,' rule to avoid accidental shootings.[37] Three destroyers were moved off the coast to provide naval gunfire support – always seen as a key for defending the base.[38] Guantánamo Bay girded itself for battle. On 23 October, two surgical teams were sent to the base from New York and Bethesda, along with 50 pints of whole blood to deal with the expected casualties.[39] Even if it wasn't the launching point for the invasion of Cuba, it was destined to become a target if/when the shooting started.

'Unmistakable Evidence'

A pivotal moment in the crisis was the United States' announcement of the presence of the missiles in Cuba and the response. Not only would this take the crisis public on the world stage and open the diplomatic and political discussions, it also would trigger a series of events militarily. The President's address was tagged as Announcement Day (A-Day).

On 21 October, the day before the announcement, a checklist of items were executed in preparation. These included plans to:

- Evacuate the dependants from Guantánamo and execute orders to reinforce the base
- Alert the 3rd Army to prepare to execute joint defense plans for the southeast United States and the Florida Keys.
- CINCLANT prepared to protect all US shipping in the Florida Straits, windward passage, and Yucatan Channel.
- Alert Strategic Air Command (SAC), the National Security Agency (NSA), the Federal Bureau of Investigation (FBI)
- Activate the Joint Battle Staff
- Inform the Secretary of Defense that the Three Pairs exercise was canceled
- Inform the Federal Aviation Administration (FAA) of the formation of a military emergency zone that would be established at A-hour
- Continue surveillance flights over Cuba
- Confirm the rules of engagement for the blockade
- Strategic Air Command (SAC) would place 1/8 of its forces on airborne alert[40]

The day of the announcement triggered a handful of events including:

- Authorizing the phased dispersal of nuclear weapons armed interceptor aircraft at A-hour - 12
- Informing all commanders in chief of the Cuban situation and the responses that would be taken.
- Alerting SAC to have its alert aircraft to depart from Homestead AFB prior to the A-hour
- Authorizing the US Army to move the Automatic Weapons Instructional Unit form Fort Bliss to Florida bases, where it would act as a nucleus of units to enhance air defense posture in the US. This move was not to take place until A-hour[41]

At 0700 hours Eastern time, President Kennedy addressed the nation and the world as to the situation in Cuba, and the US responded to it. 'Within the past week, unmistakable evidence has established the fact that a series of offensive missile sites is now in preparation on that imprisoned island. The purpose of these bases can be none other than to provide a nuclear strike capability against the western hemisphere.'[42]

He outlined the United States' next steps as:

- To halt the build-up of these weapons, a quarantine of Cuba of all offensive military equipment would be implemented
- Surveillance would be increased on Cuba
- The Armed Forces of the United States were being tasked to prepare for all eventualities
- Any nuclear missile fired from Cuba at the western hemisphere would be considered an attack by the Soviet Union on the United States and would be responded to with 'a full retaliatory response upon the Soviet Union'[43]
- The base at Guantánamo Bay had been reinforced and the dependants had been evacuated. The base was now placed under full military alert
- The President called on the Organization of American States to consider this a threat to hemispheric security and evoke articles six and eight of their charter
- The United States would be calling for an emergency session of the United Nations Security Council to address the Soviet threat
- The President called on Chairman Khrushchev to halt the construction and end this threat

The use of the word 'quarantine' was designed to soften what was in fact a partial naval blockade. Only military goods were to be blocked going to Cuba. While plans were drawn up to implement an air blockade, it was felt that the Soviets lacked the heavy-lift capability to move additional missiles or offensive hardware in place. Calling the blockade a quarantine also removed the risk of the United States being painted in the same light as the Soviets had been when they had blockaded Berlin in 1948. Quarantine sounded far less antagonistic.[44]

A series of military and political events were set off the moment that the President made his announcement. These were:

1. DEFCON 3 established for US forces world-wide.
2. Transfer operational control of all units involved to CINCLANT
3. Direct MINIMIZE plans world-wide
4. Direct implementation of Military Emergency Zone (MEZ) and Security Control of Air Traffic (SCAT) in southern Florida
5. SecDef authorizes SecNav to augment MSTS shipping to include requisition of necessary shipping required to support CINCLANT
6. Notify UK decision and start action to utilize Mayaguana Island Air Base.
7. Authorize military departments to mobilize 150,000 men, including Air Force Reserve C-119 Squadrons (to be employed in air drop) and Air National Guard units.

Army: 94,000
Navy: 40 ships, 18 squadrons
Air Force: 17,500

8. Consider other force generations world-wide
9. Direct CINCLANT implement naval blockade, as authorized by the President.
10. Direct move Marine Air Group from Cherry Point to Key West
11. Activate Opa Locka Airfield, Florida
12. Confirm to CINCLANT that if GTMO is attacked base will be defended by commander under his inherent right to defend his command
13. Direct Services provide administrative/logistic support of CINCLANT OP Plans
14. Direct Department of the Army to establish ground defense in south-east United States
15. Direct loading and movement of 5th MEB from West Coast (less one BLT already en route)
16. Request FBI apprehend all known subversives, Castro variety
17. Direct CINLANT to be prepared to execute OP Plan 312 against MRBM complex Cuba, if directed, on 23 October[45]

With the President's speech, actions were put in motion to move the US to the brink of war.

The Armored Spear-Point

The 1st Armored Division consisted of 15,605 officers and men. In October 1962, it was comprised of three brigade headquarters commanding ten combat battalions, four tanks, and six mechanized infantry. The division artillery was three 105-mm self-propelled battalions, a composite 155-mm and 8-inch self-propelled battalion, and an honest John battalion. It included an armored cavalry squadron, an aviation battalion, an armored engineer battalion with floating and fixed bridging capability, a signal battalion, and a military police company.[46] As the core of Task Force Charlie and a key unit for OP Plan 316-62, moving Old Ironsides' was of paramount priority.

The day following the President's speech, the chief of transportation of the US Army requested immediate positing of the required railroad cars necessary to move the division to Fort Stewart – home of the US Armor and Artillery Firing Center.[47] General Haines of the 1st Armored Division's father had commanded a regiment of troops at the fort during the Second World War. While the number of heavy-duty flatcars was difficult to obtain, it was not impossible. The larger challenge was in the day-coaches. The mobilization plan for the 1st Armored Division had the troops travelling with their tanks and gear to maintain unit cohesion and integrity. The number of coaches was impossible to obtain, meaning that men and vehicles were going to be arriving in a hodge-podge of order.[48]

The rapid nature of the deployment put immediate strains on the peacetime military bases. Fort Stewart was suddenly overloaded with the influx of troops – requiring an additional 1,866 tents simply to handle the transient troops.[49] Mess facilities were not stocked to handle the thousands of men coming in, nor were motor pools designed to store and dispense the large amounts of fuel needed.

Plans for the 1st Armored Division called for it to be both in the floating reserve and the on-call echelons. Initially, the floating reserve was on a 12-hour alert status for the loading of tracked vehicles, although this was later extended to 72-hour notice. Either way, the mobilization plans called for unloading of all vehicles at Fort Stewart and retaining the rail flat cars. This almost immediately caused a logistical problem. The rail sidings available measured 6.5 miles in length, which was only enough to hold 138 flatcars. The initial movement of the division used 660 cars, with the final total eventually reaching 1,945 by the end of the crisis.[50] The Army procured permission at nearby cities and requested to use Hunter AFB's sidings, only to be turned down by the Air Force. Hunter AFB was part of Strategic Air Command and was not under the command and control of the CINCLANT and they did not feel obligated to provide the siding access. The issue had to be bumped up to the Chief of Staff of the Air Force, who allowed the use of the sidings as long as it did not impede the mission of SAC at the base.[51]

Getting the division to Cuba was even more frustrating for planners. The division was to load at the Port of Savannah for the trip to Cuba aboard four US Navy LSTs (Landing Ship Tanks). On 21 October, the immediate issue was that there were no loading ramps for tanks in Savannah. An advance party there came to the conclusion that ramps were going to have to be built. While construction began immediately, they would not be completed until 31 October.[52] Any military operation on the island prior to that date would not include the 1st Armored Division.

Another problem facing planners was the weight limitations of the LSTs. In the planning for OP Plan 316-62, the Army assumed that the Navy would be using its most modern LSTs for the landings at either Mariel or in the Port of Havana. Contemporary LSTs could carry 1,000 tons. The ships to be used in the actual landing were Second World War vintage and could only carry 500 dead weight tons. Historical analysis showed they could carry 600 tons, but this would cause them to ground further out from the beach. A maximum load of 800 tons could be done, but the ship would have to halt long before reaching the beaches. The loads required to land the first (lead) elements of Task Force Charlie were 3,900 tons, meaning that the landing force would need another LST in order to make a successful landing of the full combat force possible.[53]

General Howze's staff proposed that if the ships were loaded to their maximum, they would still be able to make the assault; all that was needed was the means of getting the tanks from the ships to the shore. The solution that was proposed was a four-section causeway pier. The problem with this proposal was that assembling the pier took time, during which, the LSTs would be sitting off-shore and potentially subject to artillery attack. Also, in tests, the unloading process on the causeway pier proved to be time consuming and could be complicated by weather conditions as well. In rough surf, the assembly of the pier could take hours, or be outright impossible.

Since the Navy lacked another LST in the Caribbean or Atlantic, the decision was essentially made for the planners – they would have to include the causeway pier in their shipping. The 1st Armored Division was, on paper, ready to go with her four LSTs, albeit heavily laden with combat equipment.[54]

The support equipment was an entirely different matter. The 1st Armored Division was a modern armored division, so it included a wide range of equipment and mechanized infantry that would also have to be landed in Cuba as part of the assault. While the initial four LSTs could land the heavy tanks of the 1st Armored Division, there were still other elements that needed to be put ashore. Six M48A1 tanks of the 2nd Battalion, the 69th Armor, and the 1st Cavalry Squadron all were planned to be put ashore by D-Day +3. There was not enough time to send the LSTs back to get these units, so all eyes turned to the Navy again.[55]

The CINCLANT did not have any spare LSTs. A call was made to the Atlantic Reserve Fleet, a mothballed flotilla of ships to be tapped in such situations. They had the ships, but the time to get the rusting vessels sea worthy did not meet the timing for an invasion of Cuba. Despite this, orders were cut to begin to get the eleven LSTs of the Atlantic Fleet reactivated in case they would be needed for later operations. For the immediate need, however, this left only one other possible source: commercial ships.

The commander of the Military Sea Transport Service had the authority to charter commercial ships for military use. He stipulated that all US flag vessels would need to have operable bow doors in order to meet the loading and unloading requirements. One ship was found to meet the immediate needs, the *CAL-AGRO*, which was already in Savannah. The installation of a new bow ramp to meet the military needs would take only three days and the ship was a US flag vessel. She was provisioned, but due to a lack of suitable US Navy personnel, she would continue to use a civilian crew under Navy direction.[56]

Three other commercial LST-type vessels were located on the east coast of the US and Florida Keys: the *Inagua Foam*, the *Inagua Crest*, and the *Inagua Shipper*. These were all owned by the West India Steam Company, but were not highly desirable. Two had 40-ton crawler cranes that would have to be removed, and all required some degree of modification in order to be used properly. None would be fully ready until 20 November.[57]

The implications of this logistical issue were staggering. If OP Plan 316-62 were employed prior to the vessels being ready, they would either have to be taken as-is – potentially restricting the amount of men and material that could be taken – or they would not perform as needed, causing issues with landing the forces on the beaches. The other alternative would be a delay in the invasion, or worse yet, a delay in the D-Day +3 reinforcements by an additional four days, while the original Navy LSTs traveled back to Savannah, reloaded the reinforcements, and traveled back to Cuba. The Navy's lack of crews for the vessels would also mean that the at least some civilians would be pressed into service moving the ships to the shore for debarking.

A full decade before the Cuban Missile Crisis, the Army had developed plans for specialized shipping of combat-ready forces that called for ships to have a roll-on, roll-off capability. This meant that ships could rapidly debark their vehicles in a matter of hours as opposed to days. The Navy had two such ships, the USS *Comet* and the USS *Page*. These ships performed adequately when the weather was good, but in rough seas, the ships were unstable at best. Both of these ships were secured for use in OP Plan 316-62, but their problems were only starting to emerge. Weather would play a factor in the landings. General Howze informed CINCLANT that if the weather was bad, that elements of the 2nd Battalion, 69th Armor, would not land at Tarará as originally planned.[58] Instead, it would have to be diverted to Mariel where the port facilities might negate the rough seas. This assumed, of course, that Mariel was secured and open.

When the USS *Comet* arrived on 28 October to pre-load the 2nd Battalion, 69th Armor, issues arose. Decks three and four of the ship had a ceiling that had worked well with Second World War era trucks, but the newer 2.5-ton trucks had a higher clearance and could not fit on those decks. When the USS *Page* arrived, a loading exercise was undertaken, and it was discovered that the placement of the newer Army tanks on the ships made the vessels top heavy. The instability was so great that the master of the vessel announced he would not, on his own responsibility, put to sea until the issue was corrected. The solution proposed was to remove the periscope and guard from the tanks cupola, allowing them to fit on the lower decks, but destroying the boresight on the .50-calibre machine gun on the tank.[59] The heavy gear of a modern armored division was simply too much for the older Navy vessels to accommodate.

The USS *Page* had problems of her own. The *Page* the *Comet* were expected to marry up (dock) at sea to expedite unloading. The *Page's* stern ramp was unable to connect with the *Comet* because the *Comet*, even with a lighter load, was 18 inches too deep. In a dockside test at Savannah, the 'solution' to this was to place four tanks on the after deck of the USS *Page* to compensate. The problem was that this solution only made the top-heavy issue worse. It was determined that if fuel was removed from the USS *Page*, it then would not have enough fuel to make the trip from Savannah to Cuba and would require fuelling at sea.

No suitable resolution was found other than leaving some of the tanks behind to make the ships more stable. Given the late date and the discovery of this issue, General Howze would have been left with no other alternative. 1st Armored Division (Task Force Charlie elements) planned to debark from Savannah, Georgia, New Orleans, Louisiana, and Fort Lauderdale, Florida. The lack of suitable landing ships forces a last-minute change to OP Plan 316-62. The move caused the 69th Armored, originally scheduled to be utilized on D-Day +3, to be moved back three days to D-Day +6.[60] The net result was that the planned armored spear-point of the American invasion force would have been prematurely blunted by the time the forces eventually landed in Cuba.

Deep Water

General Howze was faced with countless logistical headaches related to moving the Army forces ashore. In early planning meetings for the invasion, the US Navy had assured him of a 'dry foot landing' at all target beaches with the exception of Mariel. The beach gradients indicated that in all case but at Mariel, the most that the Army could expect to encounter was 30 inches of water. As such, it was believed by General Howze that deep water fording kits for the vehicles were not going to be needed. These kits modified tanks, trucks, and armored cars so they could come ashore in water deeper than 30 inches. Strictly as a precaution, General Howze requested kits for the 1st Armored Division, and potentially, the 2nd Infantry Division's trucks.[61]

His suspicions proved to be correct. The US Navy corrected its estimates. Since the LSTs being used were being overloaded in capacity, they would be grounding in deeper water. The thought of a dry foot landing evaporated, at least for the 1st Armored Division.

A scramble for waterproofing kits began, and the Army discovered how woefully unprepared it was for such an operation. After just a few days of searching, no kits could be located for the M48A1 tanks or the 105-mm self-propelled howitzers. Seven kits were located for the 155-mm self-propelled howitzer and one for a M41 tank.[62] Checks were made US-wide and many were found at Fort Story, Virginia, and at Fort Hood. Of the 218 needed for tanks, 171 were eventually located. No additional kits were found for the 105-mm self-propelled artillery, and the procurement process would ensure that none would be available before the end of the year. Fort Lee, Virginia, located kits for 123 trucks; not nearly enough to support landings. Installing these kits took time and resources as well.[63]

If OP Plan 316-62 were executed before the end of November 1962, a significant number of vehicles would potentially drop into the warm waters off of Cuba and stall. While they could be recovered by engineers, it would take time and the salt water would inflict its own damage to them vehicles. The frailties of OP Plan 316-62 were emerging in a potentially nasty manner for all branches of the service.

The 2nd Division's Woes

The 2nd Divisions mobilization and prepositioning required it to relocate to port facilities at several Florida ports. It's organic tank battalion, which was slated to complete the brigade task force, would have to be relocated from Fort Benning to Fort Stewart, Georgia.[64] Also moved there were the 4th Army detachments slated for use in OP Plan 316-62.[65] From Fort Stewart, the infantry could debark from a number of different port facilities as needed.

The assumption was that the 2nd Division would land at the Tarará beaches after the Marines had secured the area. They would be reusing the marine's landing craft, but there were always losses in landing craft – damage from grounding, enemy fire, etc. These same landing craft would be used to shuttle supplies to the beaches a well. The replacement landing craft to be used were to be provisioned by the Charleston Army Depot in South Carolina. A check of the depot had thirty-one LCUs (Landing Craft Utility) with only one in operational condition. The maintenance facility in Charleston had the capacity to get three ready in two to three weeks time. The rest would have to be refit and repaired by commercial contractors, a process that was at least five weeks to complete.

The lack of suitable landing craft was beginning to strain the parameters of OP Plan 316-62 to its breaking point. The suggestion from the Commander in Chief of United States Army Forces Atlantic (CINCARLANT) that a BARC vessel might suit the needs. BARC stands for barge, amphibious, resupply, cargo, and these were a combination of trucks and amphibious craft that could carry light cargo ashore then drive on land. These craft performed both jobs marginally, but would provide the necessary landing craft to help get the troops ashore. As such, OP Plan 316-62 was modified to include the 554th Transportation Platoon, and the 14th Transportation Platoon of the 6th Army was put on standby status if it were needed.[66]

Even with these additions, landing craft needs exceeded capacity. As a result of this logistical debacle, replacement landing craft in any number would not exist if the invasion took place prior to December.

The Airborne Divisions

Given the woes of moving the 1st Armored Division, one would think that the US Army would have reacted quickly to getting the 82nd and 101st Airborne Divisions moved forward for deployment. That was simply not the case. The two airborne divisions were known to be a 'first response' asset of the US Army. If Soviet agents, who were destined to be watching these units, noticed that they were suddenly boarding transports with their gear for anything larger than a training drop, it would have tipped the United State's hand and warned everyone that something was afoot.

The other reason for not moving these divisions is that airborne divisions, by their very nature, are highly mobile. They could be assembled and moved on relatively short notice, unlike a heavy armored division. The same applied for the 1st Infantry Division, which was to be flown into Cuba on the captured airfields. Mobilizing all of these assets could be done within 72 hours of the invasion, thus reducing any intelligence lapse.

This did not mean that these forces did not face challenges. OP Plan 316-62 called for the two airborne divisions and the 1st Infantry Division to be prepositioned to McCoy, Tyndall, McDill, and Opa Locka Air Force bases.[67] What no one had considered was that the movement of this many men and equipment would put a strain on these bases, which were already over-capacity due to the prior mobilizations.

It was not just a matter of troops; there were also the large number of transport aircraft. The numbers needed to simultaneously drop both airborne divisions alone would exceed the capacity of the Air Force. The bases, filled with fighters and bombers, would be severely overloaded. The solution was a less than eloquent one. While the Army did not activate any large number of reservists for the crisis initially, the Air Force would be forced to. Only using the Air National Guard's transport aircraft, would they have the capability to move the airborne divisions in both at the same time – timed with the amphibious assault. This would also provide them with the lift capability to bring in the reinforcements that were so vital in the early phases of the invasion. The mobilization of the Air Force reservists was tagged 'Operation Sunshade', and was implemented on 24 October.[68] Sunshade called for the activation of 14,000 Air Force reservists, including twenty-one C-119 troop carrier squadrons, three C-123 troop carrier squadrons, six aerial port squadrons, and the associated support and maintenance personnel.[69]

While the airborne and infantry divisions were put on alert to be prepared to move out, the Air Force reserves began to load up the heavy equipment and supplies and move them to Florida. Pope AFB in North Carolina near the 82nd Airborne Division became filled with the C-119s picking up the heavy weapons and gear of the division and moving them down to the Florida Air Force bases.[70]

The Defense of Florida

On 21 October, the 6th Battalion, 65th Artillery (HAWK) relocated to Key West and was placed under the operational control of the commander, CONAD, Key West.[71] The first unit arrived on 24 October and was poised to provide defense of Key West and the Boca Chica Naval Air Station. The rest of the unit, loaded on twelve tractor trailer trucks had been stopped on 23 October by the Virginia State Police because the trucks exceeded the 2,000-lb overload each. They were directed to leave the state, and so they moved to Pennsylvania and restarted their trip to Florida the next day.[72]

On 24 October, additional moves were made to protect the massing Army and Air Force assets in Florida. The Joint Chiefs authorized the relocation of the 2nd Missile Battalion, 52nd Artillery (minus one battery) from Fort Bliss Texas and the 8th Missile Battalion, 15th Artillery for Fort Lewis, Washington. These units would be sent to Homestead Air Force base, except for two batteries from the 8th Missile Battalion, which were sent to Patrick and MacDill AFBs.[73]

The concerns of Cuba launching some sort of counter-attack or even a pre-emptive strike on the troops and aircraft concentrations in Florida seemed to heighten as the crisis wore on. While the Cubans (and even the Soviets) lacked the capability to launch a credible conventional attack, the fear was real as men and equipment began to pile up in the sunshine state. Additional batteries of HAWK missiles from the 65th Artillery (HAWK) were moved in at Patrick and MacDill AFBs, along with four batteries of the 2nd Missile Battalion of the 52nd Artillery (Nike-Hercules) missiles established near Homestead AFB on 29 October.[74]

The Nike-Hercules missile systems were dangerous on their own. Each of these air defense missiles was topped with a nuclear warhead. They were designed to be used against approaching enemy aircraft, guided in by radar. They would deploy above the approaching enemy and detonate in the atmosphere, creating a shockwave that would pulverize the enemy aircraft. The risks of firing nuclear weapons over your own bases to protect them was overweighed by the protection they offered.[75]

In addition to the missile defenses, the Air Force moved in a large number of 40-mm anti-aircraft guns in the event of any low-level attacks. These ringed each of the air force bases.[76]

Ammunition

OP Plane 316-62, along with Continental Army Command, dictated that all Army units would go into Cuba with their full basic loads of Class V armaments – including Chemical Corps items. For the armored elements, this meant a basic load of seventy-five rounds of ammunition per tank, which was designed to last for five days. Concerns were raised a few days after the mobilization on 23 October that this was not a sufficient number of rounds given the intelligence information known on Soviet tank numbers on the island.[77]

Detailed checks and analysis were made, and there was no way to increase the number of rounds. The movement of this amount of ammunition, and the lack of landing ships (even with the BARCs), meant that the troops would have to go into battle with what they had.[78] Ammunition replenishment for the armored units could not be expected until sometime after D-Day +5.

The other major challenge for Army was that their primary anti-tank missile, the SS-11B, was not American manufactured, but a NATO purchase from France. The supply of the missiles in the Continental United States was limited, since for years, the focus of the Pentagon had been a possible war in Europe. The stocks on hand were so low that the Department of Defense was forced to contact France to enter into negotiations to secure their stocks of such missiles. By the time of the invasion, all that was known was that France had agreed to provide 700 of the SS-11Bs for use in the invasion – pending arrival on a price. The US forces would enter the fight for Cuba with the stocks they had on hand, estimated at significantly less than what they were attempting to procure. Replenishment would not happen until long after the Army was on the ground.[79]

The Air Force, at first glance, was well-equipped for execution of the Rock Pile targeting. Beginning on 23 October they began to move large stockpiles of expendables to Florida for use in the air campaign. Over 7,000 tons of armaments, some flown in from the Philippines and Turkey, were airlifted to Florida. This included 3,849 750 lb bombs, 1,854 GAM-83's, 2.7 million rounds of 20 mm ammunition, 1,548 napalm bombs, 38,765 2.75" rockets, 2,219 launchers, 1,440 CBU bombs, and 1,020 fuel tanks and pylons.[80] While this seems ample stockpiles, one must remember the number of planned sorties, starting on D-Day with 1,190. The amount of armaments moved in would cover the start of operations, but not a sustained campaign of fifteen days or more.

This was not to say that the Air Force didn't have its own set of ammunition challenges. The demands of OP Plan 312 would consume most of the 20-mm ammunition. The Lake City Ordnance Plant in Ogden, Utah, was placed on a three-shift, seven-day-week production to attempt to keep up with the expected demands. The Army, in a mad scramble to secure ammunition, borrowed 3,000 5" Zuni rockets from the US Navy. The Navy tapped resources in the Air Force, which forced the manufacturer to accelerate production of these munitions.[81] The invasion of Cuba was going to push the logistics of all of the branches of the military to their limits, despite the fact that the enemy that they were invading was as close as 90 miles away from the US.

Tactical Air Command lacked the authorization for war reserves of conventional munitions, wing tanks, napalm tanks, and pylons, requiring the build-up of these supplies in Florida.[82] It was acknowledged at the time, the Air Force lacked a wide variety of munitions and fuses that were available to sustain a long-term campaign.[83] If the air strikes continued for a week, the options for munitions might prove less than effective in support of the ground troops.

The Floating Reserve Changes

The arrival of the floating reserves was slated for D-Day +10. The thinking by CINCLANT was that by that time, these forces could debark at four potential points – assuming, of course, that Mariel and Regla were secured. This was supposed to be the last of the armored forces landing on the island – bringing the number up to around 300.

The problems presented with the potential loss of some landing craft and the unavailability of other suitable transports made landing the last of the ground forces for the invasion potentially problematic. The solution that Admiral Dennison's staff proposed was that by D-Day +10, the need for tanks might be negated, even with an assumed number of combat losses. The need for mopping up the island was envisioned to be primarily an infantry-led mission.

Rather than resolve the issue around transporting the floating reserves tanks, a shifting between the on-call force and the floating reserve seemed to resolve the immediate issue – while potentially causing another. The proposed swap involved switching the 2nd Battalion, 81st Armor from the on-call force to the floating reserve, displacing the 2nd Battalion, 52nd Infantry. The infantry would then be made part of the on-call forces. While a last minute change, it would essentially make the armored force landing in Cuba reduced even more by the end of the planned invasion – D-Day +15.[84]

Air Force Challenges

The Air Force struggled on several fronts with the mobilization. One of the first stress points to emerge was the staffing at TAC headquarters. From the outset of the mobilization, TAC HQ was grossly undermanned, specifically in the plans, operations, and intelligence staffs. They lacked the capability to fully staff for functioning 24 hours a day. Over 200 personnel were brought into the headquarters on temporary duty to overcome this staffing gap. Even with this augmentation, the average officer put in a 15-hour work day, seven days a week.[85] With the crisis going on over thirteen days, this stress might impact the expected air campaign.

The headquarters function was not the only place that TAC was unstaffed. TAC fighter and troop carrier wings were grossly undermanned in crew authorizations to sustain the required ground alert status and at the same time accomplish the operational sorties and maintain the desired training programs.[86] TAC fighter wings were also undermanned to provide the required security, armament, and communications support in Florida. The Air Force tapped CONUS-based Air Force commands for additional staff, but the demands of rapidly changing targeting list made it difficult to ensure aircraft were readied for sorties.[87] While the initial day's worth of fighting this would not have proven to be a problem, the issue would have gotten progressively worse as the air campaign moved closer to supporting the invading ground troops.

Tactical Air Command also struggled with the number of overlapping command authorities that were needed in this kind of campaign. TAC lacked a practical organizational structure for meeting the operational command and control requirements. The various commands included the ADVON headquarters, one provisional fighter-recce-tanker air force, one provisional airlift air force, three provisional air divisions, and several provisional airlift wings had to be established in Florida.[88] All of these units were sharing a limited number of airbases and facilities, which made for potential conflicts.

Additionally, the Air Force lacked sufficient units permanently stationed in Florida to provide a satisfactory base of support for the number of units deployed to the region. The evacuation of SAC from Homestead, MacDill, and McCoy AFBs made this tolerable, but did not resolve the issue.[89]

Several concerns were raised regarding the aircraft and their outfitting as well. The Air Force lacked adequate photographic intelligence of potential Cuban targets.[90] While this would not impact the first day or two of the operations, it would potentially play a factor as the air campaign extended. There was an acknowledged lack of high-resolution aerial cameras and efficient photo-processing equipment to produce quality target photography in a timely manner.[91] If the Soviets and/or Cubans moved their assets to keep them concealed, it would be difficult to get time-sensitive targeting information for the units to respond to.

The lack of fighter-bomber forces with night and all-weather combat capability was another critical factor.[92] While the Air Force would rule the skies after the first day or two of the campaign, the night would leave US ground forces without air support, thus negating the US advantage.

Other Strains

OP Plan 316-62 only detailed the first fifteen days of the invasion; it did not even address the missiles sites beyond their targeting in the Rock Pile targeting lists. The military slowly began to come to terms with the concept that they would be in Cuba for some time. As such, they needed to count on a steady stream of replacement troops and other considerations that the invasion plans simply did not deal with. At the direction of Continental Army Command, the Army's training schools were cannibalized and support units thrown into a state of combat-readiness with little or no preparation. Among the first units that would be activated were two Army reserve units (21st and 210th Field Press Censorship Detachments) to help control the flow of information coming out of Cuba by the press corps.[93]

There was a marked lack of Spanish-speaking officers in all of the branches of the service.[94] Even the military academies were culled for both Russian and Spanish-speaking personnel. The Navy had the most immediate need on the ships poised on the Walnut Line for talking with any Soviet freighters that might attempt to cross the quarantine line.

Other supply headaches were frustrating, but also important. The Army forces to be used in the invasion were almost all assigned their winter clothing in October. While fine for American Stateside posts, these had to be traded out for summer clothing – a logistical nightmare given the rapid pace of the build-up.[95]

The Air Force mobilized its reserves, but the Army did not plan to mobilize Army reserves until the execution of OP Plan 316-62.[96] Once the invasion began, CINCLANT would need to deal with a huge influx of reserve units. Preliminary plans were devised to move these troops in to relieve the invasion forces and/or replace units assigned to Cuba, but these plans were vague at best. Much of what the US military would be doing after the invasion was best defined as 'making it up as they went along' – a dangerous proposition.

There was also the issue of the press. Any invasion would be followed with immediate requests by the media of the world to report on what was happening. OP Plan 316-62 did not have any provisions for this. Rather than deal with this,

Admiral Dennison and his staff passed this issue to Continental Army Command to cope with. As of 1 November, the first press camp (provisional) was to be established at Fort Eustis, Virginia. This unit would consist of thirteen officers, a warrant officer, and eighty-one enlisted personnel tasked with providing all media information services, facilities, security, and support for the press that would be wanting to report on the invasion.[97]

Strategic Response: the Nuclear Deterrent

The air strikes and invasion of Cuba were at the forefront of American military thinking, but they were far from alone. Attacking Cuba either by air, sea, or land would kill not only Cubans, but Soviets. It was the first time in the Cold War where the warriors of the Soviet Union and the United States would test their battlefield prowess against each other. In doing so, there was the risk of escalation. No one knew for sure what would happen once the Soviets started suffering casualties. Clearly, President Kennedy was concerned that the USSR would have to respond, just as he would have to respond if Americans were killed in military action by a foreign Government.

In 1962, the US possessed a triumvirate of nuclear weapons. The first was submarine-launched ballistic missiles. America had six submarines capable of launching nuclear weapons. These were deployed in Scotland and they put to sea in conjunction with the President's speech on 22 October.

The second leg of America's triumvirate of nuclear weapons was strategic missiles. When Kennedy ran for the presidency, it was based on the fact that there was a strategic missile gap; that the Soviets had more missiles than the United States. In reality, the US had significantly more of these delivery mechanisms than the USSR.

Missiles represented precious assets for striking at an enemy. At the same time, they were highly vulnerable. The Atlas and Titan I missiles, the heart of the American missile inventory, were liquid fueled. Many were not in protective hardened silos and required erection and time-consuming fuelling to launch. Even then, there was an assumption that a large percentage of the missiles in the US arsenal would fail, have guidance issues, etc. A war game run two years prior to the missile crisis assumed that of the 880 delivery vehicles (bombers and missiles combined) delivering 1,459 weapons on a target list of 654 targets, only 74.5 percent of the targets would actually be hit.[98]

The most potent aspect to America's nuclear arsenal was its bombers. If nuclear war broke out in 1962, it would not be as much a war of missiles, but of enemy bombers. The US missile force was less than 200, but in terms of bombers, it numbered over 800. Each of these could be configured to carry a wide range of nuclear ordnance, providing SAC with a high degree of flexibility in hitting potential Soviet targets.

When the President's speech to the world about the missiles in Cuba aired, SAC mobilized quickly to ensure that America maintained a nuclear strike option. On

22 October, SAC ordered that one-eighth of its bomber force go to alert with the setting of DEFCON 3. This maintained that one-eighth of the bombers remained in the air at all times to allow the US to counterstrike if the Soviet's launched an all-out attack. All leaves were canceled and crews were moved to staging air bases – more forward to allow for the quick turnaround of potentially returning bombers. All training and temporary duty orders were also canceled. SAC was preparing for the worse possible scenario – all-out nuclear war.[99]

AFLANT needed the use of the Strategic Air Command bases in Florida (Homestead, MacDill, and McCoy AFBs) for the Tactical Air Force aircraft in support of the Rock Pile bombing effort planned in Cuba. The decision was made to accommodate those forces by moving SAC forces to other air force bases for the duration of the crisis.[100] In many respects, this was prudent in that it moved these vital strategic nuclear defense assets out of the reach of any potential counter-attack by the Cubans.

While SAC was not expected to play a role in the invasion of Cuba, it did have a broader role in the military operations in the Atlantic. In order to support the quarantine, some SAC aircraft were designated for searching operations – locating and tracking the Soviet ships in the Atlantic, both military and commercial. These flights were dubbed 'Blue Banner' and would play a significant role in the ability to maintain the quarantine line.[101]

When the quarantine went into effect, the decision was made to increase the alert level at Strategic Air Command, since this would be the first direct friction point with the USSR. When the quarantine went into effect on Tuesday 23 October at 9.00 a.m. Eastern time, SAC was at DEFCON 3. It's readiness numbers did not alter significantly during the crisis, although its alert status would change as matters escalated. Below is a summary of aircraft and missile systems ready as of 24 October:

SAC Readiness on 24 October [102]

One-eighth airborne alert (B-52):	57
B-52 ground alert:	308
B-47 dispersal:	183
B-47 alert:	340
B-58:	6
Atlas missile alert:	89
Titan missile alert:	46

One of the final changes to OP Plan 316-62 was to give it formal operation name. The invasion of Cuba took on the name originally provided for the all-out air strike option in OP Plan 312 – Operation Scabbards. The fate of the air strikes and the invasion forces of Operation Scabbards hung on how the Soviets would respond to the US quarantine.

CHAPTER EIGHT

Showdowns and Tripwires

I believe that the Cuban missile crisis was the most dangerous crisis the world
has ever seen, because the two nuclear superpowers were at each other's jugular
veins and it was not easy to see a way out. With fumbling on either side, this
could have resulted in nuclear war.[1]

Secretary of State Dean Rusk

The Blue Moon Flights

In order to obtain better intelligence and to provide the necessary reconnaissance for
air strikes and Operation Scabbards, the decision was made to commence low-level
reconnaissance flights over Cuba. These were identified as 'Blue Moon' missions.

The first of these missions was on 23 October, led by Commander William Ecker. Six
Navy F8U-1P Crusaders flew out of Key West Florida and flew over the missile sites
at 400 mph at an altitude of 400 feet or less. The photographs that this mission and
subsequent Blue Moon missions provided was outstanding in clarity and provided a
new level of detail that the US had previously not enjoyed. Soviet and Cuban personnel
could be seen scrambling for their anti-aircraft guns or diving for cover.

The first of these Blue Moon flights showed that the four MRBM sites had
emergency launch capability, while two achieved full operational capability. The
Soviets had the capability to fire missiles. While Commander Ecker's flight was
not fired on, at least two of the Blue Moon aircraft were struck by ground bullets.[2]
A total of thirty such flights were flown during and after the missile crisis. (See
Appendix I for details of those missions during the period of this book.)

The Battle For Public Opinion at the OAS and UN

On 23 October, it was felt that the international community would find the
quarantine more palatable if they had the support of the Organization of American
States (OAS). Secretary of State Dean Rusk had hoped to secure at least two-thirds
of the members endorsing the United States' actions against Cuba.

At best, the OAS was an organization that was a toothless tiger. Having their support would give the US a thin veil of international backing. The organization was usually very disjointed and agreement took a long time and lacked any enforcement. The secretary was setting expectations high in hoping for a two-thirds majority – the OAS rarely had that kind of support. Secretary of State Rusk went in under the cover of the Rio Pact, which provided for mutual defense in the region. What he got was a stunning victory. Not only did the OAS support the US actions, but they did so unanimously; the first time they had ever done so.

Two days later, on 25 October, the US took its case to the United Nations Security Council. The American ambassador to the UN was Adlai Stevenson. An adept politician and statesman, Stevenson was often seen as a compromiser, a man that tried to arrive at a win-win situation for all parties involved. In this situation, America did not want to find a middle ground. The security council was to be the stage to present their evidence to the rest of the world.

Stevenson's opponent in this battle for world opinion was Soviet Ambassador Valerian Zorin, a bygone relic of the Stalin era. Stevenson, ever the master of the stage, laid a careful ambush for Zorin, who chaired the security council. He wanted to queue up the pivotal question: did the USSR have strategic missiles in Cuba? If Zorin answered yes, the world would know the truth. If he denied their presence, Stevenson came armed in the form of photographic evidence that would be presented on television to the entire planet. Either way, the matter would be on the table and hopefully garner the kind of support the United States needed to support the actions of the President's plan.

The presentation of the photographs was done with some degree of trepidation. There was a fear that showing them would expose some of the United States' intelligence-gathering capabilities. At the same time, the images were powerful and compelling – impossible to deny.[3] In the end, the decision was made that the risks of showing the photographs were overshadowed by the benefits they would provide.

Stevenson, on evening television, went after Zorin with a zeal that a man half of his age would have envied: 'Alright, sir, let me ask you one simple question: Do you, Ambassador Zorin, deny that the USSR has placed and is placing medium and intermediate-range missiles and sites in Cuba? Yes or no – don't wait for the translation – yes or no?'[4]

When Zorin refused to directly respond, Stevenson completed his trap. 'You can answer yes or no. You have denied they exist. I want to know if I understand you correctly. I am prepared to wait for my answer until hell freezes over, if that's your decision. And I am also prepared to present the evidence in this room.'[5] On cue, the photographs from NPIC from both the U2 and Blue Moon missions came into view for the entire world to see.

The victory was not a United Nations mandate. Instead, it was a stunning public relations success. It presented to the entire world the sly covert actions of the USSR and provided the kind of justification that the US needed on a world stage.

The Cuban Response

Fidel Castro found his island nation in the middle of a tug of war between the two superpowers – put on the world stage in the most grand manner. With the announcement by President Kennedy of the steps that he was undertaking, Castro realized that the threat of invasion was very real, and quite possibly immanent.

His reaction was to place the Cuban Armed Forces on their highest state of alert – over 270,000 men. The militia was mobilized. Castro ordered defensive measures to be taken at potential invasion sites and targets.[6] Bunkers and pillboxes were hurriedly created on some of the picturesque Cuban beaches. Anti-aircraft guns were deployed around airfields and Havana. Trenches were dug in preparation for the American attack that Fidel was sure was coming.

Tracking of Soviet Ships

Task Force 136 was already underway by the time of the President's speech, providing them with the ability to establish their picket line – the Walnut Line – by 9.00 a.m. on 23 October. The Walnut Line had been established far enough away from Cuba (800 miles) so as to prevent an air attack, specifically by the IL-28 bombers that were known to be on the island. The fear was that these aircraft, armed potentially with a nuclear warhead, could eradicate a portion of the line if the Cuban's or Soviets chose to use them. At the time, the US knew that the IL-28s were on the island, but were unsure how many were uncrated and assembled.

A special plot room, 'Saber', was established in the Pentagon for tracking all Soviet ships in the Atlantic, which fed information to the Navy's main plot room, referred to as the 'flag plot'. Even the innocent fishing trawlers were tracked carefully.[7] The tracking of these ships was done through the use of Strategic Air Command assets (Operation Blue Banner) as well a naval air assets and Tactical Air Command flights. The search area was approximately 4,500,00 square miles of ocean, with the eventual identification of over 200 ships of interest.[8] All of the data gathered on the ships were fed into a Remington Rand Univac Sea Surveillance Computer, which could provide plotting updates every 2 hours, which would be posted to the Saber board by hand. By 1962 standards, this was 'real time' data plotting.

The biggest unanswered question of the quarantine was whether the Soviets would ignore it. Would they attempt to continue on to Cuba and force the United States to take steps to prevent their trespass? If they did, what would the Soviet response be? There were more questions than answers on 23 October. The US had only one advantage; they had the privilege of more time to think through the possibilities and scenarios. The USSR was in a position of having to react to America's quarantine demands.

The Chief of Naval Operations Admiral George Anderson issued orders that all ships were to have, if possible, Russian-speaking individuals in the their communications centers to allow them to communicate with any ships that might test the line.[9]

With the President's announcement on 22 October, a significant number of the Soviet merchant ships apparently heading for Cuba were recalled or directed to neutral ports. Of the sixteen Soviet ships located en route to Cuba, nine that were east of the quarantine line reversed or altered course. Six remained close to forcing the United State's hand by continuing to move towards Cuba and the Walnut Line.[10]

Rules of engagement were established and communicated. US destroyers were to attempt to establish communications with any ship attempting to cross the line. The President's proclamation was to be transmitted. If the ship did not submit itself for boarding and inspection, a warning shot would be fired over her bow. If the vessel continued on, the destroyer would then fire a shot at non-vital parts of the ship (i.e. the ship's rudder) to disable it. Then, a boarding party would board the vessel to conduct an inspection. If the boarding party faced 'organized resistance', the ship was to be destroyed.[11] Even though such rules of engagement were fairly common, in the case of the quarantine, there was the threat of a confrontation that might lead to escalation with the USSR.

Complicating matters was that the Blue Banner flights by SAC had detected a Soviet sub-tender replenishing supplies with a submarine.[12] This opened the possibility that not only merchant ships, but submarines, would potentially be discovered.

The Walnut Line

The first tests of the quarantine came on 25 October when the Soviet tanker *Bucharest* was stopped by the US destroyer USS *Gearing*. The two ships exchanged signals and the *Bucharest* indicated that she was carrying petroleum products bound for Havana. The US, while anxious to enforce its quarantine, had been taking photographs and performing analysis of the Soviet tankers. The ships they were interested in stopping were those that were suspected of carrying nuclear missiles or other offensive weapons. Stopping such a ship would solidify the United State's position regarding the Soviet build-up in Cuba. The *Bucharest* did not meet that criteria and was allowed to continue on.

The next ship was the East German vessel *Völkerfreundschaff*, a passenger/cargo ship. Intelligence indicated that the ship was carrying 2,000 Soviet and Czech technicians and skilled laborers. There was debate in the administration as to whether such a ship should be allowed to continue. In the end, Secretary McNamara recommended that the vessel be allowed to pass. While the workers may be involved with the construction of the missile sites, it was most likely not carrying any of the banned offensive items. The *Völkerfreundschaff* was allowed to continue on.

A number of the Soviet ships were anticipated to have components on their decks needed to the missile complexes. These included the *Yuri Gargarin* and the *Komiles*. In particular, the *Komiles* had a 98-foot-long container suitable for carrying missiles or disassembled aircraft. Adding to this, a Soviet submarine was detected within 20-30 miles of the freighters.

To President Kennedy, this appeared to be the most dangerous of confrontations. With a Soviet submarine in the vicinity, would she fire in order to defend the freighters? President Kennedy asked, 'Is there some way we can avoid our first exchange with a Russian submarine – almost anything but that?' Secretary McNamara responded, 'There's no alternative. Our commanders have been instructed to avoid hostilities if at all possible, but this is what we must be prepared for, and this is what we must expect.'[13]

As the USS *Essex* and supporting destroyers closed in on the ships, it appeared that confrontation was inevitable. Just as they approached on the quarantine line, the ships slowed, halted, and turned around under orders from Moscow. 'So no ships will be stopped or intercepted,' the President said. 'If the ships have orders to turn around, we want to give them every opportunity to do so. Get in direct touch with the *Essex* and tell them not to do anything, but give the Russian vessels an opportunity to turn back. We most move quickly because the timing is expiring.'[14] The confrontation on the high seas had appeared to have reached a peak, and so far, war had been avoided.

However, Excomm members felt it important, at some point, to demonstrate America's resolve and commitment. The chance for this seemed best with the Lebanese merchant ship the *Marucla*. The ship had disappeared temporarily in the plot room, incorrectly labeled as the *Zaruwi*. Her cargo was not fully known, but seemed to be good candidate to show that the US was willing to enforce the quarantine. The destroyers the *Pierce* and the *Joseph Kennedy* were dispatched from the line to execute the intercept.[15]

Matters became muddled rather quickly. The USS *Pierce* mistakenly moved to intercept the *Völkerfreundschaff* and had to break off that pursuit to go after the *Marucla*. A report had reached the plot room that the *Marucla* had turned around and was moving away from the Walnut Line. Two hours later, a S2F from the USS *Essex* spotted the ship continuing on towards Cuba.

On Friday 26 October, the *Marucla* was intercepted by the *Pierce* and the *Kennedy*. The ship was contacted and a boarding party from the *Kennedy*, led by Commander K. C. Reynolds, was sent aboard. The ship's manifest and bills of lading were checked – she was carrying a load of sulfur, asbestos, newsprint, lathes, emery paper, and automotive parts. The holds were opened and spot inspections made. The ship was released and allowed to continue on, but the message had been sent: the US was willing and able to board ships attempting to cross the quarantine line.

Clash in the Plot Room

During 24 October, the tension of the growing crisis began to surface in the form of a confrontation at the Pentagon. Secretary of State McNamara and several staff, including two public affairs (PA) individuals visited the flag plot room where Admiral Anderson was monitoring the situation. Two versions of the momentary conflict have emerged in the years since the crisis. In one account, the Secretary of Defense asked why one of the destroyers was out of position. According to Admiral Anderson, he did not want to explain in front of the staff in the room who were not cleared for the information that the destroyer was pursuing a Soviet submarine contact. In this account, the Admiral said in a jocular tone, 'Why don't you go back to your quarters and let us handle this?'[16] According to one witness, McNamara asked what would happen if a Soviet ship refused to stop or resisted boarding. Allegedly, Admiral Anderson responded angrily, 'This is none of your goddamn business. We've been doing this since the days of John Paul Jones, and if you'll go back to your quarters Mr. Secretary, we'll handle this.'[17]

The Admiral's version differs dramatically:

One evening McNamara, Gilpatric, and an entourage of his press people came down to the flag plot, and in the course of their interrogations, they asked why that destroyer was out of line. I sort of tried to pass it off because not only were some of McNamara's people there who were not cleared for this information, but some of my own watch officers were not cleared for it in the general area of the flag plot. After some discussion, I said to McNamara – he kept pressing me, 'Come inside,' and I took him into a little inner sanctuary, where only the people who had clearance for that particular type of classified information were permitted, and explained the whole thing to him, and to his satisfaction as well. He left, and we walked down the corridor, and I said: 'Well, Mr. Secretary, you go back to your office and I'll go back to mine and we'll take care of things,' or words to that effect, which apparently was the wrong thing to say to anyone with McNamara's personality.[18]

Admiral Anderson went on to explain:

We have standardized tactical publications for almost every conceivable type of naval operation ... A command officer has those on board ship. It's his doctrine and he has to follow it, and McNamara was getting into the instructions that these people had. I said, 'They have these things, they've had them for years in the doctrine publications that they have as a basis to follow.' Somebody – it was not I and not one of the naval officers there, there was no reference on our part to John Paul Jones, but reportedly it was said that ... I said to McNamara, 'We've had them since John Paul Jones.' It was the reverse of what occurred.[19]

The Admiral further recalled that McNamara demanded to know if Russian-speaking personnel were on all of the ships. Anderson was frustrated because he had given the order that Russian speakers were supposed to be there, but had not conducted an inventory of each ship to validate it. As the Chief of Naval Operations, he was not inclined to do so. He was a man that expected his orders to be obeyed.[20]

One thing was clear: the interfacing between the Kennedy administration and the Pentagon was showing signs of strain and tension.

The Enemy Below

While the public eye was drawn to the quarantine line, the Soviet merchant ships, and the possible confrontation there, outside of the military, no one had fully realized the other naval risk unfolding in the Atlantic; the Soviets had dispatched four Project 641 (NATO Designation: Foxtrot) and one Project 611 (NATO Designation: Zulu) submarines to Cuba on 1 October 1962. Their mission was to 'reconnoiter the approaches to Mariel, to accurately log the acoustic conditions in the outer approaches, and to enter Port Mariel to make preparations for the arrival of seven ballistic missile submarines'. The submarines were designated as the 69th Brigade, and their mission was dubbed Operation Kama.[21]

Each of these subs was provided with a non-standard Type 53-58 nuclear torpedo. These weapons were blunt-nosed and tipped in purple paint, and accompanied by a special technician that literally slept with the weapon to ensure its security. These warheads had an approximate 10-kiloton yield and could be fired from the submarine's standard torpedo tube.[22] Each ship was painted with hull numbers that did not correspond to their ships, so as to further throw off American intelligence sources. Only one of the sub captains had ever fired one of the weapons in test. Depending on the range to target, there was a distinct possibility of the weapon not only destroying the target, but the firing submarine as well.

These submarines were diesel powered on the surface, and ran on batteries when submerged. In many respects, they were antiquated – more resembling late Second World War German U-Boats. Crew conditions were uncomfortable at best. For the Soviet submarine forces, this was to be one of their longest deployments undertaken at the stage of the Cold War. The strains on the crews were great. They had launched from frigid ports in the northern USSR and were being sent to a tropical environment where the heat and humidity took a toll on the crews who were inexperienced with those conditions.

When the submariners departed, they were told to avoid American and NATO anti-submarine forces, although these were not expected to be anything out of the ordinary. By the time the subs were halfway to Mariel, the situation had dramatically changed. The US had thrown up not only a quarantine line, but had significantly stepped up its anti-submarine warfare (ASW) forces. The ships and crews struggled. In the rough waters churned by Hurricane Ella, their snorkel devices, which drew in air for the diesel engines to run while the ship was submerged, closed off – sucking air instead from within in the ship. The result was a popping of eardrums and the ship constantly filling with diesel fumes. Fresh water supplies had to be distilled when they ran low. By the time the subs reached the area of US naval operations in support of the quarantine, they and their crews were already pushed to their limits. One of the Foxtrot subs was forced to return to port due to mechanical problems.

The Soviet subs, when surfaced, maintained secured contact with Moscow for orders. The guidelines for the use of the nuclear torpedoes was questionable at best. This left the discretion of use mostly in the hands of the boat captains, minus any specific orders from the Soviet Navy.

An American businessman in Moscow, William Knox, was granted an interview with Chairman Khrushchev on 24 October. The Soviet leader used Knox to informally pass on information to the Americans. His message was blunt; it was too late for the United States to take over Cuba . It implied what the US already knew – that some of the missile sites were already operational. Secondly, he said that he would eventually give orders to sink a US vessel enforcing the blockade if Soviet ships were subjected to stopping and inspection.[23] The only military assets capable of striking at the quarantine ships were the already weary men of the Soviet silent service.

A deadly game of cat and mouse unfolded between the US and Soviet Navy, with destroyers shadowing the Soviets, which limited their ability to surface to recharge their batteries. The Zulu class sub was spotted by the Navy and photographed while taking on supplies from the Soviet auxiliary supply ship the *Terek* on 22 October.[24] On 24 October, the US Navy spotted one of the subs north-east of the quarantine line. They photographed it while it recharged its batteries and covered it with destroyers.[25] On 27 October, one sub, the B-59, was forced to the surface when the level of CO_2 became unbearable and officers began to faint.[26] The captain of this vessel, Captain 2nd Rank Valentin Savitsky, ordered his nuclear torpedo to be loaded and prepared to fire. For all that he knew, the war had already begun. His actions were countered by one of his subordinate officers, which narrowly averted a nuclear confrontation. The B-59 was followed closely by two US destroyers who limited his ability to continue on to Mariel.

For over 36 hours, the B-36 (painted as number 911) was followed by the USS *Charles P. Cecil* and patrol aircraft north of Haiti and the Jamaican Channel. When his batteries were exhausted, the sub finally was forced to surface. US anti-submarine forces converged on the area to ensure that the sub could not continue on.[27]

While the US Navy could not have known it at the time, they had managed to locate all of the subs that were on their way to Cuba.

FROGS

Photographic evidence surfaced on 26 October that the Soviets did indeed have FROG (FKR) missiles in Cuba. These were designed to be tipped with a conventional or tactical nuclear warhead. There had been scant evidence prior to this date, but the photographs President Kennedy reviewed on 26 October confirmed the presence of these weapons. The CIA felt that the confirmation in the photographs was inconclusive, but they indicated that the Soviets had a tactical nuclear capability on the island. More importantly, the FROG missiles were solid fueled, unlike the R-12 and R-14 missiles. This meant that they could be launched with a few minutes' notice, as they did not require a long time to carefully prepare and fuel.[28]

Inching Towards Oblivion: the US ups the Ante

Oftentimes, accounts of the Cuban Missile Crisis tend to paint all the escalations that took place as manipulations on the part of the Joint Chiefs of Staff to attempt to initiate a broader war. These are unfair in some cases, and outright wrong in others. The Joint Chiefs were tasked with the defense of the United States, and saw the presence of Soviet offensive missiles in Cuba as unacceptable and requiring decisive action. Their actions are best framed against their responsibilities.

The White House considered military actions as potential options that could be employed if needed. President Kennedy did not clash as much with the JCS, as he saw them as consultants whose advice he could take or disregard as needed. As such, at these early stages of the crisis, the President heeded such advice.

As the drama on the high seas began to play out on 24 October, one such step was taken to defend America. General Thomas Power of Strategic Air Command ordered SAC to go to DEFCON 2 – one step away from war. This was the first time since the start of the Cold War that the United States had set this defense condition. While it only applied to SAC units, it represented not only a prudent move to ensure readiness of these forces, but a potential escalation in the eyes of the Soviets.

Going to DEFCON 2 was done with the consent of the Joint Chiefs and the President, and was within the statutory authority of the head of Strategic Air Command. Normally, it would have taken considerable time for the Soviets to have realized that the US was one step closer to war. Matters were different in this case. The order to go to DEFCON 2 was broadcast uncoded, in the open, to SAC forces: 'This is General Power speaking. I am addressing you for the purpose of re-emphasizing the seriousness of the situation this nation faces. We are in an advanced state of readiness to meet any emergencies.'[29]

Due to the way this was broadcast, the Soviets were almost instantly informed of this change of defense posture. In some cases, it could have been interpreted as an escalation, something that the United States was not deliberately signaling at this point of the crisis.[30]

The immediate effect of this escalation was that the USSR's Air Defense Command brought its level of alert to the same level as that of the United States. Under DEFCON 2, many American fighters would be equipped, per load out plans in place, to carry GAR-11's – nuclear tipped Falcon air-to-air missiles. On the surface, this seemed like a prudent move to ensure a counterstrike capability against the Soviets. Its other effect was to put in play a number of nuclear weapons that could be fired by pilots without control by the chain of command. While orders were issued to ensure that missiles would not be fired without permission, in the stress of the crisis and the increased tensions, the potential for a nuclear release had suddenly increased and had moved out of the hands of generals into the fingertips of junior officers.

Such was the case on 25 October, when at the prompting of the Joint Chiefs of Staff, President Kennedy issued National Security Action Memorandum 199. This memo authorized the Supreme Allied Commander Europe (SACEUR) to load out aircraft with multi-stage nuclear weapons.[31] These weapons had extended range to allow strikes deep into the Soviet Union in the event of attack. At the same time, it added significantly to the number of nuclear weapons in the hands of junior officers. This meant that in the event of a sudden attack by the Soviet Union, the US would have some capability to respond with theatre-based nuclear weapons. It also meant that at any time, an accident or misunderstanding might trigger a devastating response.

Tightening the Noose: the Chestnut Line

The increased U2 and Blue Moon missions provided a more detailed view of the Cuban and Soviet military on the island than had existed before. A reassessment of the Cuban Air Force indicated that only a handful of IL-28's had been uncrated and assembled, and there was no evidence that any had been flown. The distance chosen was enough to keep the task force out of range of the Soviet KOMAR missile boats as well.

As such, Admiral Dennison abandoned the Walnut Line, adopting a much more compact Chestnut Line, some 90 miles off of the Cuban coast. This meant that the ships in Task Force 136 had tighter control and less distance to travel to intercept. Given the presence of the Soviet submarines that had been detected, it was felt that moving the Navy closer to the island would provide a greater degree of control and coverage.

The Navy was having some difficulties with tracking the merchant ships on their way to Cuba. This was exasperated with the quarantine line moving closer to Cuba. Matters were made worse with the misidentification of the some of the ships still proceeding towards the line. At the same time, the CIA was leveraging its intelligence forces to learn which ships might be carrying cargo banned by the President's proclamation and which ones were not. Several of the ships were ruled out in this manner, but their presence made tracking difficult. Of the ships that remained heading for the quarantine line, the freighter the *Groznyy* was of keen interest.[32]

The USS *Lawrence*, which had been moving to intercept the Soviet tanker the *Groznyy*, was ordered to break off its efforts and assume a new position in the new quarantine line.[33] This ship was of particular interest because she had two large cylindrical tanks on her deck that were covered, potentially indicating they could possibly be missile fuel carriers. By the same token, they could very well be ammonia transport tanks. On 25 October, the Secretary of Defense had decided that the tanks were most likely ammonia tanks. On 27 October, that opinion had changed again.

The *Lawrence* and her sister ship the *Mac Donough* were ordered to reacquire the *Groznyy*, but the ship had seemingly disappeared.[34] Finally, on 27 October, a RB-47H aircraft operating under the Blue Banner missions (Strategic Air Command's 55th Strategic Reconnaissance Wing) spotted her, and she once more appeared in the flag plot room. Once she had been identified, the navy ordered in two destroyers to shadow her.

Intelligence remained split on whether the tanks were missile or ammonia transports. What was clear was that the ship had drawn the attention of Excomm. This ship would be another validation to the world that the quarantine was being enforced.[35] For the time being, the *Groznyy* was still several hundred miles from the Chestnut Line, now followed closely by the *Lawrence* and *Mac Donough*. It would reach the quarantine zone on 28 October. Excomm differed their decision until another time.

As the quarantine line pulled closer to Cuba, a series of events began to unfold, any one of which could act as a tripwire to start a war. While politicians would seek ways to prevent a conflict, the US military machine stood as prepared as it could be to bomb then invade the island nation.

U2 Issues

As diplomatic and other channels were actively trying to find a way for both the USSR and the United States to back out of the growing crisis in Cuba, matters were escalating around the world; any one of which might have provided either Government with the opportunity to escalate if they desired to do so. The U2 surveillance flights, both over Cuba and near Soviet airspace, nearly provided just that.

On Saturday 27 October, Major Rudolf Anderson took off from McCoy Air Force Base in Florida to conduct mission 3127, a flight over Cuba to photograph identified missile and military bases. U2 missions over Cuba had become an expected occurrence, but each one brought with it a wave of increased tension. Since the President's address, the overall feeling was that the United States would be invading Cuba. The low-level Blue Moon missions were reconnaissance flights – a common prelude to bombing or invasion operations. Each appearance of US aircraft might not be surveillance aircraft, but bombers signaling the start of air strikes. In one message from Moscow on 27 October, the instructions to General Pivyev read, in part, 'In the opinion of the Cuban comrades, a strike by US aircraft on our facilities in Cuba ought to be expected on the night of 26-27 October or at dawn of 27 [October].'[36] Fidel Castro had already ordered his own anti-aircraft units to fire at the Blue Moon missions. With the quarantine in place, the Soviets in Cuba were cut off and isolated from mother-Russia on an island cascading towards war.

Anderson's flight took him, in the course of 1 hour, 21 minutes, on a flight route over Yaguajay, Ciego de Avila, Camagney, Manzanillo, San Luis, Guantánamo, and Preston.[37] This time, the Soviets decided to respond with brute force. Captain N. Antonyets, the commander of the SAM battery near the port of Banes, contacted General Pliyev's headquarters requesting instructions. General Pliyev was not available, but General Stephan Grechkno, Pliyev's deputy commander, and Major General Leonid Garbuz, the chief of staff for military preparedness, fielded the call in this leave.[38]

The standing order was that none of the SAM sites were to fire without the expressed orders and permission of General Pliyev. Attempts were made to contact him, but to no avail. Fearing that not shooting might do more damage to the Soviets and Cuban than firing, permission was given to fire.[39]

The Soviets had not fired their SAMs at previous U2 flights, but the majority of those had taken place before the American denouncement of the missiles and the implementation of the quarantine. It had reached a point on 27 October where the Soviets on the ground felt they had to take matters in their own hands.

General Mikhail Titov, deputy chief of Soviet missile operations in Cuba, recounted Major Anderson's flight years later: 'American planes were literally crawling over Cuba.' He recalls that the Cubans had been urged by Castro to shoot down the Americans, which they were unable to do because the spy planes were flying far too high for Cuban anti-aircraft batteries. So Titov admits there was moral pressure on the Soviets to help. 'We requested guidance from Moscow, asking what we were supposed to do. But events were snowballing, and in Moscow, they probably did not have time to keep us informed.' Titov admits that Moscow was extremely displeased when it learnt about the U2. 'It is true that we received a reprimand, or as we say, pep-talk. But we decided that what had been done could not be undone. We thought, "let the politicians sort it out."'[40]

The 507th Anti-aircraft Missile Regiment unleashed two of its SA-2 missiles, which streaked up to an altitude of 21,000 m. At least one of them exploded near the U2, killing Major Anderson instantly and sending his U2 plummeting to the ground. The aircraft fell in the vicinity of Antilla; a search was immediately organised.[41]

The loss of the U2 brought to a head the issue of what to do about the loss of the aircraft. Since the imposition of the quarantine, the response from the Kremlin had been one of blustering threats, challenges, and accusations that the crisis was one of the United States' making. The Soviet Premier warned that the USSR saw the blockade as 'an act of aggression' and would challenge it.[42] While the Soviets had not attempted to run the quarantine line with ships carrying banned cargo, the *Groznyy* was still being tailed by the US Navy. With the contraction of the quarantine perimeter to the new Chestnut Line, it had bought the vessel some time before it would be approaching the American zone. Meanwhile, Khrushchev still was posturing loudly and publicly. It was against this context that the downed U2 was seen. As President Kennedy put it, 'This is much of an escalation by them, isn't it?'[43]

The US was not completely caught off guard by the loss of Anderson's aircraft. From early in the crisis, contingencies had been discussed as to what to do in the event of such an action. On 23 October, the thinking had been hard-lined in nature: 'It was expected, but not definitely decided, that if hostile actions should continue after such a single incident and single retaliation, it would be necessary to take action to eliminate the effectiveness of the surface-to-air missiles in Cuba.'[44]

The next day, the Joint Chiefs of Staff met on the subject and softened their response. 'They agreed that, if a U-2 was downed, one to two flights daily should continue until another U-2 loss occurred. Then, determine whether the projected attrition rate was acceptable. If so, continue the flights. If not, attack all SAM sites and then resume U-2 flights.'[45] While the White House held the final verdict as to who would deal with the matter, for the time being at least, no action was taken as a result of Anderson's shoot-down.

Oddly enough, at the same time that Excomm was attempting to digest the loss of Anderson's U2, another U2, commanded by Major Charles (Chuck) Maultsby, had created its own wave of international tension. His mission was to perform high-altitude atmospheric sample gathering near the North Pole. These missions were performed to attempt to measure radioactive residue from Soviet nuclear tests.

Major Maultsby's mission started out fine as he flew to the North Pole. But in the darkness, his magnetic compass did not give good readings given its proximity to the pole. Instead of returning straight towards Alaska and Eielson Air Force Base, he wandered into Soviet airspace. The error was detected when another aircraft reported seeing sunrise and Major Maultsby radioed that he did not – an indication that he had flown significantly to the west.

The Soviets responded, scrambling MiG 19 fighters after the U2. The Air Force responded by sending two F-102s to assist in guiding Major Maultsby back to friendly territory. What made the matter more nerve-racking was that fact that SAC had set its defense condition to DEFCON 2. The F-102s were armed with nuclear-tipped GAR-11 Falcon air-to-air missiles. Given that the Soviet Air Force had detected the US move to DEFCON 2, it is safe to assume that they too were equally armed. Major Maultsby's U2 could have been a high-altitude bomber as far as the Soviets knew.

The Major made a flight correction and managed to land on little but fumes in Alaska before any clash in the skies took place. This does not mean his simple navigational error was overlooked. On 28 October, Chairman Khrushchev wrote of the incident to President Kennedy:

A still more dangerous case occurred on 28 October when one of your reconnaissance planes intruded over Soviet borders in the Chukotka Peninsula area in the north and flew over our territory. The question is, Mr. President: how should we regard this? What is this, a provocation? One of your planes violates our frontier during this anxious time we are both experiencing, when everything has been put into combat readiness. It is not a fact that an intruding American plane could be easily taken for a nuclear bomber, which might push us to a fateful step, and all the more, since the US Government and Pentagon long ago declared that you are maintaining a continuous nuclear bomber patrol.[46]

Privately, President Kennedy's response was blunt: 'There's always some sonofabitch who doesn't get the message!'

An Incoming Nuclear Missile is Detected

One 27 October, the new long-range radar tracking station in Moorestown, New Jersey, detected an approaching lone missile launch in the Gulf of Mexico with an apparent trajectory towards Tampa, Florida. Immediately, the NORAD officers picked up their hot line and relayed the information.[47] The thinking at the moment was that Soviet submarines had been detected – what if a missile launching sub had somehow evaded the US anti-submarine efforts and was launching a pre-emptive strike at the massive conventional force build-up in Florida?

Calls were placed to Tampa after the missile was destined to land, and there was no indication that any attack had taken place. As systems were checked, it was discovered that a test tape had been fed into the computer and had detected an artificial satellite on the horizon, misinterpreting it as a missile launch.[48] For the time being, the troops in Florida were safe.

Diplomatic Wrangling

Running parallel to the military preparations, quarantine, and mobilization, the efforts to secure a diplomatic settlement to the crisis were very active. Both sides were hampered by the speed with which messages could sent. In 1962, messages were written, then encrypted, then sent via Western Union Telegraph to the embassy in the respective country. They would then be delivered, decrypted, and if necessary, translated, then delivered to the respective leader. This process meant that if an urgent message was to be sent, it could take upwards of 12 hours for the message to actually arrive for the Chairman or the President. Such a time lag in such a tense and often unfolding situation was a recipe for potential conflict.

Chairman Khrushchev's responses to the missile crisis were awkward at best. Sent on 24 October, the response did not offer a way out of the crisis, but rather, was accusatory in nature. The quarantine was called what it was – a blockade, an act of aggression. President Kennedy responded the next day, prodding the Soviets to remove the missiles from Cuba and bring about an end to the tensions. All the while, the low-level reconnaissance flights showed that the construction on the missile sites was increasing in tempo, rather than decreasing.

The President employed a personal appeal via his brother Robert Kennedy. Unknown to the members of Excomm, at the President's bidding, Robert Kennedy met with the Soviet Ambassador Dobrynin at the Soviet embassy in Washington. The meeting was hoped to drive home the point that the USSR had created the crisis with the placement of the missiles in Cuba and could end it quickly with their removal. Instead, according to Robert Kennedy, Ambassador Dobrynin maintained that he did still was unaware that missiles had been placed in Cuba.[49] Dobrynin's account varies dramatically, claiming that he defended the placement of missiles there, noting the placement of the Jupiter missiles in Turkey. According to Dobrynin, Robert Kennedy introduced the removal of the Turkish missiles as a way to end the crisis.[50]

This was not new thinking. Excomm toyed with the idea of removing the US Jupiter missiles from Turkey – something that was known to be a point of contention with Khrushchev. These short-range missiles had already been slated for replacement, as they had been obsolete for some time. Turkey saw the missiles as a sign of NATO's commitment to defend their nation.[51] The risk that the administration faced in removing these missiles as part of a swap was that Turkey greatly prized the security they provided, and it would be perceived as the US trading the security of another country for its own.

In the heat of the crisis, ABC News reporter John Scali was contacted by Aleksandr Fomin, a man known to be the KGB's Washington Station chief. The two met at the Occidental restaurant on 26 October. Fomin presented a set of criteria for ending the crisis, hoping that Scali would pass it on to the Kennedy administration. He stated that the Soviets would dismantle the missile sites under UN supervision, and Castro would pledge to not accept offensive weapons of any kind in exchange for a US pledge to not invade Cuba.[52] Scali reported to the meeting to the State Department and White House, and it was believed by some officials that this may have been a personal appeal from Chairman Khrushchev.

Later that day, a long, often rambling letter arrived from the Soviet Chairman presenting similar terms and conditions. 'I propose: we, for our part, will declare that our ships bound for Cuba are not carrying any armaments. You will declare that the United States will not invade Cuba with its troop and not support any other forces which might intend to invade Cuba.'[53] This added weight to Fomin's proposal.

27 October proved to be the crucible for the crisis. The *Groznyy* was approaching the quarantine line, Anderson's U2 was shot down – seen as a potential escalation – and Maultsby's U2 had drifted into the Soviet Union. There was hope; Khrushchev's letter on the previous day seemed to offer a way out. It was unfortunately followed with a letter on 27 October that added a new condition: the US removal of missiles from Turkey. This new condition seemed to initially squash hopes that the crisis could be abated. There was even discussion in Excomm raising questions whether the letter had actually come from Khrushchev. Perhaps a hard-line element had replaced him. Or worse, the Chairman was now simply throwing in a new demand that made matters more tense, since the US could not afford politically to be seen trading the missiles in Turkey for those in Cuba.

The solution that Excomm devised was decidedly simple. They would ignore the new request from Khrushchev received on 27 October and accept the terms and conditions in the letter of the previous day. There was no guarantee that this ploy would work. If this diplomatic approach proved unsuccessful, the military track was still open and viable. As General Taylor reported to Excomm, the Joint Chiefs had not come up with an alternative other than those they had pursued since the beginning of the crisis:

> Mr. President, the Chiefs have been in session during the afternoon on – really the same basis we have over here. The recommendation they give is as follows: that the big strike, OP Plan 312 – be executed no later than Monday morning the 29 [October] unless there is irrefutable evidence in the meantime that offensive weapons are being dismantled and rendered inoperable; that the execution of 316, the Invasion Plan [redacted] days later.[54]

Privately, the President pulled aside a small group of advisers and told them that they could *privately* assure Chairman Khrushchev that the missiles in Turkey would be removed in the next six months, but this could not be made public. The Turkish missiles were obsolete anyway, and due for removal. The full assemblage of Excomm members were not told of this alteration of the plans.

The message was delivered via two channels. One was to send John Scali back to meet with Fomin and attempt to use this 'back channel' to send a message to Khrushchev. Scali relayed that the inclusion of the Turkish missile removal was a 'stinking double cross.' Fomin considered it a result of 'poor communications'.[55] Scali told Fomin that the invasion was only hours away. He passed on word that the Chairman's letter of the 26 October would be accepted. He departed, unsure if Fomin's word would carry the weight of the urgency and need to resolve the crisis quickly.

The second course for accepting the terms was to come through Robert Kennedy personally delivering a response to Soviet Ambassador Dobrynin. The two met in the evening at the Justice Department. When the Soviet Ambassador raised the issue of the missiles in Turkey, Robert Kennedy said:

> There could be no quid pro quo or any arrangement made under this kind of threat or pressure, and that in the last analysis was a decision that would have to be made by NATO. However, I said President Kennedy had been anxious to remove those missiles from Turkey and Italy for a long time period. He had ordered their removal some time ago, and it was our judgment that, within a short period of time after this crisis was over, those missiles would be gone.

The President's brother drove home the urgency that the Soviets accept the offer. 'Time is running out. We have only a few more hours. We needed an answer immediately from the Soviet Union. I said we must have it the next day.'[56]

The implication was clear: if the Soviets continued to stall, the US would exercise its military options and rain hell on Cuba.

CHAPTER NINE

Operation Scabbards

Just consider the seriousness of deciding to invade Cuba, a densely packed area. We were up against some pretty strong ground forces, so some very drastic preparation would have to be made in the way of our bombing, gunfire; a great many people would have been killed. The Cuban beaches are really, by and large, not worth a damn, narrow entry areas and so on. So it would have been quite a bloody affair. And then, once having captured Cuba and occupied it, the United States would have had a terrible problem in rehabilitation and establishing a Government. We would have been in there for years.[1]

Admiral Robert Dennison

Introduction

In reality, the Kennedy and Khrushchev administrations arrived at a solution to the missile crisis in the late day of 27 October. The contemplation of the invasion of Cuba has been tantalizing to historians, but almost always lost in the shadow of the war escalating to a full-blown nuclear confrontation between the superpowers.

In reality, however, this was not necessarily the case. While the threat of a global nuclear war did exist, it was always held in check with the simple idea: is it worth going to full-war over Cuba – or for that matter, Berlin, if it were put in play by the Soviets? The concept of invading Cuba did not, on its own, mean a natural escalation on either side, although the risks were most assuredly there.

Other historians have tried to approach the air strikes and invasion from a counter-factual historical approach. This is tempting, but what is best is to present the facts and a summation of how the invasion might have unfolded based on the information known.

Would the US have Invaded?

One of the tantalizing questions is whether the US was seriously contemplating the invasion option of removing the missiles. At the time, this was not a point of contention; the assumption was that the air strikes and invasion was destined to occur if a diplomatic solution could not be arrived at.

This matter has become blurred over the years by revisionist views of history on the part of members of the Kennedy administration. In the atmosphere of the post-Bay of Pigs debacle, McGeorge Bundy and Robert McNamara claimed that the US had no plans in the works to invade the island, despite the fact that numerous operational plans were in the works. As McNamara said, 'We absolutely had no intention to invade Cuba … I guarantee you that President Kennedy would not have invaded …'[2] In reality, several years worth of plans would have crossed his desk regarding plans to invade Cuba.

The proverbial hawks and doves in Excomm have taken the opportunity over the years to slant their interpretation of their own support for the invasion. Even Robert Kennedy used his own recollections in his book *Thirteen Days* to paint himself as someone who was opposed to military action. As evidenced in the recordings of the Excomm meetings, the younger Kennedy made comments such as, 'I'd like to take Cuba back. That would be nice,' in reference to the invasion option.[3]

Robert McNamara, in his later years, would often represent his tough stand against the Joint Chiefs of Staff. In reality, however, as revealed in many of the Excomm meeting transcripts, he called for 'nothing short of a full invasion'.[4] McNamara argued strongly for the use of the blockade and quarantine, and in most of the meetings, he strongly supported the view of the Joint Chiefs.

In reviewing the President's own position on 27 October, when discussing the invasion in light of the downing of Anderson's U2 mission, he still was on the fence:

I would think we ought to just take a chance on reconnaissance tomorrow, without the cover, because I don't think the cover is going to really going to do you much good. You can't protect it, hide it, from ground fire, and if they're shooting tomorrow, and if we don't get an answer from U Thant, then we out to consider whether Monday morning [29 October] we [go ahead with the air attack on Cuba]. I'm not convinced yet of an invasion, because I think that's a much … I think we may.

General Taylor then chimed in: 'I agree with that. My personal view is that we should be ready to go on Monday [with the strike], and also ready to invade, but make no advance decisions.'[5] This dialogue indicates that the President still considered the invasion option viable, but simply did not want to pre-commit that the invasion would happen.

The greatest validation of the President's resolve was the signing of orders to maintain the Air Force Reservists on 27 October. These reservists served only one function – flying in the airborne troops and their reinforcements as part of the invasion.

When Would the Invasion have Started?

Prior to the resolution of the crisis, the Joint Chiefs of Staff were recommending a strike no later than 29 October.[6] The aircraft slated for the first wave of attacks were on 12-hour notice for executing the Rock Pile targeting plans.[7] This would mean that a decision to launch an attack on 29 October would have had to be made on the evening of 28 October. While possible, the reality of matters was that any hint of hope to avoid escalating the conflict would have delayed an air strike, and the history of the crisis was rife with such moments.

The problem with this is that, given the lag in time in terms of communicating between Washington and the Kremlin, it is entirely possible that the US administration would have held out for a favorable response to their proposals until the last minute. This would have delayed the decision until, most likely, the morning of 29 October. Given the Kennedy administration's lean away from rash actions, this would mean that the earliest strike time would most likely have been 30 October. This would have provided a full day of air strikes and three sorties, ensuring that the missiles and SAM sites were neutralized. Going midday on 29 October (the result of a delay in making the decision) would have limited the number of sorties that day and run the risk that the Soviets would retaliate by launching their missiles. Tactical Air Command had long stood with the concept that the first day had to ensure three full sorties to ensure that the missile sites were indeed neutralised.[8]

The risk factors in delaying from 29 to 30 October were minimal. For the most part, the medium-range missiles in Cuba were operational already, and some had been so for several days. The extra day for the Cubans and Soviets to dig in would not alter the outcome of the conflict.

Known Cuban Positions and Troop Placements

As of 27 October, the information that the US possessed regarding the disposition of Cuban and Soviet forces was incomplete at best. Most of this information came from sketchy CIA reports, with the most accurate data coming in from the Blue Moon missions.

The assumption was that during the execution of the air strikes, a significant number of Blue Moon missions would have been flown to identify additional targets. This put the invasion planners a bit in the dark. As such, several estimates had to be drawn up for what the invaders landing at the Tarará or the airborne landing zones might be facing.

The approach that Operation Scabbards planners undertook was to look at what was estimated as available in the Havana area. The estimate for the Tarará beachhead, the only location as of 25 October where intelligence estimates existed, was as follows:[9]

Estimated Tarará Beachhead Defenses
Four Infantry Battalions (Two militia, two unidentified)
One bazooka company
Three battalions and three separate companies of artillery

These Cuban assets were notably not factoring in the Soviet forces, which the US had already dramatically underestimated. The following were believed to be the reserves that the Cuban Revolutionary Army would apply to any or all of the invasion targets:[10]

Infantry
Five Regular Army Battalions
Seventeen Regular Militia Infantry Battalions
Sixteen unidentified Battalions

Artillery and Mortar Units
Regular Army
Four artillery battalions
Two separate artillery batteries
One mortar battalion
Three separate mortar batteries
Militia and Reserve
One artillery battalion
Two separate artillery batteries
One separate mortar battery

Armor
Two medium tank battalions (T34/85 or T54/100):   50 each
One heavy tank battalion (JS-2/122):   30
SU-100 Assault self-propelled gun: 50
Light tank (M3A1):   12
Medium tank (M41A1):   12
Medium tank – COMET: 15
Light armored cars (N-8): 20

Note: Some of these numbers do not jibe with other intelligence estimates as to how many of these vehicles may exist in Cuba.

As of 27 October, this was the latest intelligence on Cuban and Soviet forces in the vicinity of the invasion:

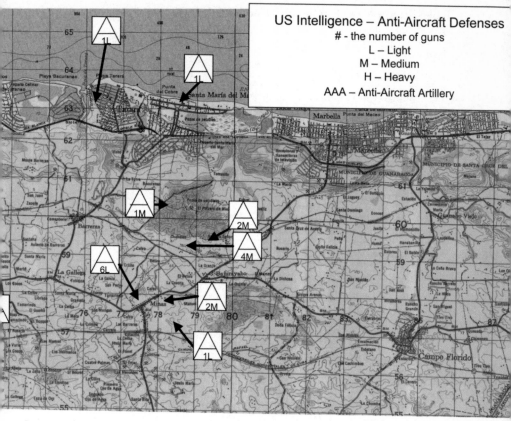

US Intelligence – Anti-Aircraft Defenses
- the number of guns
L – Light
M – Medium
H – Heavy
AAA – Anti-Aircraft Artillery

Courtesy of the Earth Sciences and Map Library, University of California, Berkeley

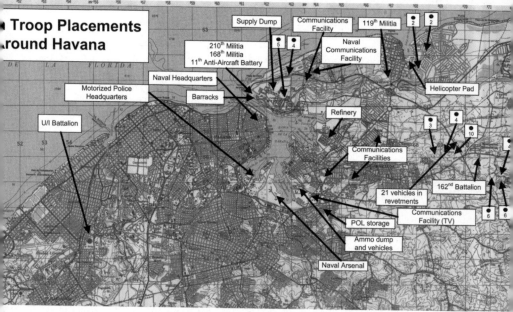

Troop Placements round Havana

Courtesy of the Earth Sciences and Map Library, University of California, Berkeley

Table 9-1: Known Cuban Infantry Units and their Placement[11]

Unit	Location
193rd Militia Battalion *	Tarará
134th Militia Artillery Battery *	Tarará
145th Militia Battalion *	South of Tarará
119th Militia Battalion	Cojimar
120th Militia Battalion *	Castle Morro
168th Militia Battalion *	Castle Morro
11th Anti-Aircraft Battery (12.7 mm) *	Castle Morro
Militia Battalion (Unidentified Code 2464)	East of Barreras
Militia Battalion (Unidentified Code 2464)	South of Minas
162nd Battalion	East of Guanabacoa
115th Militia Battalion	15 miles south and east of Havana
Navy Headquarters, Havana	West of Morro Castle (opposite side of the bay)
Motorized Police Headquarters	Havana
U/I Battalion	Havana
U/I Company, 145th Militia Battalion **	South and east of Tarará

Table 9-2: Cuban Artillery Positions[12]

Unit	Location
Two probably light dual-purpose (reveted) *	Tarará
Eleven light (reveted)	North of Bay of Pigs
Three light (under construction) (reveted) *	South Coast – Bay of Pigs
Three light (under construction) (reveted) *	South Coast – Bay of Pigs
Two light (reveted) *	Cojimar
Two light (reveted) *	Cojimar
Five light (reveted) *	South-east of Castle Morro
Four light dual-purpose (reveted) *	East of Castle Morro
Three light dual-purpose (reveted)	East of Guanabacoa
Ten light (reveted)	East of Guanabacoa
Four light (reveted)	South Coast – Bay of Pigs

Opposite: Courtesy of the Earth Sciences and Map Library, University of California, Berkeley

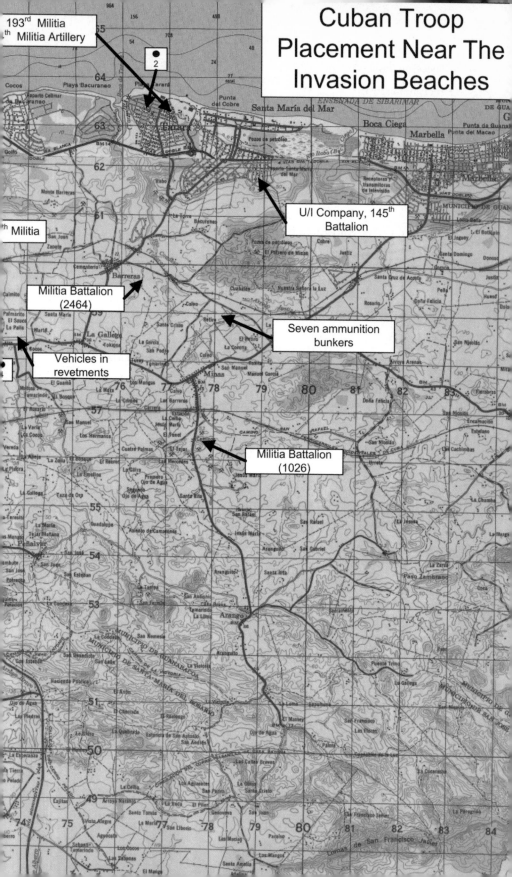

Cuban Troop Placement Near The Invasion Beaches

193rd Militia

th Militia Artillery

U/l Company, 145th Battalion

th Militia

Militia Battalion (2464)

Vehicles in revetments

Seven ammunition bunkers

Militia Battalion (1026)

Four light (reveted)	East of Guanabacoa
Six light (reveted)	East of Guanabacoa
Six light (reveted)	East of Guanabacoa
Four light (under construction) (reveted)	North of Bacuranao
Four light (reveted)	South of Bacuranao
Six light (reveted)	East of Loma de Tierra

Table 9-3: Cuban Anti-Aircraft Gun Positions[13]

Unit	Location
Six Guns (AAA) – unoccupied *	South Coast
Light (reveted) coastal defense	Santa Maria del Mar
Light (reveted)	East of Minas
Medium (reveted)	South of Santa Maria del Mar
Two medium (reveted)	South of Santa Maria del Mar
Four (possibly more) medium (reveted)	South of Santa Maria del Mar
Five medium (reveted)	Minas
Six light (reveted)	Minas
Light (reveted) *	Tarará
Seven light (reveted)	West of La Gallega
Four light (reveted) dual-purpose	East of Guanabacoa
Four light (reveted)	East of Guanabacoa
Three light (reveted)	East of Guanabacoa
Twenty-four light (reveted)	Guanabacoa
Six light (reveted) (radar controlled)*	North of Guanabacoa
Six light (reveted) (radar controlled) *	Cojimar
Six light (reveted)	East of Combre
Three light *	West of Cojimar
Three light *	South-west of Cojimar
Three light *	South-east of Castle Morro
Three light (reveted) *	South-east of Castle Morro
Two light (reveted) *	Castle Morro
Six light (reveted) *	Castle Morro

Twelve light (reveted) (radar controlled) *	Castle Morro
Three light (reveted) *	Castle Morro
Two light (reveted) *	Castle Morro
Six gun AAA (radar controlled) *	West of Tarará on the highway to Castle Morro
Six gun AAA *	West of Tarará on the highway to Castle Morro
Six gun AAA (radar controlled) *	West of Tarará on the highway to Castle Morro

Table 9-4: Cuban Automatic Weapons/AA machine guns[14]

Unit	Location
Automatic weapon (reveted) *	Tarará
Automatic weapon (reveted) *	West of Tarará
Four AA machineguns *	South of Tarará
Twelve automatic weapons (reveted)	West of Peñalver
Ten AA machineguns (under construction)	Highway east of Guanabacoa

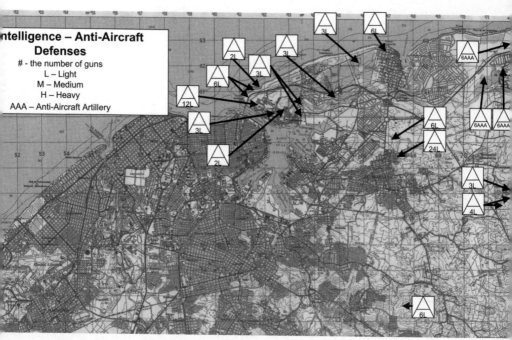

Courtesy of the Earth Sciences and Map Library, University of California, Berkeley

Ten automatic weapons (under construction) (reveted)	Highway east of Guanabacoa
Two automatic weapons (reveted) *	Highway leading to Cojimar and Castle Morro north of Cohnas de Villa Real
Two automatic weapons (reveted) *	Highway leading to Cojimar and Castle Morro north of Cohnas de Villa Real
Two automatic weapons (reveted) *	Highway leading to Cojimar and Castle Morro north of Cohnas de Villa Real
Automatic weapon (reveted) *	Highway leading to Cojimar and Castle Morro north of Cohnas de Villa Real
Four AA machineguns (reveted)	South-east of Guanabacoa
Forty-five automatic weapons (reveted)	East of Guanabacoa
Twenty-four automatic weapons (reveted)	Downtown Guanabacoa
Fourteen automatic weapons (reveted) *	West of Cojimar on the road leading to Castle Morro
Two automatic weapons (reveted) *	On the coast north-east of Castle Morro
Automatic weapon (reveted) *	Castle Morro
Two automatic weapons *	Cojimar
Two automatic weapons *	Cojimar
Two automatic weapons	Guanabacoa
Two automatic weapons	Guanabacoa

Table 9-5: Miscellaneous Cuban Unit Locations

Unit	Location
Seven ammunition bunkers	North of Minas
Vehicles in revetments	West of Gallega
Twenty-one vehicles in revetments	East of Guanabacoa
Helicopter pad *	East of Cojimar
Civilian refinery	North-west of Guanabacoa
POL storage area	Havana Harbor
Ammunition dump and vehicles	Port of Regla
Navy arsenal *	Havana Harbor
Open storage area (supply dump) *	East of Castle Morro
Barracks	South of Castle Morro
Communication facility (television)	Havana Harbor

Communication facility *	East of Castle Morro
Communication facility (Naval) *	East of Castle Morro
Communication facility	Port of Regla
Communication facility	North of Guanabacoa at the Port of Regla
Communication facility	Port of Regla

* Probably headquarters, installation and weapons positions
** This company is believed to be armed with four 50-caliber AA machine guns and three armored cars. It is believed to be the defensive unit assigned to Fidel Castro's personal residence.
AAA: anti-aircraft artillery
POL: petroleum, oil, lubricants

The Cubans had been busy establishing trench lines, some of which had firing bays established. Only a handful of these were on the landing beach at Tarará itself. Most were established to provide protection in the Castle Morro and east of Guanabacoa. Thirteen trenches had been identified, some of them extending over 150 yards in length.[15]

An analysis of the known placements of the Cuban forces and their Soviet allies reveals that they were planning resistance at the beaches of Tarará, with the bulk of their force placed deeper inland. The largest known concentration of Cuban battalions and artillery demonstrated a defense in-depth. They were concentrated at Castle Morro and Guanabacoa, which would have provided protection to the Havana/Regla ports. This is important, because both of these were Marine Corps objectives in securing Regla as a potential alternative to Mariel. The concentrations at Castle Morro alone were more than three to one odds against the Marines (BLT 3/8) assigned to seize the port entrance.

The defenses of Guanabacoa were mostly to the east, on the highway approaches to the city. This would have made for a difficult slug fest to try and enter Havana or the Regla Harbor from the east. Given the hilly terrain and thick forest areas, this ground was well suited for defensive action. With little intelligence as to the American amphibious and airborne landings, Fidel Castro had positioned his troops perfectly for defending some of the key objectives of the Marine Corps. Fidel Castro himself was establishing his own headquarters in a bunker that was rapidly under construction across from the Havana Zoo at the Almendares River. The tunnel-like bunker was far from finished, but offered Castro and his fellow military and civilian leaders ample protection.

The tunnel was about 13-feet wide, 20-feet high, and 500-feet long. Every 100 feet, on either side, were 32 x 98-foot-deep chambers, serving as work stations for various Government officials. The tunnel was strong enough to withstand a nuclear attack, but the engineers had failed to provide any ventilation system, and the resultant lack of oxygen and high humidity was almost intolerable. Nevertheless, with the imminent threat of war, the high command felt that this was the safest and most reasonable place for the main command post.[16]

Cuban intelligence on the American military build-up was remarkably accurate. 'We believe that in case of aggression against us, the possibility of mobilization of U.S. forces, serious divisions, five to six, no more. They have ten divisions, but it is impossible that all move against us.' They further asserted that the US could not deploy more than 120-130 tanks to the island.[17] Their primary concern was the American airborne divisions, specifically the 82nd Airborne Division, which they felt could be deployed against them with 5 to 6-hours notice. More importantly, the Cubans felt that they would have at least 2-hours notice if the 82nd Airborne was preparing to move out, which indicates that they had some level of intelligence in the US that could potentially alert them.[18]

The Cuban Army, while mobilized, would still need time to deploy to the landing beaches. This was estimated to be possible, depending on the locations, in approximately 3 hours. Obviously, this would be hindered greatly by the American air campaign, but this was factored into the Cuban estimates, which indicates a great confidence in responding to landings (amphibious and airborne).

In terms of anti-aircraft defense, Castro called for three concentrations of at least twenty-four batteries to be positioned in Havana itself, with one battery positioned outside of the city. Their most effective weapons were the 30-mm anti-aircraft artillery guns. The Cubans were experiencing a shortage of trucks, splitting them between the artillery batteries and the anti-aircraft emplacements. Of the 200 trucks needed for these weapons, only 85 had been allocated as of 24 October. The use of so many trucks indicated that the Cuban defense would be fluid and able to respond to a changing tactical situation.[19]

Despite being more prepared than anticipated, there were issues that the Cubans struggled with. 'Our greatest problem is communications. Much of what we should have received is still at sea or hasn't left the Soviet Union.'[20] This forced the Cubans to rely on the telephone as their primary means of communicating. Their other weakness was in aircraft detection radar. The Soviet SAM sites had tracking radar for firing missiles, but Cuba lacked the kind of long-range radar for detecting an incoming American air strike.[21] The lack of this asset meant that the Cuban Air Force would potentially be caught on the tarmac in the event of US air raids.

The Cubans organized forces near the beaches into anti-landing battalions. While the documentation is scant on these forces, it was noted that they were among those with the few radio communication sets, presumably to allow them to be quickly deployed in the event of an American beach landing, as well as direct artillery fire on the invaders.[22]

The Cuban Revolutionary Navy was busy practising torpedo launches, both during the daytime and in the evening to stay out of the eyes of the Americans. The Navy's frigates executed gunnery practice too, perhaps hoping to engage the approaching invasion fleet. Despite American air superiority after the first day of the attack, and being outnumbered by the US Navy, the Cuban Navy lacked the communications and control capabilities to coordinate with the air force and the army units.[23]

Medical capabilities for dealing with the casualties was a stress on the Cuban resources too. Castro ordered the students of the medical schools to report for duty as nurses and aides to physicians. He was as concerned about combat casualties, as he was about malaria. With his army and militia mobilized and in the field, Castro knew that malaria could be crippling for any military force operating in Cuba's forested/jungle interior. While he braced for battle, Castro ordered fumigation efforts be initiated to kill the mosquitoes before they sapped his army's strength.[24]

The American military intelligence gathered by 27 October was dangerously thin for an operation on this scale. Given the number of militia and regular army battalions, the US had managed to identify just over 3 percent of units by their designation, and had only visually identified 5 percent of the locations of Cuban Army units. Also, the estimate of response that the US military had in terms of ready-response by Cuban armored units assumed that *all* of the Cuban-owned tanks were poised in Havana, which was not the case; some were known to be positioned near Guantánamo Bay. These assumptions, while conservative, demonstrate just how vague intelligence on the island's defenders really was. What was known, was that with each passing hour, the Cubans and their Soviet allies were digging in and concealing their assets from the ever-prying eyes of the Blue Moon missions.

In reviewing the unfolding estimates of Cuban strength before the air strikes commenced, FMFLANT made his last change request of the invasion plans to Admiral Dennison on the morning of 28 October.

> In view of the increasing defensive capability of the Cuban/Soviet forces in the vicinity of the Tarará beachhead, a full-strength division effort may be required. Therefore, it is recommended that the 5th MEB be assigned to the II MEF to be available for immediate commitment to support the landing group west if required. Cruiser gunfire support for landing group west is essential.[25]

This reallocation of the 5th MEB would have removed the flexible deployment of these troops, which was what their role had intended. While discussions with the landing troops was heralded as a cake-walk, the reality was slowly emerging for US military planners that even with an air campaign of seven days, this was not going to be an easy landing.

FMFLANT's final recommendation was obviously in light of the readiness of the Soviet MRMs on the island:

> In order to provide for any contingency, recommend that an air-delivered tactical nuclear capability be available to the force commander. Specifically, the Naval Task Force Commander should have aircraft, armed with nuclear weapons, on

instant alert on carriers and on shore-based installations. The II MEF already possesses an 8-inch howitzer nuclear capable.[26]

With this request, even more nuclear weapons would be potentially introduced onto Cuba, and with them, the risk of a tragic mistake.

Soviet Preparations

While the US was aware of the presence of the Soviet motorized regiments in Cuba, they had no idea how well they were armed and equipped. There were two that would come into play with the execution of Operation Scabbards. The first was the 134th Regiment, which was stationed south of Havana near Managua. The other was the 74th Regiment, which was stationed south and west of Guanajay, which was west and south of Havana. Three other Soviet units were going to play a role in the defense of Cuba. The forces were assigned to defend the Soviet nuclear weapons at Bejucal and Manugua, and the Soviet headquarters at El Chico, south of Havana.

Up until 27 October, the Soviets had been working while wearing civilian clothing. That changed as the crisis reached its peak. The men took baths and donned their Soviet uniforms. 'Not only the Cubans were prepared to fight to the death, but the Soviets as well. This was the situation. They believed they were about to be destroyed, and they wished to behave honorably as soldiers.'[27]

The Soviets had begun a maskirovka campaign as soon as the crisis broke. This is evidenced in several of the Blue Moon images where Soviet tanks and trucks have been relocated in the evening, with the tracks obscured and hidden in the forested areas with camouflage netting. In other images, the vehicles were discovered lined up in rows, which would have certainly spelled their doom in the event of bombing runs.

The Soviet forces understood the American limitation in terms of night observation. In very few of the Blue Moon photographs do you spot Soviet vehicles on the move. The movement of vehicles was done almost exclusively at night. General Pliyev relocated the missiles themselves to 'secondary locations' near the launch sites. The Blue Moon missions concentrated on the missile launch sites and detected the majority of the attempts to conceal the missiles, but the fact remained that the Soviets were taking full advantage of the night to make any movements.

A review of the Blue Moon images shows that a remarkably small percentage of the Soviet armored vehicles were photographed, with the exception of the 74th Mechanized Regiment at Artemisa, where eleven of their tanks were observed.[28] The Soviets were obviously successfully taking advantage of concealment and camouflage to hide these assets. Even so, the US had identified 1,397 separate targets on the island, including the KOMAR missile boats, all of the Cuban Navy, and all of the target airfields not on the Scabbards land zone list.

Originally, when Operation Anadyr was provisioned discretional use of tactical nuclear weapons, it was at the discretion of General Pliyev, in keeping with standard Soviet doctrine. General Pliyev's orders as of 8 September were:

> In the situation of an enemy landing on the island of Cuba and the concentration of enemy ships with amphibious forces off the coast of Cuba in its territorial waters, when the destruction of the enemy is delaying [further actions] and there is no possibility of receiving instructions from the USSR Ministry of Defense, you are permitted to make your decision to use the nuclear means of the 'Luna,' IL-28 or FKR-1 as instruments of local warfare for the destruction of the invaders on Cuban territory and to defend the Republic of Cuba.[29]

On 22 October, the orders to General Pliyev were:

> In connection with possible landing on Cuba of Americans participating in maneuvers in the Caribbean Sea, undertake urgent measures to increase combat readiness and to repel the enemy by joint efforts of the Cuban Army and all Soviet troop units, excluding Statsenko's weapons and all of Beloborodov's cargo (the R-12 nuclear weapons).[30]

This got tempered and tightened as the crisis emerged. By the time the US had announced the quarantine, the orders from Moscow had changed. 'If there is no way to communicate with Moscow, Pliyev may use the tactical 'Luna' rockets at his discretion in the event of an American attack and if troops actually land on the coast. But there should be no haste to fire the 'Lunas'.'[31]

As the tensions increased in the stand-off between the superpowers, the message was made explicit to the General: 'We categorically confirm that you are prohibited from using nuclear weapons from missiles, FKR [cruise missiles], 'Luna', and aircraft without orders from Moscow.'[32]

This does not mean that the Soviet forces were not prepared, if pressed, to fire their missiles. General Pliyev had ordered that fuelling drills/tests be run to practice fuelling the missiles. He did these at night to avoid the prying eyes of the American Blue Moon missions, and to avoid the Americans misinterpreting his actions as actual preparation to fire the missiles.[33]

As the threat of invasion loomed closer, General Pliyev ordered one of the FKR units near Guantánamo Bay to couple their missiles with their tactical nuclear warheads. This unit had been positioned in the village of Vilorio, about 15 miles from the US naval base. On 26 October, they received orders to redeploy to the village of Filipinas with orders to be prepared to 'destroy the target,' on receipt of orders from Moscow.[34] This adjustment of position was undetected on the part of the garrison at Guantánamo Bay.

By 29-30 October, the US had a massive strike force of 576 warplanes poised to attack Cuba and secure air superiority. Guantánamo Bay was secured, although still vulnerable, with 5,858 marines. The 5th MEB was en route from the West Coast of the US. More than 150,000 American troops were mobilized and ready to pounce on whatever was left of the Cuban and Soviet defenders after the air strikes. Three aircraft carriers and a significant number of support ships and those prepared to support the invasion with shore bombardment surrounded Cuba. All that was required was the final approval from President Kennedy.

The Weather

Logistics may dominate wars, but the weather would also play a role in the air campaign and landings. The following table for the Havana area – one of the few where reporting was done at the time – provides a view of potential impacts:

Table 9-6: Havana Weather[35]

Day	Weather	Possible Impacts
29 October	Clear	
30 October	Clear	
31 October	Cloudy	Impact on reconnaissance and bombing in the afternoon sorties
1 November	Rain	Bombing sorties would be canceled or reduced, no reconnaissance
2 November	Morning Fog	Morning bombing and reconnaissance canceled
3 November	Clear – rain in the afternoon	Afternoon bombing and reconnaissance canceled or reduced
4 November	Clear	
5 November	Morning Fog	Morning bombing and reconnaissance canceled
6 November	Clear	Operation Scabbards landings unimpeded
7 November	Clear but windy	Impact on surf – landing of supplies, 2nd Infantry Division, and 1st Armored Division
8 November	Rain and afternoon thunderstorms	Bombing sorties would be canceled or reduced, no reconnaissance
9 November -12 November	Clear	

The Air War

If Operation Scabbards was employed, the air strikes would have begun at dawn on 29 October, but most likely 30 October. The aircraft would come in three waves during the day, totaling 1,190 sorties. On the first day, the targets were the missiles, the missile launch sites, the SAM installations, the KOMAR missile boats, and the airfields capable of supporting the MiG and IL-28 aircraft. Successful completion of this first day's worth of operations would ensure the neutralisation of the strategic missile threat. Subsequent days' sorties would go after the remaining SAM installations, given the US air superiority over the entire island, allowing for targeting of additional anti-aircraft emplacements, ground vehicles, command and control facilities, and identified enemy positions. Aircraft would come at Cuba from every angle, from the US task force carriers at sea, from Florida, and from Roosevelt Roads. The fighter/bombers coming from Florida cruising at 450 mph would have covered the 180 miles to the Sagua la Grande missile sites in 20-24 minutes.[36]

The plan for the first day did include all Soviet SAM sites, but the overall emphasis would concentrate instead on the five sites that protected the missiles sites. This would provide the US with the capability in those areas to operate freely to ensure that the missiles, their support equipment, and launch facilities were destroyed.[37] This is important, because it is possible that several of the SAM sites would have possibly survived the bombings on day one of Rock Pile and would be active on the second day to fire at American aircraft.

The Cubans and Soviets, for their part, were prepared. Cuban anti-aircraft guns had fired on at least two of the Blue Moon missions already, without downing an aircraft. The loss of Major Anderson's U2 demonstrated the lethality and effectiveness of the Soviet SA-2 SAMs. While they lacked long-range radar, the moment that bombing started, the network of Soviet SAMs would begin responding in a 'shoot it or lose it' approach. The skies over Cuba would have been filled for a few long, tense minutes with snaking missiles and contorting aircraft, visible through the rising smoke of bombs that had been dropped.

The largest attack on the Cuban Navy was to be against the KOMAR missile boats, the only naval targets that were to be attacked on the first day.[38] The Navy had reason to respect these small craft; their missiles were designed to be ship-killers. These ships were small and fast-moving when underway, but the Navy had insisted on making them a first day target out of concern that the Cubans would rush them out to take on the American carriers. This is one of the cases where superior fire power might not have been a factor. It is likely that most of these boats would be destroyed in the first days bombing, but it is hard to say for sure that all of them would have been sunk.

Would the rest of the Cuban Navy make a suicidal run on the American task force? With the risk of the ships being destroyed in port versus possibly inflicting some damage to the US Navy, Castro would have been hard pressed to not sortie any ships he had left. While it is doubtful they would have inflicted serious damage, there is a remote chance of US sailors being killed by a lucky torpedo shot.

The targeting accuracy of 1962 aircraft pales in comparison to their contemporary counterparts, but the first day's efforts relied on brute force in terms of the number of bombs dropped to make up for the lack of accuracy. The three waves of aircraft on the first day were designated to concentrate on the targets that posed the greatest strategic threat.

While it is impossible to ascertain what the actual losses would be, perhaps the best review of the first day came from Rear Admiral Robert F. Dunn. His oral interviews given at the US Naval Institute provides a glimpse of what the first day of Operation Scabbards would have looked like:

> Our aim was to maximize damage on the first strike, and to do so, we planned to use bombs loaded on multiple ejector racks, MERs. These MERs were fairly new and not well tested in the fleet. Yet, we planned for three MERs on each aircraft, one on the centre line, one on each wing station, and no external fuel tank. Each MER was planned to carry six Mark 81 250-lb bombs, 18 250's in toto [sic]. Overland distances to the target were short, so we intended to go in as low as we could and with a division of four aircraft. At an initial point, we would pull up and loft all seventy-two Mark 81's into the missile site. We were concerned that the big missiles were surrounded by surface-to-air missiles and by anti-aircraft artillery, and in order to avoid them, our plan was to go in low ... low and fast – 500 knots. Thank the Lord, we never had to do it because we would have all be shot down and lost. We didn't know that; we didn't learn that, though, until we began flying in Vietnam a couple of year later.[39]

The greatest risk from the first day of the air strikes is that a Soviet missile site, either known or unknown, would survive the attack and retaliate by fuelling and launching at the United States. General Charles Sweeney of the Air Force told the President on 21 October:

> That he was certain the air strikes would be 'successful'. However, even under optimum conditions, it was not likely that all of the known missiles would be destroyed ... the known missiles are probably no more than 60 percent of the total missiles on the island ... General Taylor stated, 'The best we can offer you is to destroy 90 percent of the known missiles.[40]

At 1500 hours Eastern time, in the second wave of strikes on day one, Operation Bugle Call (the psychological warfare element of Operation Scabbards) would begin. Two F105s outfitted to carry pamphlets urging the Cuban people to rise up against Castro would have begun. Over a million of the pamphlets would be dropped on Havana and the other Cuban cities from an altitude of 2,000 feet, fully exposed to any active anti-aircraft fire. The Bugle Call missions would last four days of the air campaign, in a relatively vain effort to get the Cubans to see the Americans as a solution to their Castro problem.[41]

In reality, the US *had* identified the missile launch facilities. The launch facilities themselves were fragile and dangerous. The fuel trucks near the facilities were bombs in and of themselves, and would have been easily destroyed. The launch facilities were not reinforced for air attack, and Soviet launch sites consisted of exposed cables on open ground and unprotected launch control mechanisms. The missiles themselves, while most had been moved to concealed positions, were worthless without their launch facilities, and were themselves, relatively fragile. This leaves little doubt that by the end of the day on 30 October, the missile would have been either destroyed or rendered worthless.

The MIG and IL-28 aircraft and airfields were defended by anti-aircraft batteries, but the overwhelming fire power of the American air attack would have devastated them. The Blue Moon photographs of these airfield showed that Castro had done little to protect these aircraft.[42] Day two of the air strikes of OP Plan 312-62 would have started with the remainder of the SAM sites. This would have been a bloody contest. By the second day of the air strikes, the surviving Soviet SAM sites would have been expecting an attack and would be alert and ready to fire the moment they detected any aircraft, knowing that the only planes in the sky were those of the Americans. At the end of the day, the sheer fire power of the US Air Force and US Navy would win the day, but the losses were not going to be insignificant. Also, on the second day, additional bombing strikes were called for on the missile complexes to ensure that they were not repairable.

Reconnaissance flights were also part of the first two days of action. Their goals, other than bombing damage assessment, was identification of ground targets and the Soviet mechanized regiments. The US had drastically underestimated the number of Soviet front line, armored vehicles, so these flights would have potentially identified more targets than the US thought possible. Also, the Soviets, as they had demonstrated earlier when the Blue Moon missions had begun, would use the night time to relocate and reconceal these weapons. A dangerous cat and mouse game would have begun.

After the first two days of air strikes, the Air Force and the Navy would have a targeting list that was very different – concentrating on ground targets in Cuba. Anti-aircraft batteries, artillery emplacements, trench positions, tanks and trucks – all would have been targets for bombing attacks. Additional attacks on other, non-jet capable airfields would have also begun as a precautionary measure.

The only places spared were the airfields at Baracoa, Jose Marti, and San Antonio de los Banos. The fields would have been spared any bombing, although any defenders or anti-aircraft gun emplacements there would have been pummeled. Realistically, there would have been some near-misses that would have damaged these airfields, but for the most part, these would be notably not laid waste like their sister airports. These airfields were the target for the airborne forces, and capturing them intact was critical for landing additional reinforcement troops.

The Rock Pile air strikes would have had an unexpected effect that would potentially play out in favor of the Soviets and Cubans. The immediate destruction of the missile complexes would have freed up the Soviet mechanized units for more mobile operations, including repelling the coming invasion. They had been positioned to provide defense of the missile complexes. With their destruction, General Pliyev would have been able to use his mechanized forces as what they were designed for: highly mobile operations in response to any American invasion attempts. Also, the destruction of the missile complexes would have provided Pliyev with additional troops in the form of displaced technicians and mechanics whose functions had been rendered useless by the bombing.

At the start of the air campaign, the initial landings of US Special Forces would have begun on the island. Given the nature of their missions and the flimsy planning that was in place, these two missions were almost doomed from the start. There was no indication at all that there was going to be a Cuban uprising against the Castro regime as a result of the air strikes. At best, they would have played only a minor role in the operations on the island. The one role they may have been most successful in was to act as 'eyes and ears' on the ground, relaying intelligence information to the US forces. At worst, their landings might be detected and they could end up captured or killed.

Under Siege

The start of OP Plan 312-62 would have had one immediate response from the island's defenders: an attack on the US Naval base at Guantánamo Bay. While formal Cuban plans are not forthcoming, once bombs started to fall, it is certain that Guantánamo would find itself under attack.

The first actions would be to sever the base's fresh water supply and electricity. The Yateras Water Plant would most likely be taken out in the first moments after word of the bombings reached the Cuban defenders surrounding the base. Contingency plans for this situation existed, using the ships stationed there to provide supplies. In the short term, this would work, but as a long-term solution, the base had to find itself better alternatives.

The Cubans would be able to launch artillery attacks from beyond the cactus curtain, raining shells down on the US base. A key target would be the airfields. The US defense was one of offence. Aircraft that were in the air before the airfields were shelled would have responded by bombing the attacking artillery, if they could be located. If the aircraft did not attack these positions, naval gunfire from the destroyers in the port would have shelled any suspected gun emplacements.

The Cuban's exact plans for Guantánamo have never been released. Once can only assume that they would have prepared to attack the base once the bombing of the island began. It was the one place where they could inflict American casualties before an US invasion. At least two or three divisions of troops were in the vicinity of the American base. The Cubans had a decisive advantage in terms of artillery as well.[43] While the Americans had Sea Bees that could repair damage, even a short artillery attack would have inflicted considerable damage to the defenders. An assault would have been costly for both sides. Both the US and the Cubans had sowed mines around the base. The Americans were well suited for defense, but lacked tanks and sufficient forces for any sort of decisive breakout.

If the airfields and aircraft were destroyed or damaged, it would have impacted the rest of the Rock Pile campaign. As Secretary of Defense, McNamara clarified in one of the Excomm meetings, '…How many air strikes are they likely to carry out from Guantánamo?' General Taylor's responded: 'It's maybe 200 to 300; 125 a day roughly.'[44] The loss of roughly 10 percent of the air support for Operation Rock Pile would have hurt American efforts quickly. If the attacks continued, there would have been pressure to execute the primary defense of the base, which was a limited break-out. At the same time, there were pressures to not push out. The Cuban and Soviets would only have the base as the one place to attack the Americans. Attempting to push out would have only weakened the marines stationed there and have drawn even more unwanted attention from the Cubans.

In any analysis, Guantánamo Bay would have been a base under siege, with mounting casualties each day prior to the end of hostilities.

The Invasion

On or about 6 November, the American invasion forces would have been poised for the airborne and amphibious assaults on Cuba. The day would have started with air strikes, as had every morning since the start of the air campaign. This day would have been different. The targeting on this day would have been around the beach at Tarará and the airfields that were the targets of the airborne units. This would be the first indication to the defenders that something different was unfolding. Why attack these isolated airfields that had been spared bombing up to this point unless the US felt they were needed? After the morning air strikes, there would be an increased presence of air units over the island – strike aircraft that were to be on-call by the invasion forces. Two more large waves of air strikes would have followed in the day, going after identified targets.

The shore bombardment from the cruisers off the northern Cuban coast would have commenced only 1-hour prior to the marines landing on the beach.[45] The roar of the impacting shells would have rattled windows in Havana and signaled that a new phase of the conflict was unfolding. The salvos would have lasted for only 30 minutes, chewing up the beach and the immediate areas behind it.

Just behind the beach positions at Tarará was a SAM emplacement and Spoka cruise missile launch pad. Both of these would have most likely been destroyed during Rock Pile's bombardments, but the troops there that survived would have been able to mount at least some defense once the marines landed and tried to push inland.

The marines would be coordinated by command ships off-shore. The 2nd Marine Division was had headquarters on the USS *Francis Marion*. RLT 8 was to

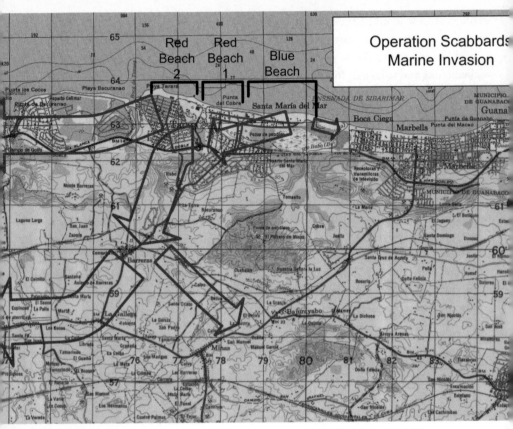

Courtesy of the Earth Sciences and Map Library, University of California, Berkeley

be directed from the USS *Boxer*. BLT 3/6 would have its floating command aboard the USS *Rockbridge*, and BLT 2/8 from the USS *San Doval*. All gunfire control would have been directed by the USS *Rockbridge*.[46]

The majority of the Cuban positions were situated at the immediate rear of the beachfront area, in easy striking distance. While most of their artillery would have been taken out in the air strikes and bombardment, some, most likely their mortars, stood a chance of surviving, although no matter what, there were bound to be some larger artillery pieces that would be serviceable. Also, the beach at Tarará had been mined, which would have played havoc on those first marines that hit the sands.

The other factor missed by American reconnaissance flights prior to 27 October was the presence of three reinforced concrete bunker/pillboxes.[47] Designed as automatic weapons positions, these were buried under the flowing sands. These would have torn away at the US landing forces while the Cuban anti-landing battalions made their way to engage them. There is no doubt that the marines would have successfully landed, but the thought of a cake-walk would be quickly fading in their minds. Underwater demolition teams (UDTs) would have been placed ashore in the early morning hours. Their job was to clear any naval mines or obstacles and mark the beach for the landing forces. Physically, the invasion forces would have been able to reach the beach, but after that, they were left to the whims of the gods of war.

The inability of the Cubans to move forces during daylight hours out of fear of air attacks meant that a concerted counter-attack would not come until the first evening or dawn the next day.

The Cuban defenses around Guanabaco were going to play havoc on two fronts. Firstly, it would dramatically slow any attempt to drive on to the Havana/Regla ports. Secondly, the planned heliborne assault on the hills outside of the city would have been met with massed anti-aircraft guns.[48] This would have forced BLT 2/8 to mount a ground assault to try and penetrate the concentration of Cuban troops in and around the city. While ultimately the US would have prevailed, the thoughts of seeing the lights of Regla Harbor the first night of the landings would have been unlikely.

BLTs 3/8 and 2/8, assigned to move along the coastal highway and seize the entrance to the harbor at the old Spanish fortress at Morro Castle, would have faced even more opposition. In the coastal town of Cojimar, defenses were established along the very road they were planning on employing, along with supporting troops. At Morro Castle itself was a concentration of anti-aircraft guns, artillery, and three known battalions of troops. Even with losses from air strikes, the fight to attempt to penetrate Havana in hopes of opening it for an alternative landing site for the 1st Armored Division would have potentially drawn out for days.

Once freed from the beachhead, the marines end-run around Havana to link up with their airborne brothers and sisters would begin, albeit delayed by the defenses they were likely to encounter in their initial landings.

The Airborne Assaults

Four hours after the marines started to land on the beaches at Tarará, the largest US airborne operation since the Second World War would have begun at the designated P-Hour, approximately 11:00 a.m. Eastern time.[49] An armada of aircraft stretching from the US to Cuba would have begun the arduous task of seizing the three target airfields outside of Havana. This airborne force would have been piloted in by less-experienced Air Force Reserve pilots. Few, if any, had ever taken part in combat missions, and none would have experience in flying in an airborne assault of this scale and scope. Worse yet, Castro's widely disbursed anti-aircraft batteries could mean that these slower transport aircraft would be subject to crippling ground fire.

The airfields, per the OP Plan 316-62 guidelines, needed to not only be taken, but be fully operational within 3 hours of being seized. If any defenders were to shell the fields either to ruin them or to shoot at the defenders, it is possible that the fields would be rendered useless. The airborne forces did have an engineering platoon in their landing, but lacked the heavy equipment for repairs. If severe damage was done to the airfields, it was assumed that the engineers and equipment of the US Marine Corps would assist in getting them repaired. That of course assumed that the marines could make their way to the airfields in light of Cuban and Soviet resistance.[50]

The easiest of the airfields to take and secure was to be Baracoa. Situated on the north shore of the island, just west of Havana, there were no trees or cover for any defending troops. It was the only airfield that could be assisted with naval off-shore bombardment for support. The attacking 101st Airborne Division would have been able to take the airfield. But Havana and the troops there were only 8 miles away. Taking the airfield was one thing, but holding it was another.

Matters were more complicated for the airfields that the 82nd Airborne Division was expected to take. San Antonio de los Banos was surrounded by sugar cane farms and irrigation ravines to the south, a thick forest area to the north, and the city of San Antonio de los Banos to the north-east, literally adjacent to the airport. All of these terrain features were going to play havoc with the forces landing. More importantly, it was only 15 miles via highway from the 74th Soviet Mechanized Regiment. This unit, unburdened with defending a missile complex thanks to the American air attacks, would be able to sweep to the east and engage the 82nd Airborne.

Jose Marti Airport was also bordered to the south by sugar cane farms, some of these with hills and valleys that would make assembly after a landing difficult. This airport was only 7 miles from where the Soviet 134th Mechanized Regiment was stationed, just south of Managua. Only 5 miles south of the airport was the Soviet nuclear warhead bunker at Bejucal. The KGB and Soviet Army personnel in this location had been detected by the American Blue Moon flights, but the significance and designation of this facility as the primary nuclear bunker on the island had not been determined. Any American landing so close could have been interpreted as the Americans knowing that the site was the Soviet bunker, which would have garnered an immediate response.

The nuclear storage bunkers at Bejucal and Managua represented another threat. Bejucal, the largest storage facility, had not been identified in the Blue Moon photographs beyond being a possible ammunition storage facility deep in a hill. Striking it would prove difficult. Managua on the other had been identified as a possible warhead storage site, making it prime for targeting lists during the Rock Pile attacks. If the US bombed the bunker where the nuclear warheads were stored, it introduced the risk of radioactive contamination of the area. While the invasion forces had protective gear against fallout, they were ill-equipped for any sort of a large scale nuclear clean-up.

The greatest threat to the 82nd Airborne's landing at Jose Marti Airport came from the fact that 4 miles from it was the village of El Chico. At a former boy's academy there was the Soviet military headquarters for Cuba. With the airport situated in the centre of this triangle of Soviet troop concentrations, the response

Opposite: Courtesy of the Earth Sciences and Map Library, University of California, Berkeley

San Antonio De Los
Banos Airfield

AIRBORNE

would have likely been immediate and vicious. The 82nd would have found seizing the airfield difficult, because defenders could have taken shelter in the adjacent town of Rancho Boyeros. The airfield literally was a part of the town centre, and urban combat favors the defenders.

If they did manage to take the airfield, the nearby Soviets would have most likely converged on the airfield as well. The men of the 82nd Airborne would have been hard-pressed to secure the field enough to allow for the landing of the reinforcement troops. While airborne troops are trained to fight in surrounded conditions, no one could have possibly anticipated the amount of pressure put on the 82nd Airborne at Jose Marti Airport.

The Swing Around Havana

The 2nd Infantry Division (and elements of the 1st Infantry Division) would have landed at Tarará, potentially delayed if the defenders on the beaches were able to slow the marines in their initial assault. The American plan called for the marines to allow the 2nd Infantry to pass through their positions, and with any available marines, drive south, then swing west, to link up with the 82nd Airborne at Jose Marti Airport, then onto the rest of the 82nd Airborne at San Antonio de los Banos Airport, then north again to link up with the 101st at Baracoa Airfield for the drive to Mariel, if they needed the support.

The presence of the Soviet 134th Mechanized Regiment was going to pose a problem. While they likely would swing to the closest American target, the 82nd Airborne at Jose Marti, they would also be imposed between the advancing American forces and the 2nd Infantry Division.

In evaluating the effectiveness of this sweep around Havana, we must remember the limited US intelligence regarding Cuban reserves in the Havana area. These could be directed in any combination of different directions. The temptation to go after the airborne forces would have been appealing, since these represented the best chance for isolating and destroying a US combat force. At the same time, throwing these at the beach-landing forces would have allowed the Soviets to engage at least two of the airborne landing forces. Directing reserves towards the 101st Airborne's airfield at Baracoa, while relatively easy, left them in the open and subject to support fire from the US Navy.

Any of the other options would have posed a problem for the sweep around Havana to relieve the Airborne forces. The 82nd was not likely to be able to receive their reinforcements on schedule because of unexpected resistance. This left the airborne elements of the invading forces lacking artillery and heavy ground armor.

Against them would be the Soviet units, as well as any Cuban reserves. While the Cubans were outfitted mostly with older tanks, some dating back to the Second World War, the Soviets were fielding T-55s – the 1962 main battle tank of the

USSR. Against these, the airborne or US Army infantry units would be severely pressed. While the Soviets would have suffered losses as a result of Rock Pile targeting, they would not have been eliminated completely.

With the 82nd Airborne Division unable to land its reinforcing artillery and tanks, these troops would be forced into defensive actions awaiting the marines and 2nd Infantry. The marines, as outlined above, were already going to be facing greater than anticipated defense by the Cubans, and the 2nd Infantry lacked any tanks.

While it is conceivable that the 2nd Infantry could reach the vicinity of the Jose Marti Airport, there would be a question if they could secure the field on D-Day or even D-Day +1 if the Soviets were well positioned. Ultimately, this would mean that the 82nd Airborne forces at San Antonio de los Banos Airport would take even longer to reach – *if* they were able to fend off whatever elements of the 74th Mechanized Regiment were launched at it.

In reality, it is conceivable that the entire operation to swing around Havana would have resulted in a crippling blow to the American 82nd Airborne Division and a substantial delay in reaching the 101st at Baracoa.

The American invasion depended on one thing: the 101st and her reinforcements reaching Mariel and securing the port for the 1st Armored Division's landing.

Mariel: the Key to the Cuban Invasion

The issues with the 101st Airborne Division in seizing the Port of Mariel were numerous, but not insurmountable. Firstly, the division's position to the east of the port was within striking distance from Havana if Castro threw any forces at them from that direction as a concerted counter-attack. The Baracoa Airfield was only 7 miles from Havana, closer to the capital of Cuba than Mariel (over 15 miles) and poised along a four-lane highway, making it vulnerable to counter-attack by the Cubans.

To get to Mariel, the airborne forces would be forced to cross four rivers to reach the port: the Rio Salado, the Rio Banes, the Rio Guefeibón, and the Rio Mosquito. Any one of these were potential choke points if militia or the Regular Army held the bridges, or worse, blew them up. Most of these rivers were flanked with swamps, making fording a slow and deadly process.

When the troops of the 101st Airborne reached the Port of Mariel, they arrived on the eastern side of the port. The port facilities were on the western side of the bay, meaning they would have to travel around the port on a road with a full view from the opposing side.

Mariel was not just a port; it was the home of the Mariel Naval Air Station. These facilities would have likely been bombed during Rock Pile, but there were several hundred Cuban naval personnel there who would be capable of defending the port facilities. It also was a SAM site for the Soviets. While this site would be damaged or destroyed in the air campaign, the personnel posted there were trained Soviet soldiers that no longer had a job to perform other than assisting the Cubans in the defense of the port.

At the start of Operation Anadyr, the Cuban's erected makeshift cinderblock walls around the Port of Mariel. The purpose of these walls was to block out the view of the Soviet equipment being unloaded.[51] These walls, while not strong protection, were still in place at the time of Operation Scabbards, awaiting the Soviet supply ships that were held off as a result of the American quarantine. These walls would provide any defenders with necessary small arms cover.

What was working in favor of the paratroopers is that they would have received at least some light tanks if their reinforcements were successfully landed – only a company's worth, but it would represent a large portion of the American armor on the island on the first day. The paratroopers had planned on moving on Mariel on D-Day, but they were 15 miles from the port. The paratroopers would have lacked any transports, and while the distance could be covered in a day, if there were any Cuban defenders, their progress could be slowed. Each hour that the 101st was delayed was an hour when the 1st Armored Division could not be brought to bear.

The only Soviet forces near to them was the 74th Mechanized Regiment. There was an equal chance that whatever remained of this force would be thrown at the 82nd Airborne Division at San Antonio de los Banos Airport. If General Pliyev split this unit against both airborne divisions, or chose to concentrate on the 101st, the odds of the Port of Mariel being opened on D-Day +1 for the American armored forces was scant. Any additional elements of the Cuban Revolutionary Army placed in Mariel or that area are unknown, since the Cuban records of the crisis remain classified.

In looking at the known Cuban troops placements around Havana with the intent to block access to the capital city Port of Regla, it can only be assumed that Castro would have realized the value of the northern coastal ports and prepared a defense appropriately.

If the Port of Mariel could not be opened by D-Day +2, the Americans on the island would be facing increasing pressure from the surviving Cuban and Soviet armor and artillery on the island. Even with one or two working airfields, the amount of troops and hardware that could be flown in were enough to allow the American's to stay in the fight, but not necessarily prevail. If the marines and the 2nd Infantry Division could not make their way around Havana to assist in securing the Port of Mariel, Admiral Dennison would have one ace up his sleeve: the 5th MEB. This force, per previous messages, was originally intended to be a resource that could be applied in several places during the invasion. CINCLANT had a request to keep it on reserve if needed at the Tarará beachhead. Chances are, it would not be needed there. But in securing Mariel, it may have proven to be the difference between a military disaster and victory. The 5th MEB could have been employed to the west of Mariel and assisted the 101st Airborne Division in securing the port facility. If this was employed, the earliest it could have been prepared for such a landing would have been D-Day +3. For the marines, paratroopers, and infantry on the island facing stiff resistance, it would have been a long wait for the much needed heavy armor.

Off-loading the 1st Armored Division, in the worst-case-scenario, would have been on D-Day +4 or later. Just because they began the debarking procedures, it does not mean the unit would be effectively engaged in battle. The inability of the Navy to provide adequate roll-on, roll-off ships, and the need to erect a temporary pier, would have meant that debarkation would have been slow, ponderous, and subject to the whims of the weather. Every hour that the 1st Armored Division was not ashore played to the advantages of the defenders.

The losses that the US suffered would have necessitated the landing of the floating reserve, most likely after D-Day +5. These additional troops would have been critical to apply pressure to any Cuban/Soviet positions that were still holding out.

The conventional fighting would have come to an end two weeks after the landing of 1st Armored Division, although it would have been a costly affair. The rugged terrain of the Cuban interior would have limited the effectiveness of armor. If the fighting dragged on into Havana, the same kind of issues would have surfaced, with the American superiority with armor on the ground being negated due to the ineffectiveness of armor when operating in the confines of urban environments. The 1st Armored Division was crucial for dealing the decisive blow against the Cuban and Soviet armored forces, but in the end, the fighting for Cuba would be decided by infantry and marine troops and the weight of air support available to them.

The Casualty Estimates

CINCLANT had his subordinate commands prepare estimates of casualties (killed and wounded) for Operation Scabbards. These estimates were seen as inflated at the time, but in light of the evidence that has surfaced since the Cuban crisis, it is clear that these estimates may have been conservative.

The following projects the casualty estimates as of 27 October:

Table 9-7: Estimated US Casualties in Operation Scabbards[52]

Day	Army	Navy	Marine	Air Force	Total
D	1,753	100	2,484	125	4,462
D+1	1,397	61	710	90	2,258
D+2	931	56	599	65	1,651
D+3	972	55	588	60	1,675

D+4	1,067	54	577	55	1,753
D+5	1,140	52	562	54	1,808
D+6	357	40	551	60	1,008
D+7	354	35	541	55	985
D+8	351	30	532	50	963
D+9	357	25	522	45	949
D+10	395	20	516	41	972
Total	9,074	528	8,182	700	18,484

It is important to note that the casualty estimates did not factor in losses as a result of Guantánamo Bay coming under attack at the start of the air campaign – something that seems inevitable given the position of the base and the circumstances of the Cubans needing to strike at the Americans wherever they could.

Also, these casualty figures only go up to D-Day +10. There is ample evidence that the losses in Cuba would not stop at that point, but could conceivably continue on for some time. As such, these estimates may have been actually low, and worse, they may have been just the start of US losses.

Endgame?

Any actions on the part of the Soviets and Cubans to defend the island would have been a bloody forestalling of the inevitable. The American control of the skies and seas, and the weight of the military might in the region, would have eventually spelled defeat in the *conventional* war for Cuba.

But conventional warfare was not the only way that the defenders of the island planned to fight. General Pliyev had plans in the event of an American victory to disburse his personnel to the mountains and fight as guerillas.[53] While the Soviet troops had not been trained in this style of warfare, the forces sent to Cuba were crack forces, and adaptation was something they had already demonstrated since their arrival.

This tactic was well suited to the Cuban military who had defeated Batista by waging a guerilla war as well, and they had done it without the benefit of the Soviet-provided arms and munitions. The concept of a guerilla campaign against the occupying American forces by the Cuban and Soviet survivors is staggering to digest. It is known now that the American forces in Vietnam were never able to fully counter the effects of a guerilla war in the jungle. It was a costly lesson that had been learned.

It is easy to see that the US would have had similar issues in occupation of Cuba; a determined enemy familiar with the terrain, who had the support of the indigenous population. The differences between the fighting in Vietnam and what the US potentially faced in Cuba was that the Vietnamese were being supplied constantly from other Communist Governments. America's blockade of Cuba would have cut off necessary supplies from reaching guerilla forces. While this did not ensure victory, it would have diminished the long-term impact of the guerilla forces.

The Americans had done little to plan for occupation of Cuba. On 26 October, Kennedy urged the State Department to establish a crash program aimed at establishing a civil Government in Cuba.[54] This was a late reaction at best, and no substantial program would have been in place by the time of Operation Scabbards. This would have left General Howze as the default civilian ruler of Cuba. He would have found himself attempting to manage a population angered by the American invasion, an infrastructure damaged by war, and with a potential guerilla war on his hands.

The Cuban population would be short of food supplies. The CINCLANT had devised a plan of how much civilian relief was needed. The estimates were as follows:

Table 9-8: Civil Relief to Cuba Post Invasion[55]

Type	D+4 to D+19 (tons)	D+20 to D+120 (tons)
Beans	114	1,450
Flour	1,824	23,200
Lard	124	1450
Rice	6,202	80,915
Milk	114	1,450
Eggs	114	1,450
Meat	1,824	23,200
Medical Supplies	4.5	125

The problem would be in getting these supplies on the island. The logistics of supporting the invasion, as shown in the previous chapter, would have been strained in simply supporting the military operations. Adding to this, getting thousands of tons of food supplies and dispersing these to the population in an organized manner would have tied up significant personnel and ships.

Ultimately, the battle of Cuba was not something that was going to conclude in a matter of two or three weeks. This was a long-term situation that the US was being drawn into; one that would potentially last years and do considerable damage to America's reputation in the region and in the world.

All of this assumes, of course, that the fighting did not turn into a nuclear contest between the super powers.

CHAPTER TEN

Escalation

Speaking in a figurative sense, Soviet artillerymen can support the Cuban people
with their rocket fire if aggressive forces in the Pentagon dare to initiative
intervention against Cuba.[1]

Nikita Khrushchev

Pulling the Trigger

There can be little doubt that the Cuban Missile Crisis was the closest we ever
came to nuclear war with the Soviet Union during the Cold War period. Were
we close to a real nuclear shooting war? In many respects, yes. Both sides had
nuclear weapons outside of the control of the generals and political leaders, and
in control of officers that were operating under extreme pressures and stress. Both
Governments had underestimated the response and reactions of each other and did
not fully understand the motivations behind the events unfolding on Cuba. Added
to the mix was Fidel Castro, a leader not really under the control of the Soviets,
who had convinced himself that the invasion was forthcoming at any time.

Ultimately, what might have sparked a larger/broader nuclear escalation? Would
the Soviets see Operation Scabbards as a prelude to a nuclear attack? Most likely
not. The US assessment at the time saw the situation as:

> Soviet assessment that a US strike on Cuba, even if Soviet nationals were among
> the casualties, was prelude to imminent US nuclear attack on the Soviet Union
> itself, seems unlikely. However, even if the Soviet concern over such an attack
> were very high, further criteria warranting the desperate act of a pre-emptive
> strike at the US would almost surely be necessary before the Soviets make a
> pre-emptive decision. Therefore, we would rate the possibility of the Soviet pre-
> emption still lower than implied.[2]

But the risk of a nuclear war still remained, despite both sides wishing to avoid it.
In short, the following summarizes what may have ignited either side considering
the nuclear option:

A technology shortcoming or failing: The most obvious example of this was the NORAD radar facility in Moorestown, New Jersey, detecting what was thought to be a missile launch on Tampa, Florida.[3] If the US had reacted to this as if it were an actual attack, it could have potentially responded with a full nuclear response on the USSR. As it was, the only detection system used to verify that an attack had not taken place was a system based on using telephones to validate that the city had not been destroyed.

Technology in 1962 had numerous failure points that could have impacted decision making and response to the crisis. Admiral Dennison and his staff struggled to establish a marginal number of communications circuits with the forward command posts.[4] This circuits were dedicated Department of Defense phone lines, and getting them in place, while vital, proved expensive and time consuming. The lack of these lines meant that information from the field could not be conveyed quickly back to the CINCLANT or the Joint Chiefs for action. If they had orders, there was a chance it would be delayed in transmitting. These communication lags and the inability to respond instantly to an ever-changing combat situation could have led to a bad decision becoming irreversible.

From even period films, such as *Dr Strangelove* or *Failsafe*, there is the illusion of technology in the war room being highly sophisticated and real-time. In reality, the display boards in the room were updated by hand with grease pencils on acetate, updating unit information, locations, status, etc. Each day, photographs were made of the charts, and these then were manually typed by clerks using typewriters who sent copies of the reports to Fort Monroe and Norfolk, taking most of the night and into the next day to arrive for CINCLANT and other commands to see the same information that was now hopelessly out of date.[5]

Human error: The most open example of this is Major Maultsby's errant flight into the Soviet Union on 27 October. If the Soviets had interpreted his U2 as a bomber, perhaps the first of many, moving to attack, their response may have been nuclear. The US sent fighters to escort the U2 back – some armed with nuclear-tipped air-to-air missiles.

With so many aircraft and ships operating in such relatively close quarters, the opportunities for a tragic mistake to be made that could be incorrectly interpreted expand dramatically. Even the best intending officers and enlisted personnel can make a mistake that can force a broader, more devastating reaction.

The pressures of combat: The shooting down of Major Rudolf Anderson is the most blatant example of this. The Blue Moon low-level reconnaissance missions had created incredible tensions on the Soviets and Cubans on the island. They had no idea when the roar of jets was a prelude to bombs falling. Despite orders to not fire without permission, the Soviet SAM site commander took matters in his own hands and shot down the U2. These men exceeded their local command authority and that of Moscow to fire their SAM. The US had established protocols for responding to attacks on a U2, which might have led to an automatic response/ escalation that could have gotten out of hand quickly.

Similarly, the strains, both physical and mental, on Soviet submarine B-59 reached a potential nuclear escalation when Captain Valentin Savitsky ordered his nuclear torpedo loaded and prepared to fire. Drenched in sweat, choking on their own CO_2 and diesel fumes, and harassed by American anti-submarine forces, the Captain's judgment was impaired. When officers were placed in such pressure-filled situations, there was an opportunity for a fatal mistake such as the one the captain nearly undertook.

The 26-27 October relocation of the FKR cruise missile to a position near Guantánamo Bay represented another example. Just before midnight on 26 October, the caravan moving in the dark jungle foliage to reposition the missile crashed into a ravine. In the rumble of the crashing truck, the men initially assumed that they were under attack by the Americans, and they prepared to respond. The crash left three dead, two Soviets and one Cuban, and fifteen wounded, but it could have resulted in a rash overreaction that could have triggered nuclear war.[6]

Once Operation Scabbards began, the Soviets on the ground would find themselves under attack daily. Soviet military doctrine was such that they were used to having discretionary control of tactical nuclear weapons – and strict orders to not allow such weapons to fall into the hands of the enemy. It is possible that under such stresses, as with the SAM crew that fired at Major Anderson, General Pliyev may have decided to use all of his assets to defend himself, including his tactical nuclear weapons.

The easiest place to respond would be to order the FKR missile near Guantánamo Bay to fire on the naval base. While it would have no direct impact on the invasion forces, it would inflict large numbers of American casualties in response to the savaging that the island's defenders were suffering. Otherwise, there was a risk that by the time he decided to use these weapons, all of his delivery mechanisms would be damaged to destroyed. The FKR near Guantánamo Bay was known to be in the area according to intelligence, but its exact position (and the fact it was armed with a nuclear warhead) was unknown.

Political pressures: There was a perception on the part of the Americans that time was running out. Each day meant that more missiles in Cuba were closer to being launch ready – according to US intelligence. The belief that the US was at much greater risk once the missiles were operational created increased pressure on the part of the Kennedy administration to act. The quarantine was not acting to provide pressure to remove the missiles, it only stopped more weapons from being sent to the island. Despite the risks of nuclear war, pressures were mounting for the US to take some sort of decisive action. This could have pushed for Operation Scabbards to begin, which may have led to escalation.

Internal politics were such that the Joint Chiefs of Staff favored a military response as the only way to be sure that the missiles were eradicated as a threat.

There were other Excomm members that also felt that attacking was the best alternative.

Once Rock Pile and Scabbards began, the USSR leadership would be immensely pressured to take action in response to the loss of Soviet lives in Cuba. There were plenty of places where the Soviets could apply pressure around the world. Berlin, always a sore spot, was the most logical. Attacking the Jupiter missile sites in Turkey was another. Both of these responses, however, risked a broader NATO response and a greater spread of the conflict.

As the crisis wore on, President Kennedy would have been facing domestic political pressures to resolve the Cuban situation, and any such response could have led to a broader nuclear war.

If the Nuclear Trigger were Pulled, Where?

The most logical known place where the escalation path to a nuclear conflict would have occurred would have been the firing of the FKR missile at Guantánamo Naval Base. There are several reasons that this is the most probable candidate for a nuclear attack. It was the only missile system mated with a nuclear warhead. Its exact location was unknown by the CIA. Until Operation Scabbards forces landed in Cuba, Guantánamo Bay represented the one place where the Soviets could inflict a significant number of American casualties. Combined with the pressures of the Soviet troops suffering bombing and strafing casualties, it is within the realm of possibility that the local commanders may have taken matters into their own hands – or that Moscow may have allowed the release of a small nuclear weapon.

Guantánamo Bay is situated at the bottom of a geographic bowl. While the warhead on a FKR is approximately over 2 kilotons, the effects would be amplified in the bay itself. The yield on such a blast would be small, but compacted by the surrounding hills. The defenses of Guantánamo Bay were barely enough for fighting a conventional siege, but were not nuclear weapons proof. The explosion would have been enough to cripple the defense of the base and cause several thousand injuries. Fires caused by the blast would have overwhelmed the base defenders.

The losses have never been estimated since; until recent years, and the work of Michael Dobbs, no one realized the threat that this missile would have posed. One thing is for sure; any destroyers or smaller ships in the bay would have been badly damaged. The defending marines would have suffered incredible losses, both from the blast and from nuclear contamination. The airfields, aircraft, and fuel storage would have been devastated in a direct hit.

Such an attack would not have hindered Operation Scabbards from taking place, but it would have removed the aircraft from the base from their ability to fly their missions – hurting the targeting schedule for operation Rock Pile.[7]

US relief to the survivors at the base would have been subject to Cuban artillery fire, adding to the injuries. While there would be thousands of survivors, the base would have been untenable as a military installation. Evacuation would have been the only short term option left to the United States. For the time being, the US would be forced to abandon its toehold on Cuba.

What Would the US Response Have Been?

Any response to a tactical nuclear attack on American forces in Cuba would not have necessarily caused an all-out nuclear war between the US and the USSR. The US nuclear war plan, SIOP-62 (System Integrated Operation Plan), as originally drawn up, had no scalability to it. In other words, it was a plan for a *complete* nuclear war against the Soviet Union and Communist China. When President Kennedy was shown this plan, he asked for alternatives other than a full-war – a way to scale a response. SIOP-62 was amended to provide for such a consideration.

The US did not have a desire to execute a full nuclear retaliation if it was not necessary. Former Secretary of Defense McNamara said that a tactical nuclear attack on the US forces in Cuba would have resulted in a US nuclear strike against Cuba.[8]

Operation Scabbards stipulated that tactical nuclear delivery systems be brought to Cuba in the form of Davy Crockett nuclear artillery pieces, and Honest John and Long John tactical missiles. On 29 October, what would have been the eve of the invasion, Admiral Dennison made the decision to have the teams responsible for these weapons remain in the US at their home stations on an on-call status. The requested tactical missiles and artillery were to be brought forward to Cuba if needed.[9] The problem was that if Guantánamo Bay or any other US unit were hit, it would take at least three to four days before these systems and crews could be debarked onto the island.

This would have meant that the response to a Soviet tactical nuclear strike would fall to either the US Navy or the US Air Force. The Navy carriers would have had nuclear weapons on-board and would have been the best quick response delivery source.

The attack would not likely be directed at a civilian target like Havana, but instead, would be directed at Soviet ground forces on the island. The 106th Mechanized Regiment would be the closest USSR unit to Guantánamo, but in reality, any concentration of Soviet troops would have potentially been a target. By this stage of the operations, however, the Soviet forces were going to be well concealed and spread out to help limit the effectiveness of American air strikes. Regardless of this, within a matter of a day, another mushroom cloud would rise up over Cuba, increasing the Soviet losses in personnel and equipment on the island.

The use of any nuclear weapons on the island would have served to slow any conventional operations in Cuba, rather than accelerate the climax of the fighting.

US forces would have taken a more defensive posture out of concern that other nuclear weapons might be employed. US military planners would be faced with the first use of battlefield nuclear weapons, and would not be sure how that could impact Operations Scabbards going forward; there were simply no models for them to follow.

The Soviet Union would not have the means to execute a tactical nuclear strike on Cuba from off-island. This would mean that if the Soviets chose to respond, their response might take place somewhere else in the world.

Berlin

From the earliest days of the crisis, the Kennedy administration assumed that Berlin was part of the overall designs of the USSR. In many of the Excomm meetings, Berlin was brought up, with the assumption that the Soviets would apply pressure there as a result to a US response against Cuba. This was easy to justify, given that just the year before, the Berlin Crisis had culminated in the building of the Berlin Wall.

Control of Berlin was seen as the impetus for any number of nuclear and conventional scenarios. In the post-Berlin Crisis days, the option was seen as executing SIOP-62, unleashing full nuclear war on the Soviets in response to any cut-off of access to the city.[10]

By the time of the crisis in Cuba, thinking had evolved on how to cope with the Soviets making a move against Berlin. 'It is a strong probability that Khrushchev would trade Berlin for Cuba any day; such a trade would be a heavy net loss for the US.'[11] The US thinking was that Berlin and Cuba were entangled. As such, there were perceived reactions on the part of the USSR against Berlin. Under the subject of possible consequences of early US military actions against Cuba:

Depending on what actions were taken, some US military forces would be engaged and hence unavailable to use in the Berlin situation. The variables are many. The stronger our action, the briefer its duration. Air action, taken alone, could rather quickly be ended and the forces moved elsewhere. The diversion of naval forces would have little impact on the Berlin situation – or to put it differently, naval action concerning Cuba would play a contributory role in the Berlin developments offsetting the thin-out of other naval measures. If ground forces were engaged on the scale of say 3 to 6 divisions, our ability to strengthen the NATO centre during phase II of a Berlin situation would be lowered. Not only would the divisions be unavailable during active operations, roll-up, and re-fit, but much of the sea-lift would be too. Besides, the allied build-up in Europe might be proportionately smaller as the US seed-crystal were smaller and slower.[12]

The Soviet reactions to the invasion of Cuba in relation to Berlin could come in several different forms:

- 'Khrushchev might simply accelerate his peace treaty procedures and let a blockade of access come as a result of this process.'
- 'More dangerous, though perhaps a shade less likely, would be an immediate interruption of access explicitly stated as a peace-loving means of controlling the Imperialist aggressors. This would take the form of interruption of the US access, allied access, or general access. It could be screwed up and down in a neat parallel to our Cuba effort.'[13]

The factors that would drive the US decisions bearing on Cuba/Berlin would include:

Soviet interests engaged in Cuba are very modest compared with those engaged in the Berlin issue. In both cases, US interests are more heavily involved. The dangers to US security are far higher in the Berlin crisis, and a Cuba success, which costs us heavily in Berlin, would be a poor bargain. To make vividly clear to the Soviets that the US is keeping its eye on the main chance, the US should make matching (in time, not necessarily size and type) deployment to Europe along with each major commitment to a Cuban operation. Some outcomes in Cuba would make more military forces available for Berlin use than would be prudent today; some others might tie up forces now available, i.e. an air threat had to be matched by air defense, or if occupation duties tied up several divisions.'[14]

The 1962 defense of Berlin, from a conventional build-up perspective, called for two Army divisions to be transported to Europe from the US to 'marry-up' with duplicate equipment there. A third Army division would be pulled from another part of the world to augment this build-up. Ten Tactical Air Command fighter squadrons would also be sent to Europe. The problem was that if Operation Scabbards was executed, these forces would have to be drawn from reservists. The ability to sea-lift or air-lift the personnel and equipment were also strained, requiring additional reserve resource, or even commercial sources.[15]

This build-up was to be a prelude to attempting to force a relief of Berlin via highways through East Germany if the city were indeed cut-off.[16] This would almost certainly precipitate a conventional war on the European continent.

The Dogs of War: Nuclear War 1962-Style

Details of SIOP-62 are still classified, especially the targeting lists, which still are considered to pose a risk in this era of the War on Terror. Some aspects of the plan can be gleaned from the portions of earlier plans that have been declassified over the years, and other sources where the elements of the plan have been incorporated into documents that are publicly available.

The key to understanding a nuclear confrontation in 1962 is that it would not be primarily a war fought with missiles. Both sides had a limited number of strategic intercontinental nuclear-tipped missiles. The US and her NATO allies possessed a large number of tactical missiles in Europe and the UK, which were well-within range of the USSR. On both sides, the real damage would be delivered not via missiles, but by bombers.

In the event of a 'massive retaliation' or all-out US attack, the United States had full force of 2,300 vehicles carrying 3,400 weapons.[17] Strategic Air Command was at DEFCON 2, but by 5 November, that force had been flying at full alert for a week. There were concerns regarding the strains on the personnel, especially air crews, who were not used to being pressed into service for this period of time.

The air crew hours spent at nuclear alert were staggering:

Table 10-1: Tactical Hours Flown by Strategic Air Command During the Missile Crisis[18]

Aircraft	1-31 October	22-31 October	1-7 November	8-14 November	14-21 November	22 October – 21 November
B-52	35,903	13,823	11,667	11,775	14,827	52,092
B-52 A/A	(18,810)	(13,423)	(11,576)	(11,572)	(10,597)	(47,168)
KC-135	19,478	3,000	2,064	2,658	4,188	11,910
B-47	28,700	1,000	641	1,737	4,827	7,205
KC-97	16,186	600	259	363	1,899	3,121
B-58	1,823	30	15	93	276	414

One wonders if SAC had a contingency in place for having its airborne alert force at DEFCON 2 for so long. If the attack came after 5 November, there was a worry that SAC would have to start standing down upwards of 20 percent of its alert force.[19]

The impact of a full nuclear strike on the USSR under SIOP-62 would have been devastating.

If the SIOP were executed as planned, the alert force would be expected (in the statistical sense) to kill 37 percent of the population of the Soviet Union (including 55 percent of the urban population), and the full force (Author: All nuclear assets), 54 percent (including 71 percent of the urban population), and the two forces, respectively, to destroy 75 percent and 82 percent of the buildings, as measured by floor space.[20]

This assumed an attrition rate of approximately 25 percent, mostly in the form of bombers shot down by fighters and SAMs, as well as Soviet defensive missile networks.[21]

The bottom-line of this scenario is that in a matter of a few hours, the Soviet Union would have been left a flaming nuclear shadow of its former self.

SIOP-62 estimated the Soviet capabilities as follows:

Table 10-2: Assumptions of Soviet Nuclear Attack on the US[22]

Vehicle	Number	Weapon Yield	Number Per Vehicle	Total Megatons
Bison Bomber	80	1 Megaton	4	320
Bear Bomber	40	1 Megaton	4	160
Badger Bomber	400	1 Megaton	2	800
ICBM	52	7 Megatons	1	364
			Total:	1,644

The US Department of Defense did conduct studies to determine probable Soviet targets in the United States, but these too have remained classified. In order to determine how an attack against the United States would have potentially appeared, the best source of material comes from the records of the Federal Civil Defense Administration.

In March 1962, a few months prior to the crisis, the Civil Defense Administration generated a simulated attack on the United States, which can serve as a good working model for a probable Soviet attack; it is titled Operation Sentinel. The weaknesses of this approach include the fact that there is no way to fully know what targets the USSR were planning on attacking, and that some statistical models had to be applied to the attack factoring in near misses, some targets being hit twice, and the effectiveness of the missile defense systems that the US employed at the time. Operation Sentinel, while providing a sound model for the impact of an attack, was not designed as a full military simulation, although the military had input to its results.

Keeping in mind that a nuclear war in 1962 would be bomber-based, any large airport that could potentially service strategic bombers would appear on the Sentinel target lists too. As such, the cities hit in the simulated attack were as follows:

Table 10-3: Operation Sentinel – US Nuclear Target List and Blast Radius'[23]

State	City	Targets (including probable miss distances)	Blast Radius
Maine			
	Caribou-Presque Isle	Loring AFB	4 miles
		Loring AFB (2 miles west)	4 miles
		Presque Isle AFB	4 miles
	Augusta	Dow AFB	4 miles
		Augusta	4 miles
	Brunswick	Brunswick NAS	3 miles
New Hampshire			
	Portsmouth	Portsmouth Navy Yard	3 miles
		Portsmouth Navy Yard (2 miles SSW)	3 miles
Vermont			
	Burlington	Burlington Municipal Airport	3 miles
		Burlington Municipal Airport (1 mile south-east)	3 miles
Massachusetts			
	Boston	Logan International Airport	5 miles
		Boston Common	5 miles
	Springfield-Holyoke	Westover AFB	4 miles
		Westover AFB (2 miles north)	4 miles
	Fall River	Fall River	4 miles
Rhode Island			
	Providence	Providence	5 miles
Connecticut			
	Hartford	Hartford	5 miles
	New Haven	New Haven	5 miles
	New London	Submarine Base	3 miles
		Submarine Base (4 miles west)	3 miles
New York			
	New York	Grand Central Area	5 miles

		Idlewind International Airport	5 miles
		Jersey City	5 miles
	Plattsburg	Plattsburg AFB	4 miles
		Plattsburg AFB (3 miles north)	4 miles
	Buffalo	Buffalo	4 miles
		Niagara Fall Airport	4 miles
	Rochester	Rochester	4 miles
	Syracuse	Syracuse	4 miles
	Utica	Griffiss AFB (2 miles west)	4 miles
	Newburgh	Stewart AFB	3 miles
		West Point	3 miles
	Riverhead	Suffolk County AFB	4 miles
		Suffolk County AFB (4 miles west-south-west)	4 miles
New Jersey			
	Atlantic City	Atlantic City NAS	3 miles
	Trenton	McGuire AFB	4 miles
		McGuire AFB (2 miles south-south-east)	4 miles
Pennsylvania			
	Erie	Erie	3 miles
		Erie (5 miles south)	3 miles
	Harrisburg	Harrisburg	3 miles
		Olmstead AFB	3 miles
	Reading	Reading (2 miles east)	3 miles
	Allentown	Allentown	3 miles
	Philadelphia	Philadelphia	5 miles
		Philadelphia International Airport	5 miles
		Trenton (4 miles west-north-west)	5 miles
Delaware			
	Wilmington	Wilmington	3 miles
Maryland			
	Baltimore	Harbor Area	5 miles
District of Columbia			

	Washington	Federal Triangle	5 miles
		Washington International Airport	5 miles
		Andrews AFB	5 miles
Virginia			
	Norfolk	Norfolk	5 miles
		Hampton (3 miles north)	5 miles
West Virginia			
	Wheeling	Wheeling	3 miles
Ohio			
	Cleveland	Cleveland	5 miles
	Akron	Akron	3 miles
	Youngstown	Youngstown Airport	3 miles
	Canton	Canton (3 miles south-east)	3 miles
	Columbus	Lockborne AFB	4 miles
		Lockbourne AFB (3 miles north-east)	4 miles
		Port Columbus Airport	4 miles
	Cincinnati	Cincinnati	5 miles
Kentucky			
	Lexington	Lexington	3 miles
	Hopkinsville	Campbell AFB	4 miles
	Louisville	Louisville	3 miles
		New Albany, IN	3 miles
North Carolina			
	Greensboro-Highpoint	Greensboro	3 miles
		Highpoint	3 miles
	Cherry Point	Cherry Point MCAS	4 miles
South Carolina			
	Columbia	Columbia (3 miles west-south-west)	3 miles
	Charleston	Charleston Harbor	5 miles
Georgia			
	Augusta	Augusta (4 miles north-east in S. Carolina)	4 miles

	Savannah	Hunter AFB	4 miles
	Atlanta	Atlanta	5 miles
		Dobbins AFB (1 mile north)	5 miles
	Macon	Robins AFB	4 miles
	Albany	Turner AFB	4 miles
	Albany	Turner AFT (6 miles east)	4 miles
	Columbus	Columbus	3 miles
		Fort Benning	3 miles
Florida			
	Jacksonville	Jacksonville NAS	4 miles
	Miami	Miami International Airport	4 miles
		Homestead AFB	4 miles
	Tampa	Tampa	4 miles
		MacDill AFB	4 miles
		MacDill AFB (2 miles south)	4 miles
Alabama			
	Mobile	Mobile	3 miles
		Brookley AFB	3 miles
Tennessee			
	Knoxville	Oak Ridge	3 miles
		Oak Ridge (3 miles east)	3 miles
	Chattanooga	Chattanooga	3 miles
		Chattanooga (3 miles south-east)	3 miles
	Memphis	Memphis	5 miles
		Memphis (3 miles south-east)	5 miles
Michigan			
	Oscoda	Wursmith AFB	3 miles
	Detroit	Detroit (north-east)	5 miles
		Detroit	5 miles
		Wayne Major Airport	5 miles
		Selfridge AFB	4 miles
		Selfridge AFB (3 miles north-west)	4 miles
	Flint	Flint	3 miles
	Lansing	Lansing (2 miles south-west)	3 miles

	Grant Rapids	Grand Rapids	3 miles
	Battle Creek	Kellogg Field	4 miles
Wisconsin			
	Madison	Truax Field	4 miles
	Milwaukee	Milwaukee	4 miles
		General Billy Mitchell Field	4 miles
Indiana			
	Indianapolis	Indianapolis	3 miles
		Indianapolis (1 mile north-east)	3 miles
Illinois			
	Chicago	Chicago (south)	5 miles
		O'Hare Field	5 miles
		Gary, Indiana	5 miles
	Rockford	Rockford (2 miles north)	3 miles
	Springfield	Springfield	3 miles
Missouri			
	St. Louis	St. Louis (south-west)	5 miles
		St. Louis	5 miles
		Scott AFB (Belleville IL)	5 miles
	Kansas City	Kansas City, MO	3 miles
		Kansas City, Kansas	3 miles
		Kansas City, Kansas (4 miles north)	3 miles
Arkansas			
	Little Rock	Little Rock AFB	4 miles
		Little Rock AFB	4 miles
Louisiana			
	New Orleans	New Orleans	5 miles
		New Orleans (1 mile north-west)	5 miles
		Moisant International Airport	3 miles
	Shreveport	Barksdale AFB	4 miles
		Shreveport	4 miles
	Lake Charles	Lake Charles AFB	4 miles
		Lake Charles AFB	4 miles
		Lake Charles AFB (20 miles north-north-east)	4 miles

Oklahoma			
	Tulsa	Tulsa	3 miles
	Oklahoma	Oklahoma City	3 miles
		Tinker AFB	3 miles
	Altus	Altus AFB	4 miles
		Altus AFB	4 miles
		Altus AFB (3 miles north-west)	4 miles
Texas			
	Lubbock	Reese AFB	3 miles
		Reese AFB (3 miles south-east)	3 miles
	El Paso	Biggs AFB	4 miles
		Biggs AFB (3 miles north-west)	4 miles
	Pecos	Pecos Airport	3 miles
	San Angelo	Goodfellow AFB	3 miles
		Goodfellow AFB (6 miles east)	3 miles
	Wichita Falls	Wichita Falls	3 miles
	Gainesville	Gainesville (8 miles west)	5 miles
	Ft. Worth	Carswell AFB	4 miles
		Carswell AFB (3 miles south-east)	4 miles
	Bryan	Bryan AFB	3 miles
	Houston	Houston	5 miles
		Houston (5 miles south)	5 miles
	Galveston	Galveston Harbor	5 miles
	Austin	Austin	3 miles
		Bergstrom AFB	3 miles
	San Antonio	San Antonio	5 miles
	Laredo	Laredo AFB	3 miles
		Laredo AFB (4 miles north)	3 miles
New Mexico			
	Mosquero	Mosquaro (10 miles east-north-east)	4 miles
	Los Alamos	Los Alamos	3 miles
	Albuquerque	Kirtland AFB	3 miles
		Albuquerque	3 miles

	Roswell	Walker AFB	4 miles
		Roswell (6 miles north)	4 miles
	Deming	Deming Airport	3 miles
Minnesota			
	Duluth	Duluth	4 miles
	Minneapolis	St. Paul	4 miles
		Minneapolis-St. Paul International Airport	4 miles
Iowa			
	Davenport	Davenport (4 miles west)	3 miles
		Rock Island, IL	3 miles
	Des Moines	Des Moines	3 miles
	Sioux City	Sioux City Airport	3 miles
		Sioux City (3 miles east)	3 miles
North Dakota			
	Minot	Minot	4 miles
	Bismarck	Bismarck	3 miles
South Dakota			
	Aberdeen	Aberdeen	3 miles
	Mason	Mason (12 miles east-north-east)	4 miles
	Rapid City	Ellsworth AFB	4 miles
		Ellsworth AFB	4 miles
	Sioux Falls	Foss Airport	3 miles
	Pierre	Pierre	3 miles
Nebraska			
	Omaha	Offutt AFB	4 miles
		Offutt AFT (4 miles north)	4 miles
	Lincoln	Lincoln	4 miles
		Lincoln AFB	4 miles
	Grand Island	Grand Island	3 miles
	Kearney	Kearney Airport	3 miles
		Kearney Airport (3 miles south-south-west)	3 miles
	McCook	McCook Airport	3 miles
Kansas			

	Salina	Smoky Hill AFB	4 miles
		Smoky Hill AFB	4 miles
		Smoky Hill AFB (2 miles south-east)	4 miles
Wyoming			
	Rock Spring	Rock Springs	3 miles
	Cheyenne	Cheyenne Airport	3 miles
Colorado			
	Denver	Buckley NAS	4 miles
		Denver	4 miles
		Stapleton International Airport	4 miles
	Colorado Spring	Ent AFB	4 miles
		Ent AFB (1 mile west)	4 miles
	Pueblo	Pueblo Memorial Airport	3 miles
Arizona			
	Phoenix	Phoenix Sky Harbor	4 miles
		Williams AFB (2 miles west)	4 miles
	Tucson	Davis-Monthan AFB	3 miles
		Davis-Monthan AFB	3 miles
Utah			
	Ogden	Hill AFB	3 miles
	Salt Lake City	Salt Lake City	3 miles
		Salt Lake City (8 miles east)	3 miles
Idaho			
	Mountain Home	Mountain Home AFB	4 miles
		Mountain Home AFB	4 miles
Montana			
	Great Falls	Malmstrom AFB	4 miles
		Malmstrom AFB	4 miles
		Great Falls Airport	4 miles
	Billings	Billings Airport	3 miles
		Billings Airport (4 miles south-east)	3 miles

Nevada			
	Fallon	Fallon NAS	3 miles
Washington			
	Addy	Addy	4 miles
	Spokane	Spokane (1 mile west)	4 miles
		Fairchild AFB	4 miles
	Richland	Richland (8 miles north-north-west)	3 miles
	Everett	Paine AFB	3 miles
		Paine AFB (3 miles north)	3 miles
	Bremerton	Bremerton Navy Yard	4 miles
	Seattle	Seattle	5 miles
		Boeing Field	5 miles
	Olympia	Olympia	3 miles
Oregon			
	Portland	Portland	5 miles
		Portland International Airport	4 miles
California			
	San Francisco	San Francisco	5 miles
		Oakland	5 miles
		Alameda NAS	4 miles
		San Francisco International Airport	4 miles
	Sacramento	McClellan AFB	3 miles
		Sacramento (10 miles south-south-east)	3 miles
	Stockton	Sharpe General Depot	3 miles
	Merced	Castle AFB	4 miles
	Los Angeles	Los Angeles	5 miles
		San Pedro	5 miles
		Burbank	4 miles
		March AFB (Riverside)	4 miles
		March AFB (2 miles west)	4 miles
		Long Beach	3 miles
		El Toro MCAS (Santa Ana)	3 miles
	San Diego	San Diego Naval Base	4 miles

		Brown Field NAS (Chula Vista)	4 miles
		Camp Pendleton	3 miles
		Camp Pendleton (6 miles east)	3 miles

According to Operation Sentinel's projections, the losses to the United States in a 1962 nuclear war with the USSR would be reflected as follows:

Table 10-4: US Estimated Losses in Nuclear War – Operation Sentinel (in millions)[24]

Day	Dead	Dead from Fallout	Total Dead	Total Surviving Casualties
1	40.8		40.8	64.6
7	10.2	6.8	17	47.6
14	4.5	7.4	11.9	35.7
60	4.8	7.1	11.9	23.8
Total:	60.3	21.3	81.6	23.8

Note: This model is based on the population of 170,000,000

Total killed and injured:	105.4
Surviving population:	64.6
Surviving casualties from the initial attack at day 60:	7.9
Surviving casualties from fallout at day 60:	15.9

In the event of a nuclear war with the USSR, one of the biggest losers would be the countries of Europe. With both NATO and Warsaw Pact nations brimming with tactical nuclear weapons, both sides would unleash these more numerous tactical nuclear weapons on their nearby neighbors. While SIOP-62 looked at a US versus USSR conflict, it did not factor in damage inflicted as a result of a full NATO nation response and retaliation.

Ultimately, there would be no winners in the event of a full nuclear exchange. Both of the superpowers would have been crippled to the point where they may never have fully recovered. Europe would have been left ablaze. Attempting to contemplate how the world would have appeared after such a catastrophic war is best left to fiction writers and counterfactual historians. One thing is certain: stepping back from the brink was the right choice, not just for the US and USSR, but for the world as a whole.

Epilogue

Once the United States is in Cuba, who will drive it out?

Cuban revolutionary José Martí[1]

Operation Scabbards was a plan that was thankfully never executed. Many young men going into Cuba from the US and USSR never would have returned from the air strikes and invasion. Even more Soviets and Cubans would have perished as well.

I interviewed a number of men who were part of the planned invasion force. All felt that the invasion was going to be a walk in the park for the US. The reality is that the United States would have been badly bloodied in such an operation. Matters would have been even worse if tactical nuclear weapons were deployed.

In the 'real world,' a diplomatic solution was arrived at. The US used the first week of November to undertake a number of military maneuvers using the forces they had already mustered for the invasion. The 1st Armored Division stormed a beach, but instead of Tarará, it was the sands of Fort Lauderdale. The 101st Airborne Division executed a massive air drop, not to secure airfields in Cuba, but training fields at several military bases in the south. The marines too stormed the beaches of Florida. It provided a glimpse of the battle-that-never-was while demonstrating to the world the forces that had been assembled that *could* have taken down the Castro Government.

One overriding concern voiced during the crisis was that if we had gone into Cuba, it would have limited our capability to go anywhere else in the world. This fear was well founded. The two US airborne divisions would have been badly mauled, especially the 82nd Airborne Division. The marines as well would have suffered more losses than projected. These losses would not be quickly made up.

Worse yet, the Cubans and Soviets both had plans to fight on after the battle for Cuba was lost, waging a guerilla war. The US occupation of Cuba was not a one or three month effort; it was destined to drag on potentially for years with a long string of mounting casualties. With no plans to win over the 'hearts and minds' of the civilian population, the American invaders would be playing out a scenario similar to what it faced in South East Asia only years earlier.

The impact of such a prolonged war would impact our influence in the hemisphere. While the OAS supported US intervention in Cuba, the images of US soldiers occupying a sister nation for years smacks of Yankee Imperialism, and over time, would have raised the ire of other central and South American countries.

The impact of Cuba influenced how the US undertook matters in Vietnam. The US took a hesitant role in committing forces after the Cuban Missile Crisis. But would Vietnam have even happened if Operation Scabbards had been undertaken? Many of the key units that would have been slated to go to Vietnam were the same ones that would have been involved with the Cuban invasion. With the US facing a possibly prolonged guerilla war in Cuba, it may not have had the manpower to intervene in Vietnam. Even more importantly, would the American people have endorsed *another* bloody jungle war to liberate people that did not desire us to be there? While it is difficult to say, if the lessons of Vietnam can be used, it is possible to see that Vietnam would not have happened for the US, at least not in the manner that occurred. As such, the invasion of Cuba would have altered the face of the Cold War.

How hard is it to think of the Vietnam Memorial Wall in Washington DC as being the Cuban War Memorial? It could have very well been dedicated to the men and women that died in a very different jungle in a struggle against Communism, only one much closer to home. Americans might never have mentioned the Siege of Kae Sanh; instead, they may have talked about the Siege of Guantánamo Bay.

Operations Scabbards and Rock Pile are fascinating studies in a war that never happened. They are one of the very rare instances where a conceptual contingency plan was almost put into use. It revealed the best of the American military, and exposed flaws that were important to change and correct.

While we are all thankful that it never occurred, especially the families of those that would have become casualties, one cannot help but wonder at the speed and complexity of mobilizing such a military force in such a short period of time.

Let us hope we never have to explore such options ever again.

Appendices

Appendix One
Chronological List of Photographic Missions Over Cuba[1]

Date	Missions Flown	Joint Evaluation	Significant Conclusions
14 October 1962	U2 3101		San Cristobal, MRBM Sites one, two, and three identified. In retrospect, deployment activity in this area was negated by photo coverage of 29 August 1962
15 October 1962	U2 3102, 3103		San Cristobal MRBM Sites one, two and three are covered again and Guanajay IRBM Sites one and two identified
16 October 1962	None	GMAIC Evaluation forwarded to the White House at 1830 hours. Based on evaluation of photo missions of 14 and 15 October	Same as above
17 October 1962	U2 3104, 3105, 3106, 3107, 3108, 3109		Same as above

18 October 1962	U2 3110, 3111	GMAIC, JAEIC (Joint Atomic Energy Intelligence Committee), NPIC 2100 hours, based on evaluation of photo missions of 14 and 15 October plus very preliminary assessment of photo missions of 17 October	All previous identified sites covered. In addition Sagua La Grande MRBM Sites one and two identified for the first time. No missile deployment activity noted in Sagua La Grande Area on 5 September 1962
19 October 1962	U2 3112, 3113, 3114	GMAIC JAEIC, NPIC 2100 hours, based on evaluation of photo missions of 14, 15, and 17 October	Probable nuclear storage bunker identified for the first time. All previously identified MRBM and IRBM site observed under construction
20 October 1962	U2 3115, 3116, 3117	GMAIC, JAEIC, NPIC, 2200 hours	Continued construction activity was evident at all sites. San Cristobal Site Four identified for the first time. Three MRBM sites had reached an emergency operational capability and two MRBM sites had achieved a full operational capability
21 October 1962	None	GMAIC, JAEIC, NPIC, 2200 hours, Based on evaluation of all photographic missions 14 October through 19 October	Remedios RIBM Site observed on 18 October photography under construction. Construction activities at the six MRBM sites. Three had an emergency operational capability; two a full operational capability, and one was still developing

22 October 1962	U2 3118, 3119, 3120	GMAIC, JAEIC, NPIC, 2200 hours, Based on evaluation of all photographic missions 14 October through 20 October	No significant change
23 October 1962	U2 3121, 3122, 3123 Low-level missions (Code Named: Blue Moon) 5002-5006	GMAIC, JAEIC, NPIC, 0100 hours 24 October. Based on evaluation of all U2 photographic missions 14 October through 22 October, plus preliminary analysis of Blue Moon mission 5002	Four MRBM sites had emergency capability; two achieved full operational capability
24 October 1962	None	GMAIC, JAEIC, NPIC, 0200 hours, Based on evaluation of all U2 photographic missions 14 October through 22 October, plus low level Blue Moon Missions 5002-5006	Increase use of camouflage
25 October 1962	U2 3125, Low-level missions 5007-5016	GMAIC, JAEIC, NPIC, 0200 hours, 26 October. Based on all U2 missions through 25 October and preliminary analysis of all low level missions	No significant changes relative to capability. Construction continuing
26 October 1962	Low-level missions 2622, 2623, and 2624	GMAIC, JAEIC, NPIC, 0200 hours, 27 October. Based on all U2 and low level missions through 25 October and preliminary analysis of low level missions of 26 October	Five of six MRBM sites achieved full operational capability. Construction continuing at a rapid pace

27 October 1962	U2 Mission 3126 (shot down) Low-level missions 5013-5017	GMAIC, JAEIC, NPIC, 0200 hours, 28 October. Based on all U2 and low level missions through 26 October and preliminary analysis of photography of low-level missions on 27 October	All six MRBM sites (24 launchers) fully operational. Construction continuing at a rapid pace. AA weapon being deployed and camouflage used extensively
28 October 1962	None	GMAIC, JAEIC, NPIC, 2200 hours. Based on low-level photography of 27 October	No significant changes
29 October 1962	Low-level missions 5031, 5032, and 29211	GMAIC, JAEIC, NPIC, 0900 Hour 30 October. Based on preliminary analysis of low-level photography of 29 October	Clear evidence of continued construction and no indication of dismantling or vacating any of the MRBM or IRBM sites
30 October 1962	None	GMAIC, JAEIC, NPIC, 2200 hours, 30 October. Based on complete analysis of low-level photography of 29 October	Same as above. The extensive use of natural concealment and camouflage was evident
31 October 1962	None	GMAIC, JAEIC, NPIC	No significant changes

Appendix Two
An Enduring Myth of the Missile Crisis: Special Forces

When working on this book, I was coached by an army historian regarding individuals who claim they were in the special forces (Green Beret, Rangers, Navy SEALs) during the missile crisis. 'I get several requests a year to validate that someone's father or grandfather was dropped into Cuba prior to the invasion to perform some sort of secret mission. Many are looking to claim to the VA they were in a combat situation.' As it turns out, he is right; I did get such a contact. I also spoke with fellow author and MWSA member Dwight Zimmerman, who has written articles on the history of the SEALs, and he told me quite a bit about the culture and personalities of the men at that time.

In working on this book, I found references in a magazine article, a book, and on the web, of Navy SEALS from SEAL Team One going into Cuba at the start of the missile crisis. The claim was that the submarine USS *Sea Lion* deposited the team in Cuba and their photographs of the missile sites were instrumental in the US policy making, and even appeared in *Time* magazine. As a military historian, this was something that appealed to me, since it would mean we had US combat troops in Cuba ahead of the invasion.

With all due respect to the authors and men making these claims, however, the evidence does not hold water.

A check of the SEAL mission chronology at the time shows that that SEAL Team One was in Europe, Norway, and Greece, conducting joint exercises.[1] The USS *Sea Lion* was one of the two submarines specially outfitted to take underwater demolition teams (UDTs) and SEALs to their mission sites. In this case, the records for this sub show that it was on patrol between St Thomas, Miami, and the Florida Keys at the time.[2] While it was in the vicinity of Cuba, there is no record whatsoever that the sub undertook a mission to deposit SEALs off the coast of the island.

Furthermore, the claims that there were photographs in *Time* magazine holds no water. The images *Time* used were from the U2, and in one case, a Blue Moon flight. All were aerial photographs; none were taken by a ground-based team. Navy SEAL Team Two was on its way to Vietnam during the period in question, at least according to the documentation.

The *Sea Lion* and Navy SEAL Team One *did* take part in an exercise off of Puerto Rico in April 1962, where the team went ashore, cleared obstacles for a landing, and tested communication gear with the shore. This took place as part of a broader amphibious landing exercise and was months before the crisis emerged.[3] In fairness, a half-century has passed, and it is possible that someone confused the dates and locations, mistaking the landings in Puerto Rico with a raid on Cuba.

There are pundits that will say the records are deliberately concealing the mission given its sensitive nature. That is a possibility, but it is remote. It would have been more prudent to simply omit the records. It is also possible that the men making this claim were convinced that this was in reality a UDT exercise. That may be the case, but there was no plan to put UDT forces in Cuba until just prior to the invasion landings.

In terms of the Army Special Forces, many of their records from the time of the invasion, in many cases, are still classified. The 3rd Army summary of the events (published in 1963) confirms what other documents state, that there was *no* plan to deposit Special Forces until the start of the Rock Pile air campaign.

Ultimately, there is no tangible documented evidence that any American military units were actually on the island of Cuba during the crisis. That does not mean that such evidence will not surface in the coming years; it simply means that there is nothing now to substantiate any such claims.

Endnotes

Foreword

1. Flaherty, '...How the Invasion Would Have Been Made'. *Life* (7 December 1962) p. 38
2. 'Notes taken from the Joint Chiefs of Staff, October-November 1962,' Entries for 7 and 12 November. National Security Archives
3. Records Group 127, Records of the US Marine Corps, Entry A1 1009. US National Archives

Chapter One

1. Perry. 'Latin America, 1999-1849'. *The New Cambridge Modern History,* Chapter VIII (Cambridge UK: New Cambridge, 1960)
2. 'Mikoyen Winds Up His 9-Day Visit To Cuba,' *The St Petersburg Times* (13 February 1960) p. 2
3. Joint Chiefs of Staff. 'Unified Action Armed Forces'. *JCS Pub.* 2 (November 1959) p. 39
4. Dennison Admiral Robert L. and Harry S. Truman. Biographical Sketch, Harry S. Truman Library and Museum. http://www.trumanlibrary.org/hstpaper/dennisonhst.htm#bio
5. 'Admiral With 2 Hats'. *New York Times* (23 October 1962) p. 20
6. Kugler. *The Army's Role in the Cuban Crisis: 1962.* US Army Center of Military History. pp. III-4
7. Loomis. *US Army Command the Control In the Cuban Missile Crisis: Comments on Organization, Information Flows, and Relationships.* Stanford Research Institute, HMC-2 No. 115. US Army Center of Military History (June 1963) p. 10
8. Loomis. *US Army Command and Control In the Cuban Missile Crisis: Comments on Organization, Information Flows, and Relationships.* Stanford Research Institute, HMC-2 No. 115. US Army Center of Military History (June 1963) p. 11
9. Kugler. *The Army's Role.* pp. III-5
10. Kugler. *The Army's Role.* pp. III-6
11. Kugler. *The Army's Role.* p. III-7. Taken from 'The Role of the XCIII Airborne Corps in the Cuban Crisis'. HQ XVIII Airborne Corps. pp. III-3
12. Kugler. *The Army's Role.* p. III-8. Taken from 'US Policy Toward Cuba and Related Events: 1903 to May 1961'. prepared by the OCHM
13. Kugler. *The Army's Role.* pp. III-10. Taken from 'The Role of the XCIII Airborne Corps in the Cuban Crisis'. HQ XVIII Airborne Corps. pp. II:1-12
14. Foreign Relations of the United States, 1958-1960, Cuba, Vol. VI. p. 850
15. '75 Die In Havana As Munitions Ship Explodes At Dock: Government Said to Suspect Sabotages – Castro Paper Hints at US Role'. *The New York Times* (Retrieved 21 July 2012)
16. 'The Bay of Pigs: 40 Years After Chronology'. National Security Archive http://www.gwu.edu/~nsarchiv/bayofpigs/chron.html
17. 'The Bay of Pigs: 40 Years After Chronology'. National Security Archive http://www.gwu.edu/~nsarchiv/bayofpigs/chron.html
18. Fursenko Naftali. *One Hell of a Gamble* (New York: W.W. Norton & Company, 1997) p. 92
19. Joint Chiefs of Staff and Chairman L. L. Lemnitzer. Memorandum for the Secretary of Defense, Military Evaluation of the CIA Paramilitary Plan: Cuba. National Security Archive (2 March 1961)
20. 'The Bay of Pigs: 40 Years After Chronology'. National Security Archive http://www.gwu.edu/~nsarchiv/bayofpigs/chron.html
21. 'The Bay of Pigs: 40 Years After Chronology'. National Security Archive http://www.gwu.edu/~nsarchiv/bayofpigs/chron.html
22. Telegram to Admiral Dennison. Naval Historical Center (12.06 p.m. 19 April 1961)

23. Chang and Korblub. *The Cuban Missile Crisis: 1962* (New York: The New Press, 1992). Letter from W. W. Rostow. 'Notes on Cuba Policy' (24 April 1961) pp. 16-17
24. Chang and Korblub. *The Cuban Missile Crisis: 1962* (New York: The New Press, 1992). Letter from W. W. Rostow. 'Notes on Cuba Policy' (24 April 1961) pp. 32-38
25. 'The Bay of Pigs: 40 Years After Chronology'. National Security Archive http://www.gwu. edu/~nsarchiv/bayofpigs/chron.html
26. 'The Bay of Pigs: 40 Years After Chronology'. National Security Action Memorandum 181, on Actions and Studies in Response to New Soviet Bloc Activity in Cuba (23 August 1962) Recollection of Intelligence Prior to the Discovery of Soviet Missiles and of Penkovsky Affair, n.d. Chronology of John McCone's Suspicions on the Military Build-up in Cuba Prior to Kennedy's 22 October Speech. National Security Archive (11 November 1962) http://www.gwu.edu/~nsarchiv/ bayofpigs/chron.html
27. Loomis. *US Army Command and Control.* p.10
28. Kugler. *The Army's Role.* pp. III-10-12.
29. Loomis. *US Army Command and Control.* p.11
30. Operational Narrative, Cuban Emergency, United States 3rd Army, 26 June 1963, Appendix 6 (Quartermaster) to Annex C (Logistics) US Army Center of Military History. p. 2
31. Kugler. *The Army's Role.* p. III-12

Chapter Two

1. Blight and Welch. *On the Brink, Americans and Soviets Re-examine The Cuban Missile Crisis.* (New York: Hill and Wang, 1989) p. 294
2. 'Eisenhower on the Russians'. *Corpus Christi Times* (12 December 1961) p. 14
3. Young. *When the Russians Blinked: The US Marine Response to the Cuban Missile Crisis.* History and Museums Divisions, Headquarters, US Marine Corps, Washington DC (1990) Appendix IV: Guantanamo Estimates of Cuban Forces, OP-PLAN 316-62, and Investigation of the Preparedness Program, Interim Report on the Cuban Military Build-up by the Preparedness Investigating Subcommittee, Committee on Armed Services, U.S. Senate, 88th Congress, 1st Session, Washington DC (1963) pp. 4-5. Note: These figures vary in different accounts, especially the tank numbers
4. Freedman. *Kennedy's Wars: Berlin, Cuba, Laos, and Vietnam* (New York: Oxford University Press, 2000) p. 128
5. Young. *When the Russians Blinked.* pp. J-III-1
6. 'RLT_Blue Beach, Operation Plan 314-62 (Modified 316-62)'. Records Group 127, Records of the US Marine Corps, National Archives, Washington DC. pp. B-1-5
7. Young. *When the Russians Blinked: The US Marine Response to the Cuban Missile Crisis,* History and Museums Divisions, Headquarters, US Marine Corps, Washington DC (1990) Appendix IV: From Commander Guantanamo Sector, Caribbean Sea Frontier. Appendix III: Enemy Ground Forces. pp. J-III-1
8 'RLT_Blue Beach, Operation Plan 314-62 (Modified 316-62)'. Records Group 127, Records of the US Marine Corps, National Archives, Washington DC. pp. B-1-5
9. 'RLT_Blue Beach, Operation Plan 314-62 (Modified 316-62)'. Records Group 127, Records of the US Marine Corps, National Archives, Washington DC. pp. B-1-5
10. Young, *When the Russians Blinked.* pp. J-III-1
11. 'RLT_Blue Beach, Operation Plan 314-62 (Modified 316-62)'. Records Group 127, Records of the US Marine Corps, National Archives, Washington DC. pp. B-1-8
12. 'RLT_Blue Beach, Operation Plan 314-62 (Modified 316-62)'. Records Group 127, Records of the US Marine Corps Washington DC: National Archives pp. B-1-6
13 'RLT_Blue Beach, Operation Plan 314-62 (Modified 316-62)'. Records Group 127, Records of the US Marine Corps, National Archives, Washington DC. pp. B-1-9
14. Young. *When the Russians Blinked.* pp. J-II-1, J-II-2
15. Young. *When the Russians Blinked.* pp. J-II-1, J-II-2
16. Young. *When the Russians Blinked.* pp. J-II-3
17. Young. *When the Russians Blinked.* pp. J-II-3
18. 'RLT_Blue Beach, Operation Plan 314-62 (Modified 316-62)'. Records Group 127, Records of the US Marine Corps, National Archives, Washington DC. pp. B-1-7
19. Young. *When the Russians Blinked.* pp. J-II-1-J-II-2
20. Young. *When the Russians Blinked.* pp. J-I-2 J-I-5
21. 'RLT_Blue Beach, Operation Plan 314-62 (Modified 316-62)'. Records Group 127, Records of the US Marine Corps, National Archives, Washington DC. pp. B-1-7
22. Khruschchev. *Kruschchev Remembers,* (New York: Little Brown Publishing, 1971) p. 493
23. Gribkov and Smith. *Operation ANADYR* (Chicago: Edition q., Inc 1994) p. 13
24. Gribkov and Smith. *Operation ANADYR* (Chicago: Edition q., Inc 1994) p. 27

25. Kugler. *The Army's Role.* pp. II-14
26 'New Evidence on the Cuban Missile Crisis: Khrushchev, Nuclear Weapons, and the Cuban Missile Crisis'. *Cold War International History Project.* Bulletin 11 (Winter 1998) p. 258
27. 'New Evidence on the Cuban Missile Crisis: Khrushchev, Nuclear Weapons, and the Cuban Missile Crisis'. *Cold War International History Project.* Bulletin 11 (Winter 1998) p. 255
28. Volkogonov Papers, Library of Congress, reprinted in *Cold War International History Project.* Bulletin 11. Trans. by Raymond Garthoff. The Wilson Center (20 July 1962) Cold War International History Project
29. Khrushchev. *Nikita Khrushchev and the Creation of a Superpower* (Pennsylvania: Pennsylvania State University Press, 2000) p. 512
30. 'New Evidence on the Cuban Missile Crisis: Khrushchev, Nuclear Weapons, and the Cuban Missile Crisis'. *Cold War International History Project.* Bulletin 11. (Winter 1998) pp. 251-253
31. Gribkov and Smith. *Operation ANADYR* (Chicago: Edition q., Inc. 1994) p. 25
32. 'New Evidence on the Cuban Missile Crisis: Khrushchev, Nuclear Weapons, and the Cuban Missile Crisis'. *Cold War International History Project.* Bulletin 11 (Winter 1998) p. 259
33. Gribkov and Smith. *Operation ANADYR* (Chicago: Edition q., Inc., 1994) p. 28
34. 'New Evidence on the Cuban Missile Crisis: Khrushchev, Nuclear Weapons, and the Cuban Missile Crisis'. *Cold War International History Project.* Bulletin 11 (Winter 1998) pp. 259-260. From the General Staff archives now in the Volkogonov papers, Reel 6 (Library of Congress, Manuscript Division) translated for this article
35. Gribkov and Smith. *Operation ANADYR* (Chicago: Edition q., Inc., 1994) p. 40
36. Gribkov and Smith. *Operation ANADYR* (Chicago: Edition q., Inc., 1994) p. 40
37. Polmar and Gresham. *Defcon-2, Standing on the Brink of Nuclear War During the Cuban Missile Crisis* (New York: John Wiley & Sons, Inc., 2006) pp. 311-312
38. Gribkov and Smith. *Operation ANADYR* (Chicago: Edition q., Inc., 1994) pp. 59-62. And 'Night Session Of The Presidium Of The Central Committee, 22-23 October 1962'. Alexander Fursenko. Trans. by Yuri M. Zhukov in *Naval War College Review.* Vol. 59. No. 3 (Summer 2006) p.135

Chapter Three

1. Young. *When the Russians Blinked.* pp. 212-122
2. 'RLT_Blue Beach, Operation Plan 314-62 (Modified 316-62)'. Records Group 127, Records of the US Marine Corps, National Archives, Washington DC. pp. B-1-2
3. 'The Invasion of Cuba'. *MHQ.* Vol. 4, No. 2. (Winter 1992) p. 93. And 'RLT_Blue Beach, Operation Plan 314-62 (Modified 316-62)'. Records Group 127, Records of the US Marine Corps, National Archives, Washington DC. pp. B-1-3
4. 'RLT_Blue Beach, Operation Plan 314-62 (Modified 316-62)'. Records Group 127, Records of the US Marine Corps, National Archives, Washington DC. pp. B-1-1
5. 'RLT_Blue Beach, Operation Plan 314-62 (Modified 316-62)'. Records Group 127, Records of the US Marine Corps, National Archives, Washington DC. pp. B-1-1
6. 'RLT_Blue Beach, Operation Plan 314-62 (Modified 316-62)'. Records Group 127, Records of the US Marine Corps, National Archives, Washington DC. pp. B-1-1
7. 'RLT_Blue Beach, Operation Plan 314-62 (Modified 316-62)'. Records Group 127, Records of the US Marine Corps, National Archives, Washington DC. pp. B-1-2
8. 'RLT_Blue Beach, Operation Plan 314-62 (Modified 316-62)'. Records Group 127, Records of the US Marine Corps, National Archives, Washington DC. pp. B-1-2
9. Varner. *The History of Guantanamo Bay 1964.* US Naval Base, Guantanamo Bay, Cuba, 1964 (USN) p. 87
10. Varner. *The History of Guantanamo Bay 1964.* US Naval Base, Guantanamo Bay, Cuba, 1964 (USN) p. 87
11. Varner. *The History of Guantanamo Bay 1964.* US Naval Base, Guantanamo Bay, Cuba, 1964 (USN) p. 88
12. 'RLT_Blue Beach, Operation Plan 314-62 (Modified 316-62)'. Records Group 127, Records of the US Marine Corps, National Archives, Washington DC. pp. B-1-2
13. 'RLT_Blue Beach, Operation Plan 314-62 (Modified 316-62)'. Records Group 127, Records of the US Marine Corps, National Archives, Washington DC. pp. B-1-2
14. Varner. *The History of Guantanamo.* pp. 2-6
15. 'A US Base in Trouble 500 Miles From Home'. *US News and World Report* (11 April 1960) p. 83
16. 'Traffic into Base Halted'. *New York Times* (13 May 1961) p. 5
17. Young. *When the Russians Blinked.* p. 120
18. Young. *When the Russians Blinked.* pp. 121-122
19. Young. *When the Russians Blinked.* pp. 122-123
20. Young. *When the Russians Blinked.* pp. 160-161
21. Young. *When the Russians Blinked.* pp. 160-162

22. 'CINCLANT Historical Account of the Cuban Crisis: 1963 (U)'. National Security Archive. pp. 55-56
23. 'CINCLANT Historical Account of the Cuban Crisis: 1963 (U)'. National Security Archive. p. 5
24. Varner. *The History of Guantanamo.* p. 60

Chapter Four

1. Polmar and Gresham. *Defcon-2,* p. 82. Taken from Statement by Soviet Union that a US Attack on Cuba Would Mean Nuclear War. National Security Archive (11 September 1962)
2. McNamara, Robert S. Statement before a Subcommittee of the Committee on Appropriations, House of Representatives, 88th Congress, 1st Session, on Department Defense Appropriations for 1964. Part I. pp. 2-3
3. 'CINCLANT Historical Account of the Cuban Crisis: 1963 (U)'. National Security Archive. pp. 6-7
4. 'CINCLANT Historical Account of the Cuban Crisis: 1963 (U)'. National Security Archive. p. 10
5. Brugioni. *Eyeball to Eyeball, The Inside Story of the Cuban Missile Crisis* (New York: Random House, 1990) p. 17.9
6. 'A Highly Compressed Narrative Account and Assessment of "The Tactical Air Command and the Cuban Crisis"'. Air Force Historical Research Agency, K417.042-21 (1 December 1962) p. 2
7. Kugler. *The Army's Role.* pp. III-1-III-5. And 'CINCLANT Historical Account of the Cuban Crisis: 1963 (U)'. National Security Archive p. 101. There are discrepancies between these two published versions. The author has attempted to reconcile these differences. OP Plan 312-62 remains classified, so it is necessary to reconstruct it from a wide range of other sources.
8. 'CINCLANT Historical Account of the Cuban Crisis: 1963 (U)'. National Security Archive. p. 41-42
9. Nathan. *The Cuban Missile Crisis Revisited* (New York: St Martin's Press, 1992). And Hershberg. 'Before the Missiles of October Did Kennedy a Military Strike Against Cuba?'. p. 250
10. 'CINCLANT Historical Account of the Cuban Crisis: 1963 (U)'. National Security Archive. pp. 2-3
11. 'CINCLANT Historical Account of the Cuban Crisis: 1963 (U)'. National Security Archive. p. 40
12. 'CINCLANT Historical Account of the Cuban Crisis: 1963 (U)'. National Security Archive. p. 40-41
13. Brugioni. *Eyeball to Eyeball.* p. 181
14. Brugioni. *Eyeball to Eyeball.* p. 196
15. Brugioni. *Eyeball to Eyeball.* p. 200
16. Brugioni. *Eyeball to Eyeball.* p. 214
17. Kugler. *The Army's Role.* pp. II-24-II-25
18. Abel. *The Missile Crisis* (Philadelphia: Lippincott, 1966) pp. 44-45
19. Chang and Kornbluh. *The Cuban Missile Crisis.* p. 359
20. 'Transcript of the second Executive Committee meeting, 16 October 1962 6.30—7.55 p.m.' US National Archives, JFK Library via the National Security Archive
21. 'Transcript of the second Executive Committee meeting, 16 October 1962 6.30—7.55 p.m.' US National Archives, JFK Library via the National Security Archive
22. 'Transcript of the second Executive Committee meeting, 16 October 1962 6.30—7.55 p.m.' US National Archives, JFK Library via the National Security Archive
23. 'Transcript of the second Executive Committee meeting, 16 October 1962 6.30—7.55 p.m.' US National Archives, JFK Library via the National Security Archive
24. 'Transcript of the second Executive Committee meeting, 16 October 1962 6.30—7.55 p.m.' US National Archives, JFK Library via the National Security Archive
25. Kennedy. *Thirteen Days* (New York: W. W. Norton & Company, 1969) p. 31
26. 'CINCLANT Historical Account of the Cuban Crisis: 1963 (U)'. National Security Archive. p. 3
27. Chang and Kornbluh. *The Cuban Missile Crisis.* p. 361
28. Chang and Kornbluh. 'Document 17, Theodore Sorensen, Summary of Agreed Facts and Premises, Possible Course of Action and Unanswered Questions, October 17, 1962'. *The Cuban Missile Crisis.* p. 114
29. Chang and Kornbluh. 'Document 17, Theodore Sorensen, Summary of Agreed Facts and Premises, Possible Course of Action and Unanswered Questions, October 17, 1962'. *The Cuban Missile Crisis.* pp. 114-115
30. 'CINCLANT Historical Account of the Cuban Crisis: 1963 (U)'. National Security Archive. p. 11

Chapter Five

1. Zelikow and May. *The Presidential Recordings of John F. Kennedy: The Great Crisis.* Vol. III (New York: W. W. Norton & Company, 2001) p. 409
2. Kugler. *The Army's Role.* pp. II-5

3. Kugler. *The Army's Role*, pp. III-15. And 'History of the Tactical Air Command, July–December 1962'. Narrative Vol. II. Chapter IV. The Tactical Air Command and the Cuban Crisis. p. 678
4. 'CINCLANT Historical Account of the Cuban Crisis: 1963 (U)'. National Security Archive. pp. 41-44
5. 'CINCLANT Historical Account of the Cuban Crisis: 1963 (U)'. National Security Archive. p. 44
6. Kugler. *The Army's Role*. pp. III-20
7. Kugler. *The Army's Role*. pp. III-20-III-21
8. Kugler. *The Army's Role*. pp. III-22
9. Message from Joint Chiefs of Staff to CINCLANT, 261624Z Oct 1962. Records Group 218, US National Archives
10. 'The Air Force Response to the Cuban Crisis'. US Air Force Historical Division Liaison Office. p. 8
11. 'The Air Force Response to the Cuban Crisis'. US Air Force Historical Division Liaison Office, p. 8. And 'A Highly Compressed Narrative Account and Assessment of The Tactical Air Command and The Cuban Crisis'. US Air Force Historical Division Liaison Office. p. 14
12. '2nd Marines, OP Plan 316-62: Blue Beach'. Records Group 127, Records of the US Marine Corps, National Archives, Washington DC. p. 3
13. 'RLT_Blue Beach, Operation Plan 314-62 (Modified 316-62)'. Records Group 127, Records of the US Marine Corps, National Archives, Washington DC. p. 5
14. Kugler. *The Army's Role*. pp. III-29. Note: This was compiled from the working papers of Lt. Colonel G. K. Anderson, Western Hemisphere Division, ODCSOPS
15. Kugler. *The Army's Role*, pp. III-30
16. House, Major Jonathan M. *The United States Army in Joint Operations, 1950-1983* (US Army: 1984) US Army Center for Military History. p. 80
17. Author's Note: I have located some indication that in an earlier rendition of OP Plan 316-62 that the 101st was slated to execute an airborne assault on the Naval Air Station at Mariel. This seems to have been scrubbed in the final rendition of the plans, most likely due to the fact that adequate landing zones were not located close enough to Mariel
18. Kugler. *The Army's Role*. pp. III-26
19. 'RLT_Blue Beach, Operation Plan 314-62 (Modified 316-62)'. Records Group 127, Records of the US Marine Corps, National Archives, Washington DC. p. 1
20. 'CINCLANT Historical Account of the Cuban Crisis: 1963 (U)'. National Security Archive. pp. 65-66. Note: Additional details such as D-Day assignments have been gleaned from a number of different sources
21. 'CINCLANT Historical Account of the Cuban Crisis: 1963 (U)'. National Security Archive. pp. 64-66
22. US Navy and Marine Corps Squadron Designations and Abbreviations, US Navy Web Site http://www.history.navy.mil/download/history/app16.pdf
23. 'RLT_Blue Beach, Operation Plan 314-62 (Modified 316-62)'. Records Group 127, Records of the US Marine Corps, National Archives, Washington DC. pp. 4-6
24. '5th Marine Expeditionary Brigade Embarkation Plan 316-62'. Records Group 127, Records of the US Marine Corps, National Archives, Washington DC. pp. 1-2
25. '5th Marine Expeditionary Brigade Embarkation Plan 316-62'. Records Group 127, Records of the US Marine Corps, National Archives, Washington DC. Map and debarkation plans for Guantanamo reinforcement. P.A-1-A-3 and accompanying overlay map
26. '5th Marine Expeditionary Brigade Embarkation Plan 316-62'. Records Group 127, Records of the US Marine Corps, National Archives, Washington DC. pp. E-1
27. '5th Marine Expeditionary Brigade Embarkation Plan 316-62'. Records Group 127, Records of the US Marine Corps, National Archives, Washington DC. p. 2
28. '5th Marine Expeditionary Brigade Embarkation Plan 316-62'. Records Group 127, Records of the US Marine Corps, National Archives, Washington DC. Annex Tango. p. 1
29. Ibid. pp. F1-F2
30. 'RLT_Blue Beach, Operation Plan 314-62 (Modified 316-62)'. Records Group 127, Records of the US Marine Corps, National Archives, Washington DC. pp. B-2-A-1
31. 'RLT_Blue Beach, Operation Plan 314-62 (Modified 316-62)'. Records Group 127, Records of the US Marine Corps, National Archives, Washington DC. pp. B-2-A-1
32. 'RLT_Blue Beach, Operation Plan 314-62 (Modified 316-62)'. Records Group 127, Records of the US Marine Corps, National Archives, Washington DC. pp. B-2-A-1
33. 'RLT_Blue Beach, Operation Plan 314-62 (Modified 316-62)'. Records Group 127, Records of the US Marine Corps, National Archives, Washington DC. pp. B-1-2
34. 'RLT_Blue Beach, Operation Plan 314-62 (Modified 316-62)'. Records Group 127, Records of the US Marine Corps, National Archives, Washington DC. pp. B-2-2
35. 'RLT_Blue Beach, Operation Plan 314-62 (Modified 316-62)'. Records Group 127, Records of the US Marine Corps, National Archives, Washington DC. pp. 1
36. 'RLT_Blue Beach, Operation Plan 314-62 (Modified 316-62)'. Records Group 127, Records of

the US Marine Corps, National Archives, Washington DC. pp. B2-B-3
37. 'RLT_Blue Beach, Operation Plan 314-62 (Modified 316-62)'. Records Group 127, Records of the US Marine Corps, National Archives, Washington DC. Map Overlay of Objectives
38. 'RLT_Blue Beach, Operation Plan 314-62 (Modified 316-62)'. Records Group 127, Records of the US Marine Corps, National Archives, Washington DC. pp. B-2-B-2, B-2-B-1
39. 'RLT_Blue Beach, Operation Plan 314-62 (Modified 316-62)'. Records Group 127, Records of the US Marine Corps, National Archives, Washington DC. pp. II-1
40. 'RLT_Blue Beach, Operation Plan 314-62 (Modified 316-62)'. Records Group 127, Records of the US Marine Corps, National Archives, Washington DC. pp. C-2-C-3
41. 'RLT_Blue Beach, Operation Plan 314-62 (Modified 316-62)'. Records Group 127, Records of the US Marine Corps, National Archives, Washington DC. pp. D-1
42. 'RLT_Blue Beach, Operation Plan 314-62 (Modified 316-62)'. Records Group 127, Records of the US Marine Corps, National Archives, Washington DC. pp. B-1
43. 'RLT_Blue Beach, Operation Plan 314-62 (Modified 316-62)'. Records Group 127, Records of the US Marine Corps, National Archives, Washington DC. pp. C-3
44. 'RLT_Blue Beach, Operation Plan 314-62 (Modified 316-62)'. Records Group 127, Records of the US Marine Corps, National Archives, Washington DC. p. 2
45. 'RLT_Blue Beach, Operation Plan 314-62 (Modified 316-62)'. Records Group 127, Records of the US Marine Corps, National Archives, Washington DC. pp. C-3
46. 'RLT_Blue Beach, Operation Plan 314-62 (Modified 316-62)'. Records Group 127, Records of the US Marine Corps, National Archives, Washington DC. pp. B-1
47. 'RLT_Blue Beach, Operation Plan 314-62 (Modified 316-62)'. Records Group 127, Records of the US Marine Corps, National Archives, Washington DC. p. 2
48. 'RLT_Blue Beach, Operation Plan 314-62 (Modified 316-62)'. Records Group 127, Records of the US Marine Corps, National Archives, Washington DC. p. 2
49. 'RLT_Blue Beach, Operation Plan 314-62 (Modified 316-62)'. Records Group 127, Records of the US Marine Corps, National Archives, Washington DC. pp. NR-13, D-1. Note: There are conflicting numbers provided in the operational plans, most likely reflective of the constant changes to the plan
50. 'RLT_Blue Beach, Operation Plan 314-62 (Modified 316-62)'. Records Group 127, Records of the US Marine Corps, National Archives, Washington DC. pp. Appendix E-2
51. 'RLT_Blue Beach, Operation Plan 314-62 (Modified 316-62)'. Records Group 127, Records of the US Marine Corps, National Archives, Washington DC. pp. Appendix E-3
52. 'RLT_Blue Beach, Operation Plan 314-62 (Modified 316-62)'. Records Group 127, Records of the US Marine Corps, National Archives, Washington DC. pp. Appendix E-3
53. 'RLT_Blue Beach, Operation Plan 314-62 (Modified 316-62)'. Records Group 127, Records of the US Marine Corps, National Archives, Washington DC. pp. Appendix E-3
54. 'RLT_Blue Beach, Operation Plan 314-62 (Modified 316-62)'. Records Group 127, Records of the US Marine Corps, National Archives, Washington DC. pp. G-2-1
55. 'RLT_Blue Beach, Operation Plan 314-62 (Modified 316-62).' Records Group 127, Records of the US Marine Corps, National Archives, Washington DC. p. 2
56. 'RLT_Blue Beach, Operation Plan 314-62 (Modified 316-62)'. Records Group 127, Records of the US Marine Corps, National Archives, Washington DC. pp. I-3-I-4
57. 'RLT_Blue Beach, Operation Plan 314-62 (Modified 316-62)'. Records Group 127, Records of the US Marine Corps, National Archives, Washington DC. pp. C-5
58. 'RLT_Blue Beach, Operation Plan 314-62 (Modified 316-62)'. Records Group 127, Records of the US Marine Corps, National Archives, Washington DC. pp. C-4-C-5
59. 'RLT_Blue Beach, Operation Plan 314-62 (Modified 316-62)'. Records Group 127, Records of the US Marine Corps, National Archives, Washington DC. pp. C-5
60. 'RLT_Blue Beach, Operation Plan 314-62 (Modified 316-62)'. Records Group 127, Records of the US Marine Corps, National Archives, Washington DC. pp. C-5
61. 'RLT_Blue Beach, Operation Plan 314-62 (Modified 316-62)'. Records Group 127, Records of the US Marine Corps, National Archives, Washington DC. pp. B-3-5-1 (amended)
62. 'RLT_Blue Beach, Operation Plan 314-62 (Modified 316-62)'. Records Group 127, Records of the US Marine Corps, National Archives, Washington DC. pp. B-1
63. Rawlins. *Marines and Helicopters 1946-1962* (Washington DC: History and Museums Division Headquarters, US Marine Corps 1976) p. 106
64. 'RLT_Blue Beach, Operation Plan 314-62 (Modified 316-62)'. Records Group 127, Records of the US Marine Corps, National Archives, Washington DC. pp. C-2-B-1, C-2-B-6
65. 'MAG 26, TE-129.1.2.1, Operation Plan 316-62'. Records Group 127, Records of the US Marine Corps, National Archives, Washington DC. pp. D-2-1
66. 'MAG 26, TE-129.1.2.1, Operation Plan 316-62'. Records Group 127, Records of the US Marine Corps, National Archives, Washington DC. pp. B-1
67. 'MAG 26, TE-129.1.2.1, Operation Plan 316-62'. Records Group 127, Records of the US Marine

Corps, National Archives, Washington DC. pp. B-1
68. Kugler. *The Army's Role.* pp. III-41
69. Kugler. *The Army's Role.* pp. III-35-36
70. Kugler. *The Army's Role.* pp. III-35-36
71. Kugler. *The Army's Role.* pp. III-36
72. Kugler. *The Army's Role.* p. III-36
73. Post 1946 Commands, UDT Files (Declassified) October 1962, File 1559, Naval History and Heritage Command
74. 'CINCLANT Historical Account of the Cuban Crisis: 1963 (U)'. National Security Archive, pp. 47-48
75. Kugler. *The Army's Role.* pp. III-38
76. The Joint Chiefs of Staff. 'Unified Action Armed Forces' *JCS* Pub. 2, Paragraph 40708. US Army Center of Military History
77. Kugler. *The Army's Role.* Headquarters XVIII Airborne Corps. 'History of the XVIII Airborne Corps in the Cuban Crisis, 1962'. p. VII, 1, 4. US Army Center of Military History. p. III-39
78. Kugler. *The Army's Role.* Headquarters XVIII Airborne Corps, 'History of the XVIII Airborne Corps in the Cuban Crisis, 1962,' p. VII, 1, 4. US Army Center of Military History. p. III-39
79. 'RLT_Blue Beach, Operation Plan 314-62 (Modified 316-62)'. Records Group 127, Records of the US Marine Corps, National Archives, Washington DC. pp. B-3-2
80. 'RLT_Blue Beach, Operation Plan 314-62 (Modified 316-62).' Records Group 127, Records of the US Marine Corps, National Archives, Washington DC. pp. B-3-2

Chapter Six

1. 'The Might We Had Aimed at Cuba'. *Life* (7 December 1962) p. 33
2. Yarmolinsky. 'Department of Defense Operations During the Cuban Crisis'. *Set and Drift: Naval War College Review. No.* 32 (June-July 1979) p. 90
3. Yarmolinsky. 'Department of Defense Operations During the Cuban Crisis,' *Set and Drift: Naval War College Review. No.* 32 (June-July 1979) p. 90. And House. 'Joint Operational Problems in the Cuban Missile Crisis'. *Parameters* (Spring 1991) p. 96
4. Loomis. *US Army Command and Control In the Cuban Missile Crisis: Comments on Organization, Information Flows, and Relationships.* Stanford Research Institute, HMC-2 No. 115. US Army Center of Military History (June 1963) p. 14
5. Loomis. *US Army Command and Control In the Cuban Missile Crisis: Comments on Organization, Information Flows, and Relationships.* Stanford Research Institute, HMC-2 No. 115, US Army Center of Military History (June 1963) pp. 14-15
6. Kugler. *The Army's Role.* pp. V-14
7. House. 'Joint Operational Problems in the Cuban Missile Crisis'. *Parameters* (Spring 1991) p. 95
8. House. 'Joint Operational Problems in the Cuban Missile Crisis'. *Parameters* (Spring 1991) p. 97
9. House. 'Joint Operational Problems in the Cuban Missile Crisis'. *Parameters* (Spring 1991) p. 97
10. House. 'Joint Operational Problems in the Cuban Missile Crisis'. *Parameters* (Spring 1991) p. 97
11. House. 'Joint Operational Problems in the Cuban Missile Crisis'. *Parameters* (Spring 1991) p. 97
12. House. 'Joint Operational Problems in the Cuban Missile Crisis'. *Parameters* (Spring 1991) p. 99
13. House. 'Joint Operational Problems in the Cuban Missile Crisis'. *Parameters* (Spring 1991) p. 99. And Kugler. *The Army's Role.* pp. IV-15, IV-54
14. House. 'Joint Operational Problems in the Cuban Missile Crisis'. *Parameters* (Spring 1991) p. 101
15. Kugler. *The Army's Role.* pp. IV-17
16. Kugler. *The Army's Role.* pp. IV-19
17. Kugler. *The Army's Role.* pp. IV-20
18. Kugler. *The Army's Role.* pp. IV-21
19. Kugler. *The Army's Role.* pp. IV-23
20. Kugler. *The Army's Role.* pp. IV-24-IV-25
21. Kugler. *The Army's Role.* pp. IV-30. And Fact Sheet, Headquarters USSTRICOM, 'The United States Strike Command'. Office of Center of Military History
22. Kugler. *The Army's Role.* pp. IV-31
23. Kugler. *The Army's Role.* pp. IV-35
24. Kugler. *The Army's Role.* Message JCS 6806, JCS to CINCSTRIKE, 201209Z Oct 1962. pp. IV-38
25. Kugler. *The Army's Role.* pp. IV-40-IV-42
26. Kugler. *The Army's Role.* pp. IV-40-IV-43-IV-47
27. Kugler. *The Army's Role.* pp IV-40-IV-48
28. Kugler. *The Army's Role.* pp. IV-48-IV-50
29. Kugler. *The Army's Role.* pp. V-1-V-3
30. Kugler. *The Army's Role.* pp. V-4-V-5

31. Kugler. *The Army's Role.* pp. V-5-V-6
32. Kugler. *The Army's Role.* pp. V-8-V-9
33. Kugler. *The Army's Role.* pp. V-11
34. Kugler. *The Army's Role,* p.V-12
35. House. 'Joint Operational Problems in the Cuban Missile Crisis'. *Parameters* (Spring 1991) p. 96. And Wisnack. 'Old Ironsides' Response to the Cuban Crisis'. *Army* (April 1963) p. 26
36. Wisnack. 'Old Ironsides' Response to the Cuban Crisis'. *Army* (April 1963) p. 27
37. Wisnack. 'Old Ironsides' Response to the Cuban Crisis'. *Army* (April 1963) p. 29
38. 'Tactical Air Command Chronology of the Cuban Crisis, 1962'. Air Force Historical Research Agency (29 January 1963) pp. 3-9
39. 'Tactical Air Command Chronology of the Cuban Crisis, 1962'. Air Force Historical Research Agency (29 January 1963) pp. 3-4
40. 'Tactical Air Command Chronology of the Cuban Crisis, 1962'. Air Force Historical Research Agency (29 January 1963) p. 3
41. 'Tactical Air Command Chronology of the Cuban Crisis, 1962'. Air Force Historical Research Agency (29 January 1963) p. 9
42. 'CINCLANT Historical Account of the Cuban Crisis: 1963 (U)', National Security Archive, p. 12 (II)
43. 'CINCLANT Historical Account of the Cuban Crisis: 1963 (U)'. National Security Archive. p. 62
44. 'Tactical Air Command Chronology of the Cuban Crisis, 1962'. Air Force Historical Research Agency (29 January 1963) p. 2
45. 'Tactical Air Command Chronology of the Cuban Crisis, 1962'. Air Force Historical Research Agency, (29 January 1963) p. 10
46. 'CINCLANT Psychological Leaflet Program'. Records of the Secretary of Defense, Records Group 200, US National Archives. p. 1

Chapter Seven

1. Notes taken from transcripts of meetings of the Joint Chiefs of Staff, October-November 1962, Dealing with the Missile Crisis, National Security Archive
2. Kennedy. *Thirteen Days.* pp. 36-38
3. Naftali and Zelikow. *The Presidential Records of John F. Kennedy, September-21 October 1962.* Vol. II (New York: W. W. Norton & Company, 2001) p. 588
4. Naftali and Zelikow. *The Presidential Records of John F. Kennedy, September-21 October 1962.* Vol. II (New York: W. W. Norton & Company, 2001) p. 588
5. Naftali and Zelikow. *The Presidential Records of John F. Kennedy, September-21 October 1962.* Vol. II (New York: W. W. Norton & Company, 2001) p. 590
6. Naftali and Zelikow. *The Presidential Records of John F. Kennedy, September-21 October 1962.* Vol. II (New York: W. W. Norton & Company, 2001) p. 591
7. Naftali and Zelikow. *The Presidential Records of John F. Kennedy, September-21 October 1962.* Vol. II (New York: W. W. Norton & Company, 2001) p. 589
8. Naftali and Zelikow. *The Presidential Records of John F. Kennedy, September-21 October 1962.* Vol. II (New York: W. W. Norton & Company, 2001) p. 586
9. Naftali and Zelikow. *The Presidential Records of John F. Kennedy, September-21 October 1962.* Vol. II (New York: W. W. Norton & Company, 2001) pp. 586-589
10. Naftali and Zelikow. *The Presidential Records of John F. Kennedy, September-21 October 1962.* Vol. II (New York: W. W. Norton & Company, 2001) pp. 593-594
11. Kennedy. *Thirteen Days.* pp. 36-37. Note: Kennedy misquoted the quote as coming from General Shoupe
2. Kennedy. *Thirteen Days.* pp. 36-37. Note: Kennedy misquoted the quote as coming from General Shoupe
3. Naftali and Zelikow. *The Presidential Records of John F. Kennedy, September-21 October 1962.* Vol. II (New York: W. W. Norton & Company, 2001) pp. 597-598
4. Naftali and Zelikow. *The Presidential Records of John F. Kennedy, September-21 October 1962.* Vol. II (New York: W. W. Norton & Company, 2001) pp. 604-605
5. Naftali and Zelikow. *The Presidential Records of John F. Kennedy, September-21 October 1962.* Vol. II (New York: W. W. Norton & Company, 2001) p. 614
6. 'CINCLANT Historical Account of the Cuban Crisis: 1963 (U)'. National Security Archive. p. 103
7. 'CINCLANT Historical Account of the Cuban Crisis: 1963 (U)'. National Security Archive. p. 103-104
8. 'CINCLANT Historical Account of the Cuban Crisis: 1963 (U)'. National Security Archive, p. 109-110
9. 'CINCLANT Historical Account of the Cuban Crisis: 1963 (U)'. National Security Archive. p. 111
20. 'CINCLANT Historical Account of the Cuban Crisis: 1963 (U)'. National Security Archive. pp.

110-113
21. 'CINCLANT Historical Account of the Cuban Crisis: 1963 (U)'. National Security Archive. p. 114
22. 'CINCLANT Historical Account of the Cuban Crisis: 1963 (U)'. National Security Archive. p. 113
23. 'CINCLANT Historical Account of the Cuban Crisis: 1963 (U)'. National Security Archive. p. 9.1
24. 'CINCLANT Historical Account of the Cuban Crisis: 1963 (U)'. National Security Archive. p. 92
25. Young. *When the Russians Blinked.* pp. 126-127
26. Young. *When the Russians Blinked.* p. 128. And 'CINCLANT Historical Account of the Cuban Crisis: 1963 (U)'. National Security Archive. p. 93
27. Young. *When the Russians Blinked.* p. 129
28. Varner. *The History of Guantanamo Bay.* p. 62
29. 'CINCLANT Historical Account of the Cuban Crisis: 1963 (U)'. National Security Archive. p. 95
30. Varner. *The History of Guantanamo Bay.* p. 62
31. Berhow. *US Strategic and Defensive Missile Systems: 1950-2004* (Oxford UK: Osprey Publishing, 2004) p. 29
32. Young. *When the Russians Blinked.* p. 130
33. Young. *When the Russians Blinked.* p. 131
34. Young. *When the Russians Blinked.* p.131
35. 'CINCLANT Historical Account of the Cuban Crisis: 1963 (U)' .National Security Archive. p. 96
36. Guantanamo Special Equipment List, Chief of Naval Operations Files, Col 552, File 9A, Naval History and Heritage Command
37. Varner. *The History of Guantanamo Bay.* p. 61
38. 'CINCLANT Historical Account of the Cuban Crisis: 1963 (U)'. National Security Archive. p. 101
39. 'CINCLANT Historical Account of the Cuban Crisis: 1963 (U. National Security Archive. p. 94
40. Checklist of Activities, A-Day-1, Chief of Naval Operations Files, Col 552, File 9A, Naval History and Heritage Command
41. Checklist of Activities, A-Day, Chief of Naval Operations Files, Col 552, File 9A, Naval History. And Heritage Command 42 'Transcript, President Kennedy's Address, 22 October 1962'. John F. Kennedy Library
43. 'Transcript, President Kennedy's Address, 22 October 1962'. John F. Kennedy Library
44. Carpenter. 'When the Right Words Counted'. *Naval History.* Vol. 15. Issue 5 (October 2001) p. 46
45. Checklist of Activities, A-Hour, Chief of Naval Operations Files, Col 552, File 9A, Naval History and Heritage Command
46. Wisnack. 'Old Ironsides' Response to the Cuban Crisis'. *Army* (April 1963) pp. 27-28
47. Wisnack. 'Old Ironsides' Response to the Cuban Crisis'. *Army* (April 1963) p. 28
48. Kugler. *The Army's Role.* pp. VI-9-VI-10
49. 'Historical Narrative of the Cuban Crisis of 1962'. US Army Center of Military History. p. 11
50. Kugler. *The Army's Role.* pp. VI-14. And Wisnack. 'Old Ironsides' Response to the Cuban Crisis'. *Army* (April 1963) p. 29
51. Kugler. *The Army's Role.* pp. VI-12-VI-13. And 'CINCLANT Historical Account of the Cuban Crisis: 1963 (U)'. National Security Archive. pp. 50-51
52. Kugler. *The Army's Role.* pp. VI-22-VI-23
53. Kugler. *The Army's Role.* pp. VI-23-VI-24. And 'CINCLANT Historical Account of the Cuban Crisis: 1963 (U)'. National Security Archive. pp. 50-51
54. Kugler. *The Army's Role.* pp. VI-25. And 'CINCLANT Historical Account of the Cuban Crisis: 1963 (U)'. National Security Archive. pp. 50-52
55. Kugler. *The Army's Role.* pp. VI-26
56. Kugler. *The Army's Role.* pp. VI-28
57. Kugler. *The Army's Role.* pp. VI-29
58 Kugler, *The Army's Role,* pp. VI-34
59. Kugler. *The Army's Role.* pp. VI-36
60. 'CINCLANT Historical Account of the Cuban Crisis: 1963 (U)'. National Security Archive. p. 67
61. Kugler. *The Army's Role.* pp. VI-31
62. Kugler. *The Army's Role.* pp. VI-32
63. Kugler. *The Army's Role.* pp. VI-33
64. Kugler. *The Army's Role.* pp. V-13
65. 'CINCLANT Historical Account of the Cuban Crisis: 1963 (U)'. National Security Archive. p. 63
66. 'CINCLANT Historical Account of the Cuban Crisis: 1963 (U)'. National Security Archive, p. 74
67. 'CINCLANT Historical Account of the Cuban Crisis: 1963 (U)'. National Security Archive. p. 47
68. Keefe. 'Operation Sunshade: The Air Force Reserve Plays A Key Role in the Cuban Missile Crisis'. *Journal: American Aviation Historical Society* (Winter 2006) p. 306
69. 'The Air Force Response to the Cuban Crisis'. US Air Force Historical Division Liaison Office.

p. 10
70. Keefe. 'Operation Sunshade: The Air Force Reserve Plays A Key Role in the Cuban Missile Crisis'. *Journal: American Aviation Historical Society* (Winter 2006) pp. 309-310
71. 'CINCLANT Historical Account of the Cuban Crisis: 1963 (U)'. National Security Archive. p. 60
72. 'CINCLANT Historical Account of the Cuban Crisis: 1963 (U)'. National Security Archive. p. 66
73. 'CINCLANT Historical Account of the Cuban Crisis: 1963 (U)'. National Security Archive. p. 53, 66
74. 'CINCLANT Historical Account of the Cuban Crisis: 1963 (U)'. National Security Archive. p. 72
75. Berhow. *US Strategic and Defensive Missile Systems.* p. 32
76. 'The Air Force Response to the Cuban Crisis'. US Air Force Historical Division Liaison Office. p. 6
77. Kugler. *The Army's Role.* pp. VI-4
78. Kugler. *The Army's Role.* pp. VI-4
79. Kugler. *The Army's Role.* pp. VI-5
80. 'The Air Force Response to the Cuban Crisis'. US Air Force Historical Division Liaison Office. p. 7
81. 'The Air Force Response to the Cuban Crisis'. US Air Force Historical Division Liaison Office. p. 10
82. 'A Highly Compressed Narrative Account and Assessment of the Cuban Crisis'. Air Force Historical Research Agency. p. 19
83. 'A Highly Compressed Narrative Account and Assessment of the Cuban Crisis'. Air Force Historical Research Agency. p. 19
84. 'CINCLANT Historical Account of the Cuban Crisis: 1963 (U)'. National Security Archive. p. 78
85. 'A Highly Compressed Narrative Account and Assessment of the Cuban Crisis'. Air Force Historical Research Agency. p. 17
86. 'A Highly Compressed Narrative Account and Assessment of the Cuban Crisis'. Air Force Historical Research Agency. p. 17
87. 'A Highly Compressed Narrative Account and Assessment of the Cuban Crisis'. Air Force Historical Research Agency. p. 17
88. 'A Highly Compressed Narrative Account and Assessment of the Cuban Crisis'. Air Force Historical Research Agency. p. 18
89. 'A Highly Compressed Narrative Account and Assessment of the Cuban Crisis'. Air Force Historical Research Agency. p. 18
90. 'A Highly Compressed Narrative Account and Assessment of the Cuban Crisis'. Air Force Historical Research Agency. p. 19
91. 'A Highly Compressed Narrative Account and Assessment of the Cuban Crisis'. Air Force Historical Research Agency. p. 19
92. 'A Highly Compressed Narrative Account and Assessment of the Cuban Crisis'. Air Force Historical Research Agency. p. 19
93. 'CINCLANT Historical Account of the Cuban Crisis: 1963 (U)'. National Security Archive. p. 62
94. 'CINCLANT Historical Account of the Cuban Crisis: 1963 (U)'. National Security Archive. p. 65
95. 'CINCLANT Historical Account of the Cuban Crisis: 1963 (U)'. National Security Archive. p. 80
96. 'CINCLANT Historical Account of the Cuban Crisis: 1963 (U)'. National Security Archive. p. 60
97. 'CINCLANT Historical Account of the Cuban Crisis: 1963 (U)'. National Security Archive. p. 77
98. 'JCS Weekly Status Report, SIOP 14'. National Security Archive. p. 2
99. 'Chronology of SAC Participation in the Cuban Crisis'. Air Force Historical Research Agency. p. 6
100. 'Chronology of SAC Participation in the Cuban Crisis'. Air Force Historical Research Agency. p. 6. And 'CINCLANT Historical Account of the Cuban Crisis: 1963 (U)'. National Security Archive. p. 47
101. 'Chronology of SAC Participation in the Cuban Crisis'. Air Force Historical Research Agency. p. 10
102. Kugler. *The Army's Role.* pp. VI-3. From ', Chief, Battle Staff' for *JCS* (24 October 1962) Supplemental SITREP Information as of 241200Z. p. 7

Chapter Eight

1. Blight and Welch,. *On the Brink, Americans and Soviets Re-examine the Cuban Missile Crisis* (Hill and Wang: New York, 1989) p. 179
2. 'Reminiscences of Admiral Robert Lee Dennison'. US Naval Institute Oral Histories. p. 416
3. Brugioni. *Eyeball to Eyeball.* p. 394
4. Adlai Stevenson. Statement by Ambassador Adlai Stevenson to the UN Security Council (UN press release 4074) (25 October 1962) p. 737-740
5. Adlai Stevenson, Statement by Ambassador Adlai Stevenson to the UN Security Council (UN press release 4074) (25 October 19620 p. 737-740
6. 'Chronology of the Cuban Missile Crisis'. National Security Archive. p. 370

7. Records of the Office of Chief of Naval Operations, 1946-200, Coll 552, Naval History and Heritage Command. Box 1
8. 'CINCLANT Historical Account of the Cuban Crisis: 1963 (U)'. National Security Archive, p. 104
9. Carpenter. 'When the Right Words Counted'. *Naval History.* Vol. 15. Issue 5 (October 2001) p. 52
10. Records of the Office of Chief of Naval Operations, 1946-200, Coll 552, Naval History and Heritage Command, Box 1, Summary of CNO Participation in the Cuban Crisis. p. 57
11. Records of the Office of Chief of Naval Operations, 1946-200, Coll 552, Naval History and Heritage Command, Box 1, Summary of CNO Participation in the Cuban Crisis. p. 48
12. 'Chronology of SAC Participation in the Cuban Crisis'. Air Force Historical Research Agency. p. 5
13. Kennedy. *Thirteen Days.* p. 70
14. Kennedy. *Thirteen Days.* p. 71-72
15. Records of the Office of Chief of Naval Operations, 1946-200, Coll 552, Naval History and Heritage Command, Box 1, Summary of CNO Participation in the Cuban Crisis. p. 58
16. Poole. 'The Cuban Missiles Crisis: How Well Did the Joint Chiefs of Staff Work?' p. 18
17. Poole. 'The Cuban Missiles Crisis: How Well Did the Joint Chiefs of Staff Work?' p. 18
18. Anderson, George W. Vol. II. US Naval Institute. p. 559
91. Carpenter. 'When the Right Words Counted'. *Naval History.* Vol. 15. Issue 5 (October 2001) p. 48
20. Carpenter. 'When the Right Words Counted'. *Naval History.* Vol. 15. Issue 5 (October 2001) p. 48
21. Huchthausen. *October Fury* (Hoboken NJ: John Wiley & Sons, Inc., 2002) p. 62. And 'Recollections of Vadim Orlov (USSR Submarine B-59) We Will Sink Them All, But We Will Not Disgrace Our Navy'. National Security Archive. p. 1
22. Huchthausen. *October Fury.* p. 47
23. Chang and Kornbluh. *The Cuban Missile Crisis.* p. 372
24. Records of the Office of Chief of Naval Operations, 1946-200, Coll 552, Naval History and Heritage Command, Box 1, Summary of CNO Participation in the Cuban Crisis. p. 64
25. Records of the Office of Chief of Naval Operations, 1946-200, Coll 552, Naval History and Heritage Command, Box 1, Summary of CNO Participation in the Cuban Crisis. p. 60
26. 'Recollections of Vadim Orlov (USSR Submarine B-59) We Will Sink Them All, But We Will Not Disgrace Our Navy'. National Security Archive. p. 2
27. Records of the Office of Chief of Naval Operations, 1946-200, Coll 552, Naval History and Heritage Command, Box 1, Summary of CNO Participation in the Cuban Crisis. p. 66
28. Dobbs. *One Minute to Midnight* (New York: Alfred A. Knopf, 2008) p. 145
29. Dobbs. *One Minute to Midnight* (New York: Alfred A. Knopf, 2008) pp. 94-96
30. Dobbs. *One Minute to Midnight* (New York: Alfred A. Knopf, 2008) pp. 94-96
31. 'The Air Force Response to the Cuban Crisis 14 October–24 November 1962'. Air Force Historical Research Agency. p. 27
32. Author's Note: The spelling of the ship's name as *Grozneyy* is as it appears in multiple naval records. Other records record the name as *Grozney.* I have opted for the spelling used by the US Navy in this text
33. Records of the Office of Chief of Naval Operations, 1946-200, Coll 552, Naval History and Heritage Command, Box 1, Summary of CNO Participation in the Cuban Crisis. p. 63
34. Records of the Office of Chief of Naval Operations, 1946-200, Coll 552, Naval History and Heritage Command, Box 1, Summary of CNO Participation in the Cuban Crisis. p. 64
35. Transcript of Executive Committee Meetings 27 October 1962 from Chang and Kornbluh. *The Cuban Missile Crisis.* pp. 209-210
36. CPSU Instructions to General Pivyev, 27 October. National Security Archive. p. 1
37. Garthoff. 'New Evidence on the Cuban Missile Crisis: Khruschchev, Nuclear Weapons and the Cuban Missile Crisis'. *Cold War International History Project.* Bulletin 11. National Security Archive. p. 262
38. Polmar and Gresham. *Defcon-2.* p. 150
39. Polmar and Gresham. *Defcon-2.* p. 150
40. Freeman. 'To The Brink of Nuclear War'. *World Magazine* (October 1992) pp. 48-49
41. Garthoff. 'New Evidence on the Cuban Missile Crisis: Khruschchev, Nuclear Weapons and the Cuban Missile Crisis'. *Cold War International History Project.* Bulletin 11. National Security Archive. p. 262
42. Message from Premier Khrushchev, 24 October 1962. National Security Archive
43. Chang and Kornbluh. *The Cuban Missile Crisis.* p. 210
44. Bundy. Executive Committee Minutes, 23 October 1962 from Chang and Kornbluh. *The Cuban Missile Crisis.* p. 158
45. Notes Taken from Transcripts of the Meetings of the Joint Chiefs of Staff, October-November 1962, Dealing with the Cuban Missile Crisis. National Security Archive. p. 16
46. Kennedy. *Thirteen Days.* p. 210
47. 'Chronology of SAC Participation in the Cuban Crisis'. Air Force Historical Research Agency. p. 14

48. Dobbs. *One Minute to Midnight.* p. 336
49. Kennedy. *Thirteen Days.* p. 64
50. Chang and Kornbluh. *The Cuban Missile Crisis.* p. 375
51. Turkish Position With Regard to Trading Jupiters for Soviet Missiles in Cuba, 25 October 1962. National Security Archive.
52. John Scali's Notes of the First Meeting With Soviet Embassy Counsellor and KGB officer Alexsandr Fomin, 26 October 1962 from Chang and Kornbluh. *The Cuban Missile Crisis.* p. 375
53. Khrushchev Letter to Kennedy, 26 October 261962 from Chang and Kornbluh. *The Cuban Missile Crisis.* p. 375
54. Transcript of Executive Committee meeting, 27 October 1962. John F. Kennedy Library. p. 16
55. Chang and Kornbluh. *The Cuban Missile Crisis.* p. 378
56. Kennedy. *Thirteen Days.* p.109

Chapter Nine

1. 'The Reminiscences of Robert Lee Dennison'. Oral Interview Transcripts. US Naval Institute (August 1975) pp. 416-417
2. Nathan. *The Cuban Missile Crisis Revisited.* p. 239
3. Stern. 'The Cuban Missile Crisis ExComm Meetings: Getting it Right After 50 Years'. *HNN* (15 October 2012) http://hnn.us/articles/cuban-missile-crisis-excomm-meetings-getting-it-right-after-50-years
4. Stern. 'The Cuban Missile Crisis ExComm Meetings: Getting it Right After 50 Years'. *HNN* (15 October 2012) http://hnn.us/articles/cuban-missile-crisis-excomm-meetings-getting-it-right-after-50-years
5. Zelikow and May. *The Presidential Recordings of John F. Kennedy.* p. 441
6. Notes Taken from Transcripts of the Meetings of the Joint Chiefs of Staff, October-November 1962, Dealing with the Cuban Missile Crisis. National Security Archive. p. 23
7. 'Timing Factors'. General Maxwell Taylor, 25 October 1962. National Security Archive p. 1
8. 'A Highly Compressed Narrative Account and Assessment of the Cuban Crisis'. Air Force Historical Research Agency. pp. 6-11
9. 'RLT_Blue Beach, Operation Plan 314-62 (Modified 316-62)'. Records Group 127, Records of the US Marine Corps, National Archives, Washington DC. pp. C-1-9
10. 'RLT_Blue Beach, Operation Plan 314-62 (Modified 316-62)'. Records Group 127, Records of the US Marine Corps, National Archives, Washington DC. pp. B-1-8
11. 'RLT_Blue Beach, Operation Plan 314-62 (Modified 316-62)'. Records Group 127, Records of the US Marine Corps, National Archives, Washington DC. pp. B-1-A-1, B-1-A-5
12. 'RLT_Blue Beach, Operation Plan 314-62 (Modified 316-62)'. Records Group 127, Records of the US Marine Corps, National Archives, Washington DC. pp. B-1-A-1, B-1-A-5
13. 'RLT_Blue Beach, Operation Plan 314-62 (Modified 316-62)'. Records Group 127, Records of the US Marine Corps, National Archives, Washington DC. pp. B-1-A-1, B-1-A-5
14. 'RLT_Blue Beach, Operation Plan 314-62 (Modified 316-62)'. Records Group 127, Records of the US Marine Corps, National Archives, Washington DC. pp. B-1-A-1, B-1-A-5
15. 'RLT_Blue Beach, Operation Plan 314-62 (Modified 316-62)'. Records Group 127, Records of the US Marine Corps, National Archives, Washington DC. pp. B-1-A-3
16. Lima. 'Fifty Years Later: Cubans Remember Preparing to Fight the Americans'. *Air & Space Magazine* (November 2012) p. 10
17. Aspectos Importantes Contenidos En Los Informes Ofrecidos, 24 October 1962. National Security Archive (1992) p. 1
18. Aspectos Importantes Contenidos En Los Informes Ofrecidos, 24 October 1962. National Security Archive (1992) p. 2
19. Aspectos Importantes Contenidos En Los Informes Ofrecidos, 24 October 1962. National Security Archive (1992) pp. 2-3
20. Aspectos Importantes Contenidos En Los Informes Ofrecidos, 24 October 1962. National Security Archive (1992) p. 3
21. Lima. 'Fifty Years Later: Cubans Remember Preparing to Fight the Americans'. *Air & Space Magazine* (November 2012) p. 11
22. Aspectos Importantes Contenidos En Los Informes Ofrecidos, 24 October 1962. National Security Archive (1992) p. 4
23. Aspectos Importantes Contenidos En Los Informes Ofrecidos, 24 October 1962. National Security Archive (1992) p. 5
24. Aspectos Importantes Contenidos En Los Informes Ofrecidos, 24 October 1962. National Security Archive (1992) p. 6
25. Operation Scabbards, CINCLANT from FMFLANT, 28 October 1962, Recommendations. Record Group 127, Records of the US Marine Corps, National Archives, Washington DC.

26. Operation Scabbards, CINCLANT from FMFLANT, 28 October 1962, Recommendations. Record Group 127, Records of the US Marine Corps, National Archives, Washington DC.
27. Blanton and Blight. 'A Conversation in Havana'. *Arms Control Today* (November 2002) 32, 9: Social Science Module,. p. 7
28. Review of photographs on file at the US National Archives
29. Gribkov and Smith. *Operation ANADYR* (Chicago: Edition q., Inc., 1994) p. 182
30. Gribkov. *On the Brink of the Nuclear Abyss* (Moscow: Gregory Page, 1998) p. 363. Trans. by Svetlana Savranskaya. The National Security Archive
31. Gribkov and Smith. *Operation ANADYR* (Chicago: Edition q., Inc., 1994) p. 13
32. Archive of the President of the Russian Federation, Special Declassification (April 2002) Trans. by Svetlana Savranskaya. The National Security Archive
33. Gribkov and Smith. *Operation ANADYR*. p. 63
34. Dobbs. *One Minute to Midnight*. pp. 178-179
35. El Mundo, Revolucio, and Noticias de Hoy Newspapers, Library of Congress. Note: Only Noticias de Hoy actually printed any weather, and that was only when there was projected rain or storm. The remaining information had to be extracted from information provided in the three newspapers such as photographs, etc
36. Blight and Welch. *On the Brink Americans and Soviets Re-examine The Cuban Missile Crisis* (New York: Hill and Wang, 1989) p. 211
37. Notes of Secretary of Defense, Robert McNamara, 21 October 1962, Meeting with the President. National Security Archive. pp. 1-2
38. 'CINCLANT Historical Account of the Cuban Crisis: 1963 (U)'. National Security Archive. p. 39
39. Vice Admiral Robert F. Dunn, Interview No. 3. US Naval Institute, (23 April 1990) pp. 191-192
40. Notes of Secretary of Defense, Robert McNamara, 21 October 1962, Meeting with the President. National Security Archive. p. 2
41. 'CINCLANT Psychological Leaflet Program'. Records of the Secretary of Defense. US National Archives. p. 1
42. Review of Photographs from 25-28 October of airfields San Antonio de Los Banos, Holguin, and Jose Marti International. US National Archives. And 'CINCLANT Historical Account of the Cuban Crisis: 1963 (U)'. National Security Archives. p. 10
43. Young. *When the Russians Blinked*. pp. 160-161
44. Timothy Naftali, Philip Zelikow. *The Presidential Records of John F. Kennedy, September-21 October 1962*. Vol. II (New York: W. W. Norton & Company, 2001) p. 596
45. 'RLT_Blue Beach, Operation Plan 314-62 (Modified 316-62)'. Records Group 127, Records of the US Marine Corps, National Archives, Washington DC. p. 3
46. 'RLT_Blue Beach, Operation Plan 314-62 (Modified 316-62)'. Records Group 127, Records of the US Marine Corps, National Archives, Washington DC. D1-D2
47. Dobbs. *One Minute to Midnight* (New York: Alfred A. Knopf, 2008) p. 102
48. 'RLT_Blue Beach, Operation Plan 314-62 (Modified 316-62)'. Records Group 127, Records of the US Marine Corps, National Archives, Washington DC. pp. B-1-A-1, B-1-A-5
49. '2nd Marines, OP Plan 316-62: Blue Beach'. Records Group 127, Records of the US Marine Corps, National Archives, Washington DC. p. 3
50. The Air Force Response to the Cuban Crisis, US Air Force Historical Division Liaison Office. p. 8. And 'A Highly Compressed Narrative Account and Assessment of The Tactical Air Command and The Cuban Crisis'. US Air Force Historical Division Liaison Office. p 14
51. Lima. 'Fifty Years Later: Cubans Remember Preparing to Fight the Americans'. *Air & Space Magazine* (November 2012) p. 10
52. 'CINCLANT Historical Account of the Cuban Crisis: 1963 (U)'. National Security Archive. pp. 55-56
53. Gribkov and Smith. *Operation ANADYR* (Chicago: Edition q., Inc., 1994) pp .64-65
54. Chang and Kornbluh. *The Cuban Missile Crisis: A National Security Archive Documents Reader* (The New Press: New York, 1992) p. 373
55. 'CINCLANT Historical Account of the Cuban Crisis: 1963 (U)'. National Security Archive. p. 54

Chapter Ten

1. 'Kruschchev on Cuba'. *New York Times* (10 June 1960) p. 3
2. Comments on State Paper on Possible Soviet Actions by Soviets and Others in Event of Surprise Air Strike, Col. Wolfe, 20 October 1962. Records Group 200, US National Archive. p. 1
3. 'Chronology of SAC Participation in the Cuban Crisis'. Air Force Historical Research Agency. p. 14
4. 'CINCLANT Historical Account of the Cuban Crisis: 1963 (U)'. National Security Archive. pp. 24-30
5. Kugler. *The Army's Role*. pp. 33-35
6. Dobbs. *One Minute to Midnight*. pp. 179-181

7. Naftali and Zelikow. *The Presidential Records of John F. Kennedy.* p. 596
8. Nathan. *The Cuban Missile Crisis Revisited.* p. 193
9. 'CINCLANT Historical Account of the Cuban Crisis: 1963 (U)'. National Security Archive. p. 68
10. Memo From General Taylor, 6 September 1961, Strategic Air Planning and Berlin'. National Security Archive. p. 1
11. White House Memorandum, The Defense of Berlin if Cuba is Blockaded, 19 October 1962, Records Group 200. US National Archives. p. 1
12. Cuba and Berlin, 19 October 1962, Records Group 200. US National Archives. pp. 3-4
13. White House Memorandum, The Defense of Berlin if Cuba is Blockaded, 19 October 1962, Records Group 200. US National Archives. pp. 1-2
14. Cuba and Berlin, 19 October 1962, Records Group 200. US National Archives. pp. 5-6
15. Comments on State Paper on Possible Soviet Actions by Soviets and Others in Event of Surprise Air Strike, Col. Wolfe, 20 October 1962, Records Group 200. US National Archive. Appendix
16. Comments on State Paper on Possible Soviet Actions by Soviets and Others in Event of Surprise Air Strike, Col. Wolfe, 20 October 1962, Records Group 200. US National Archive. Appendix
17. Memo From General Taylor, 6 September 1961, Strategic Air Planning and Berlin'. National Security Archive. p. 1
18. 'Strategic Air Command Operations in the Cuban Crisis of 1962'. Historical Study 90, Reel 34530, Air Force Historical Agency
19. 'Strategic Air Command Operations in the Cuban Crisis of 1962'. Historical Study 90, Reel 34530, Air Force Historical Agency. And 'Chronology of SAC Participation in the Cuban Crisis'. Air Force Historical Research Agency. pp. 12-33
20. 'Memo From General Taylor, 6 September 1961, Strategic Air Planning and Berlin'. National Security Archive. p. 2
21. 'Memo From General Taylor, 6 September 1961, Strategic Air Planning and Berlin'. National Security Archive. p. 4
22. Memo From General Taylor, 6 September 1961, Strategic Air Planning and Berlin'. National Security Archive, p. 8
23. Operation Sentinel, Target City List, Federal Civil Defense Administration, 26 March 1962, Records Group 397. US National Archives. pp. E1-E17
24. Operation Sentinel, Casualties Summary, Federal Civil Defense Administration, 26 March 1962, Records Group 397. US National Archives

Epilogue

Perez. *Cuba: Between Reform and Revolution* (New York: Oxford University Press, 1988) p. 147

Appendix One

Post 1946 Reports, Chief of Naval Operations, Cuba, Box 10, Document No. 7. Naval History and Heritage Command

Appendix Two

1. SEAL Team Chronology, 1962, Post 1946 Reports, Chief of Naval Operations, Cuba, Box 10, Document No. 7. Naval History and Heritage Command.
2. Ship File, USS *Sea Lion*, Cruise Summary 1961-1963. US Navy Historical Research Center
3. SEAL Team Chronology, 1961, Post 1946 Reports, Chief of Naval Operations, Cuba, Box 10, Document No. 7. Naval History and Heritage Command

Acronyms

AFB:	Air Force Base
AFLANT:	Air Force Atlantic
AFR:	Air Force Refueling
ANTCOM:	Antilles Command
ARLANT:	Army Component, Atlantic
ASW:	Anti-Submarine Warfare
ASW:	Anti-Submarine Warfare
BLT:	Marine Designation for Battalion Landing Team
CAP:	Combat Air Patrol
CAS:	Combat Air Strike
CCTW:	Combat Crew Training Wing
CINCLANT:	Commander in Chief of the Atlantic Command – Admiral Dennison
CINCLANTFLT:	Commander in Chief of the Atlantic Fleet
CONARC:	Continental Army Command
DCSOPS:	Deputy Chief of Staff for Military Operations
ECM:	Electronic Countermeasures
FKR:	Frontoviye Krilatiye Raketi – Soviet cruise missiles (NATO designation SSC-2a Salish)
FMFLANT:	Fleet Marine Force Atlantic
FROG:	Free Rocket Over Ground
FTC:	The Revolutionary Army of Cuba
GMAIC:	The Guided Missile and Astronautics Intelligence Committee
HAWK:	Homing, All-The-Way Killer surface-to-air missile
HEAT:	High Velocity Anti-Tank
HMM:	Marine designation for Helicopter – Marine Medium – a squadron designator
HVAR:	High Velocity Aircraft Rocket
ICBM:	Intercontinental Ballistic Missile
JAEIC:	Joint Atomic Energy Intelligence Committee
JCS:	Joint Chiefs of Staff
JUWTFA:	Joint Unconventional Warfare Task Force Atlantic
LAAM:	Light Anti-Aircraft Missile
LCT:	Landing Craft Tanks
LST:	Landing Ship Tanks
LZ:	Landing Zone
LZ:	Landing Zone
MATS:	Military Air Transit Service
MATS:	Military Air Transit Services
MAW:	Marine Air Wing
MEB:	Marine Expeditionary Brigade
MEZ:	Military Emergency Zone
MRBM:	Medium Range Ballistic Missile
NAS:	Naval Air Station
NAVPIC:	Naval Photographic Intelligence Center
NORAD:	North American Aerospace Defense Command
NPIC:	National Photographic Interpretation Center
NSA:	National Security Agency
PHIBRIGLEX-62:	Amphibious Brigade Landing Exercise known as 'Three Pairs'

RLT:	Marine designation for Regimental Landing Team
RLT:	Regimental Landing Team
SAC:	Strategic Air Command
SACEUR:	Supreme Allied Commander Europe
SAM:	Surface-to-Air Missile
SAP:	Semi-Armor Piercing
SAR:	Search and Rescue
SEAL:	Sea, Air, and Land Teams
SGA:	Special Group Augmented – the inter-agency task force tasked with managing Operation Mongoose
SIOP:	System Integrated Operation Plan
SRW:	Strategic Reconnaissance Wing
STRAC:	Standards in Training Commission
STRICOM:	Strike Command – also known as United States Strike Command USSTRICOM
TAC:	Tactical Air Command
Task Force 125:	The Army elements of Op Plan 312-61, 314-62, and 316-62
TFW:	Tactical Fighter Wing
TRW:	Tactical Reconnaissance Wing
UDT:	Underwater Demolition Teams
VA:	Attack Squadron
VAH:	Heavy Attack Squadron
VMA:	Marine Attack Squadron
VMF:	Marine Fighter Squadron

Bibliography

Books

Berhow, Mark A. *US Strategic and Defensive Missile Systems: 1950-2004* (Oxford: Osprey Publishing, 2004)

Blight, James G. and Welch, David A. *On the Brink: Americans and Soviets Reexamine the Cuban Missile Crisis* (New York: Hill and Wang, 1989)

Brugioni, Dino A. *Eyeball to Eyeball: The Inside Story of the Cuban Missile Crisis* (New York: Random House, 1990)

Chang, Laurence and Peter Korblub. *The Cuban Missile Crisis: 1962* (New York: The New Press, 1992)

Department of the Army. *FM 57-10 Army Forces in Joint Airborne Operations* (Washington DC: Department of the Army, 1962)

Dobbs, Michael. *One Minute to Midnight* (New York: Alfred A. Knopf, 2008)

Freedman, Lawrence. *Kennedy's Wars: Berlin, Cuba, Laos, and Vietnam* (New York: Oxford University Press, 2000)

Fursenko Aleksandr and Timothy Naftali. *One Hell of a Gamble* (New York: W. W. Norton & Company, 1997)

Gribkov, General Anatoli I. and General William Y. Smith. *Operation ANADYR* (Chicago, Edition q., Inc., 1994)

House, Major Jonathan M. *The United States Army in Joint Operations: 1950-1983* (US Army, 1984)

Huchthausen, Peter. *October Fury* (Hoboken New Jersey: John Wiley & Sons, Inc., 2002)

Johnson, Haynes. *The Bay of Pigs* (New York: W. W. Norton & Company, 1964)

Kennedy, Robert F. *Thirteen Days* (New York, W. W. Norton & Company, 1969)

Khrushchev, Nikita S. *Khrushchev Remembers*. Trans. and ed by Strobe Talbott (New York: Little Brown Publishing, 1971)

Khrushchev, Sergei N. *Nikita Khrushchev and the Creation of a Superpower* (Pennsylvania: Pennsylvania State University Press, 2000)

Kugler, Richard. *The Army's Role in the Cuban Crisis: 1962* (US Army Center of Military History, 1963)

Naftali, Timothy and Philip Zelikow. *The Presidential Records of John F. Kennedy, September-21 October 1962.* Vol. II (New York: W. W. Norton & Company, 2001)

Nathan, James A. *The Cuban Missile Crisis Revisited* (New York: St Martin's Press, 1992)

Perez, Louis A. Jr. *Cuba: Between Reform and Revolution* (New York: Oxford University Press, 1988)

Perry, J. H. *Latin America: 1999-1849* (Cambridge UK: The New Cambridge Modern History, 1960)

Polmar, Norman and John D. Gresham. *Defcon-2: Standing on the Brink of Nuclear War During the Cuban Missile Crisis* (New York: John Wiley & Sons, Inc., 2006)

Varner, Commander B. D. *The History of Guantanamo Bay 1964* (Guantanamo Bay: US Naval Base, 1964 (USN))

Young, John M. *When the Russians Blinked: The US Marine Response to the Cuban Missile Crisis* (Washington DC: US Marine Corps, 1990)

Zelikow, Philip and Ernest May. *The Presidential Recordings of John F. Kennedy: The Great Crisis.* Vol. III (New York: W. W. Norton & Company, 2001)

Periodicals

'A US Base in Trouble 500 Miles From Home'. *US News and World Report* (11 April 1960)

Brugioni, Dino A. 'The Invasion of Cuba'. *MHQ.* Vol. 4. No. 2 (Winter 1992)

Blanton, Thomas S. and James G. Blight. 'A Conversation in Havana'. *Arms Control Today* (November 2002)
Carpenter, Ronald H. 'When the Right Words Counted'. *Naval History.* Vol. 15. Issue 5 (October 2001)
Flaherty, Tom. 'How the Invasion Would have Been Made'. *Life* (7 December 1962)
Freeman, Simon. 'To The Brink of Nuclear War'. *World Magazine* (October 1992)
Fursenkko, Alexander. 'Night Session Of The Presidium of the Central Committee' (22-23 October 1962) Trans. by Yuri M. Zhukov in *Naval War College Review.* Vol. 59. No. 3 (Summer 2006)
Garthoff, Raymond L. 'New Evidence on the Cuban Missile Crisis: Khrushchev, Nuclear Weapons, and the Cuban Missile Crisis'. *Cold War International History Project.* Bulletin 11 (Winter 1998)
Gribkov, General A. I. *On the Brink of the Nuclear Abyss:* Moscow. (Gregory Page, 1998)
House, Jonathan M. 'Joint Operational Problems in the Cuban Missile Crisis'. *Parameters* (Spring 1991)
Joint Chiefs of Staff. 'Unified Action Armed Forces'. *JCS.* Pub. 2 (November 1959)
Keefe, Major General Stephen T. 'Operation Sunshade: The Air Force Reserve Plays A Key Role in the Cuban Missile Crisis' *Journal: American Aviation Historical Society* (Winter 2006)
Luce, Henry Robinson. 'The Might We Had Aimed at Cuba'. *Life* (7 December 1962)
Stern, Sheldon M. 'The Cuban Missile Crisis ExComm Meetings: Getting it Right After 50 Years'. *HNN* (15 October 2012)
Wisnack, Major Joseph R. 'Old Ironsides' Response to the Cuban Crisis'. *Army* (April 1963)
Yarmolinsky, Adam. 'Department of Defense Operations During the Cuban Crisis,' *Set and Drift: Naval War College Review.* No. 32 (June-July 1979)

Newspapers

'Mikoyen Winds Up His 9-Day Visit To Cuba'. *The St Petersburg Times* (13 February 1960)
'75 Die In Havana As Munitions Ship Explodes At Dock'. *New York Times* (5 March 1960)
'Kruschchev on Cuba'. *New York Times* (10 June 1960)
'Traffic into Base Halted'. *New York Times* (13 May 1961)
'Admiral With 2 Hats'. *New York Times* (23 October 1962)
'Eisenhower on the Russians'. *Corpus Christi Times* (12 December 1961)

Archival Sources

'2nd Marines, OP Plan 316-62 – Blue Beach'. Records Group 127, Records of the US Marine Corps. US National Archives
'A Highly Compressed Narrative Account and Assessment of the Cuban Crisis'. Air Force Historical Research Agency
'A Highly Compressed Narrative Account and Assessment of The Tactical Air Command and the Cuban Crisis'. Air Force Historical Research Agency, K417.042-21 (1 December 1962)
'Archive of the President of the Russian Federation, Special Declassification'. Trans. by Svetlana Savranskaya for the National Security Archive (April 2002)
'Aspectos Importantes Contenidos En Los Informes Ofrecidos'. National Security Archive (24 October 1962)
'Checklist of Activities, A-Day'. Chief of Naval Operations Files. Col 552. File 9A. Naval History and Heritage Command
'Checklist of Activities, A-Day-1,' Chief of Naval Operations Files. Col 552. File 9A. Naval History and Heritage Command
'Chronology of SAC Participation in the Cuban Crisis'. Air Force Historical Research Agency
'CINCLANT Historical Account of the Cuban Crisis – 1963 (U)'. National Security Archives (1963)
'CINCLANT Psychological Leaflet Program'. Records of the Secretary of Defense. Records Group 200. US National Archives
'Comments on State Paper on Possible Soviet Actions by Soviets and Others in Event of Surprise Air Strike'. Col. Wolfe. Records Group 200. US National Archive (20 October 1962)
'CPSU Instructions to General Pivyev'. National Security Archive (27 October 1962)
'Cuba and Berlin'. Records Group 200. US National Archives (19 October 1962)
'Guantanamo Special Equipment List'. Chief of Naval Operations Files. Col 552. File 9A. United States Naval Historical Association
'JCS Weekly Status Report, SIOP 14'. National Security Archive
'MAG 26, TE-129.1.2.1, Operation Plan 316-62'. Records Group 127, Records of the US Marine Corps. US National Archives
'Memo From General Taylor, 6 September 1961, Strategic Air Planning and Berlin'. National Security Archive
'Message from Joint Chiefs of Staff to CINCLANT, 261624Z Oct 1962'. Records Group 218. US National Archives

'Message from Premier Khrushchev, 24 October 1962'. National Security Archive

'NORAD Participation in the Cuban Crisis'. Historical Reference Paper 8. Air Force Historical Research Agency

'North American Air Defense Command and Continental Air Defense Command'. Historical Summery. Air Forces Historical Research Agency (1 April 1963)

'Notes of Secretary of Defense, Robert McNamara, 21 October 1962, Meeting with the President'. National Security Archive

'Notes taken from the Joint Chiefs of Staff, October-November 1962'. Entries for 7 and 12 November. National Security Archive.

'Notes Taken from Transcripts of the Meetings of the Joint Chiefs of Staff, October-November 1962, Dealing with the Cuban Missile Crisis'. National Security Archive

'Operation Scabbards'. CINCLANT from FMFLANT. Recommendations. Record Group 127. Records of the US Marine Corps. National Archives (28 October 1962)

'Operation Sentinel'. Casualties Summary. Federal Civil Defense Administration. Records Group 397. US National Archives (26 March 1962)

'Recollections of Vadim Orlov (USSR Submarine B-59): We Will Sink Them All, But We Will Not Disgrace Our Navy'. National Security Archive

'Reminiscences of Admiral Robert Lee Dennison'. US Naval Institute Oral Histories

'RLT_Blue Beach, Operation Plan 314-62 (Modified 316-62)'. Records Group 127. Records of the US Marine Corps. National Archives, Washington DC

'Robert S. McNamara, Statement before a Subcommittee of the Committee on Appropriations'. House of Representatives, 88th Congress, 1st Session, on Department Defense Appropriations for 1964, Part I

'SEAL Team Chronology, 1961'. Post 1946 Reports, Chief of Naval Operations, Cuba, Box 10, Document No. 7, Naval History and Heritage Command

'SEAL Team Chronology, 1962'. Post 1946 Reports, Chief of Naval Operations, Cuba, Box 10, Document No. 7, Naval History and Heritage Command

'Strategic Air Command Operations in the Cuban Crisis of 1962'. Historical Study 90, Reel 34530, Air Force Historical Agency

'Summary of CNO Participation in the Cuban Crisis'. Records of the Office of Chief of Naval Operations, 1946-200, Coll 552, Naval History and Heritage Command, Box 1

'Tactical Air Command Chronology of the Cuban Crisis, 1962'. Air Force Historical Research Agency (29 January 1963)

'The Air Force Response to the Cuban Crisis 14 October-24 November 1962'. Air Force Historical Research Agency

'The Air Force Response to the Cuban Crisis'. US Air Force Historical Division Liaison Office (1963)

'The Cuban Missiles Crisis: How Well Did the Joint Chiefs of Staff Work?' US National Security Archive

'Timing Factors'. General Maxwell Taylor, National Security Archive (25 October 1962)

'Transcript of Executive Committee meeting, October 27, 1962'. John F. Kennedy Library

'Transcript of the second Executive Committee meeting, 16 October 1962 6:30-7:55 p.m.' US National Archives, JFK Library via the National Security Archive

'Turkish Position With Regard to Trading Jupiters for Soviet Missiles in Cuba'. National Security Archive (25 October 1962)

'UDT Files (Declassified)'. Post 1946 Commands, File 1559. Naval History and Heritage Command (October 1962)

'US Army Command the Control In the Cuban Missile Crisis: Comments on Organization, Information Flows, and Relationships'. Richard T. Loomis, Stanford Research Institute, HMC-2 No. 115. US Army Center of Military History (June 1963)

'Vice Admiral Robert F. Dunn Interview No. 3'. US Naval Institute (23 April 1990)

'Volkogonov Papers'. Library of Congress

'White House Memorandum, The Defense of Berlin if Cuba is Blockaded'. Records Group 200. US National Archives (19 October 1962)

Adlai Stevenson, Statement by Ambassador Adlai Stevenson to the UN Security Council. UN press release 4074 (25 October 1962)

ADM George W. Anderson Jr. Vol. II. US Naval Institute

Foreign Relations of the United States, Cuba, Volume VI (1958-1960)

JCS, Chairman L. L. Lemnitzer, Memorandum for the Secretary of Defense, Military Evaluation of the CIA Paramilitary Plan Cuba. National Security Archive (2 March 1961)

Operational Narrative, Cuban Emergency, United States 3rd Army Appendix 6 (Quartermaster) to Annex C (Logistics) US Army Center of Military History (26 June 1963)

Ship File, USS *Sea Lion*, Cruise Summary 1961-1963 (Naval History and Heritage Command)

Telegram to Admiral Dennison (CINCLANT) Naval History and Heritage Command (12.06 p.m. 19 April 1961)

Index